The Paradox of Scale

The Paradox of Scale

How NGOs Build, Maintain, and Lose Authority
in Environmental Governance

Cristina M. Balboa

The MIT Press
Cambridge, Massachusetts
London, England

This book was set in ITC Stone Sans Std and ITC Stone Serif Std by Toppan Best-set Premedia Limited. Printed and bound in the United States of America.

Library of Congress Cataloging-in-Publication Data

Names: Balboa, Cristina M., author.
Title: The paradox of scale : how NGOs build, maintain, and lose authority in environmental governance / Cristina M. Balboa.
Description: Cambridge, MA : MIT Press, [2018] | Includes bibliographical references and index.
Identifiers: LCCN 2018008757| ISBN 9780262038775 (hardcover : alk. paper) | ISBN 9780262535854 (pbk. : alk. paper)
Subjects: LCSH: Environmental policy--International cooperation--Case studies. | Environmental policy--Decision making--Case studies. | Non-governmental organizations--Case studies. | Environmental sciences--Societies, etc.--Case studies. | Conservation International. | International Marinelife Alliance. | Community Conservation Network.
Classification: LCC GE170 .B35 2018 | DDC 363.7/0561--dc23 LC record available at https://lccn.loc.gov/2018008757

10 9 8 7 6 5 4 3 2 1

For Jake

Contents

Acknowledgments

It seems every acknowledgments section from an author's first book talks about how long the book took to write. This book is no different. As my neighbor, the esteemed scholar Jessica Blatt, jokes: we're from Brooklyn where everything is increasingly artisanal and handmade, and that kind of work takes time. Over time, this "artisanal" scholarly endeavor has accumulated a debt of thanks to many people.

This book would not be possible were it not for the communities and organizations that opened their doors to me and whose members entrusted me with their stories. To all of these individuals: I am humbled by your openness and I hope this work contributes only good things to your work and lives.

This project began in my doctoral program at Yale University, and there were many people there for whose support, critiques, and comaraderie I am grateful, including Ben Cashore, Jonathan Koppell, Brad Gentry, Graeme Auld, Cecilia Blasco, Anastasia O'Rourke, Becca Barnes, Helen Poulos, Barry Muchnick, Monica Araya, and Weslynne Ashton. I wrote some of the preliminary analysis for this project at the Hauser Center—thank you to Mark Moore, David Brown, and Alnoor Ebrahim for the opportunity. Thanks also to the staff, board, and fellows of the Environmental Leadership Program who "dreamed a world in color when our outlook was so gray."

I am grateful for the many organizations have entrusted their funds to me, including Yale University, the Yale Institute for Biospheric Studies, the Yale Council on Southeast Asian Studies, the Yale Center for the Study of Globalization, the Yale Tropical Resources Institute, the Switzer Foundation, the Environmental Protection Agency's Science to Achieve Results (STAR) program, the International Studies Association (ISA), the Association for Research on Nonprofit Organizations and Voluntary Associations

(ARNOVA), Central European University, the Eugene M. Lang Foundation, the Faculty Fellowship Publication Program of CUNY (City University of New York), the Marxe School Dean's Research Award, and the Baruch Provost's Book Completion Award. Support for this project was also provided by a PSC-CUNY Award, jointly funded by the Professional Staff Congress and the City University of New York. I hope you find this research worthy of your support.

Thank you, also, to the people who housed and supported me during field work: John Parks and family in Honolulu and the Puyat family in the Philippines, especially Berna, and my late Tita and cousin: Baby and Dave.

I have been welcomed and encouraged by many faculty at the City University of New York, Baruch College, and the Marxe School of Public and International Affairs in particular. Leading this group of kind critics is my writing group of Susan Chambre, Hilary Botein, and Nicole Marwell (now at the University of Chicago) who have read more of my work than anyone except my dad and my husband. Rob Smith was a great sounding board for strategizing revisions and big conceptual thinking. Others generously commented on the proposals and chapters, and helped protect my writing time, including John Casey, Jack Krauskopf, George Mitchell, Ryan Smith, Rachel Smith, Don Waisanen, and the entire Center for Nonprofit Strategy and Management at the Marxe School; and my insightful and inspiring cohort at the CUNY Faculty Fellowship Publication Program including Jennifer Johnson, Mark Lewis, Teresita Levy, Megan Moran, Isabel Martinez, and Virginia Sanchez-Korrol.

I was extremely fortunate that the MIT Press commissioned three thoughtful scholars to anonymously review the manuscript; their questions and comments paved a clear path to a more compelling and concise argument. I am grateful to Beth Clevenger and Anthony Zannino for finding these reviewers and for general guidance in this process. Others have generously offered comments on iterations of the proposal, the manuscript, and the process of revisions including Bill Demars, Dan Magaziner, Paloma Raggo; Maryam Deloffre (whom I owe triply for reviewing the same chapter three times!); Ben Cashore, Stefan Renckens, Matto Mildenberger, and the members of the Yale Governance, Environment, and Markets Initiative; Roger Hayden of Cornell University Press and one reviewer from Oxford University Press; and the discussants and chairs at Association for Research on Nonprofit Organizations and Voluntary Action (ARNOVA) and the International Studies Association (ISA). Els de Graauw, Sarah Bush, and Alnoor Ebrahim gave solid publishing advice. Seth Fisher's editing notes and advice taught me more about writing and telling a story than all my years in graduate school. Daniela Vizcano helped me rethink the figures in the book. The Academic Ladder Social Science/Humanities Writing Group 11 has been an incredible source of encouragement, advice, and sage insight into the strange workings of academia. To my "circle of academic niceness" everywhere: I thank you all.

I am grateful for my neighbors and friends who were supportive by helping with childcare and just being great people to be around for a full life—thanks Armory Crew. Rachel, Erin, and Amy—who also wrote their work during the "naps, nights, and weekends" of early parenthood—and our FGCH Babysitting Co-op helped me maintain favorable status as both mom and scholar.

I thank my family for supporting me in this process. Jaime Balboa and Todd Presner, my family-academic mentors, always answered my questions with calm and encouragement; Elizabeth Balboa's editing was invaluable on chapters 4 and 5; my siblings Miguel, Roberto, Juan, and Maria happily helped brainstorm book titles; my stepmother TJ and my late mother Sharon were incredible role models for strength and discovery; and my father Ronaldo Balboa instilled in me the Balboa traditions of civic duty and unrelenting questioning.

To Matilda, Fernanda, and Carly: Thank you for being wonderful human beings, for your empathy and encouragement on the writing process, and for working with me to be kinder, smarter, and healthier every day.

I am most grateful for the constant support, intellect, humor, competence, and gourmet cooking of my husband Jake—a true partner in the adventure, even when the adventure isn't too exciting. I promise we will visit amazing places together some day. Thanks for it all: everything from taking the girls on trips so I could write to helping me become who I want to be. You bring both meaning and joy to my life. I dedicate this work to you.

1   Introduction: NGO Authority, Effectiveness, and the Paradox of Scale

It didn't matter that the snow leopard was listed as endangered by the Convention on International Trade in Endangered Species of Wild Fauna and Flora (CITES). Farmers in northern Pakistan had to defend their livestock and livelihoods. Once these big cats had feasted on an animal, they wouldn't stop there—one leopard could kill up to twenty goats or sheep. In the poor region of Balistan in Pakistan, these predatory killings could significantly reduce an already meager income. Killing that predator would end the loss of livestock, and selling the cat's carcass—although rare for farmers to do—could also make up for the financial loss of dead livestock. These retaliatory killings have been a primary threat for the snow leopard since before the animals were classified as endangered in 1975 (Hussain 2000).[1]

In 1998, the organization Project Snow Leopard created an innovative program to convince farmers not only to stop the retaliatory killings, but also to protect the predators. The project was two-pronged: (1) create an insurance scheme so that farmers could be compensated for any livestock losses created by the big cats; and (2) create an alternative income—an ecotourism trekking company—dependent on the protection of these wild animals. This approach to snow leopard conservation was both groundbreaking in its approach, and tailor-made for the communities of Balistan, based on the understanding the project's founder, Shafqat Hussain, accumulated while living in the area for five years. The pilot program in the village of Skoyo required households to pay a premium—1 percent of a goat's current value—to gain coverage. Following the project plan, in the first year the Village Insurance Committee verified one livestock killing and paid that claimant (Hussain 2000). Word spread throughout the region: this peculiar scheme actually compensated herders and reduced retaliatory killing. The project expanded to two more villages (Strauss 2016). Since

1998, the project has expanded to cover more than ten thousand families in nineteen villages in Northern Pakistan (Ebrahim 2010; Strauss 2016; Rosen et al. 2012).

But the range of the snow leopard reaches far beyond the Northern Areas of Pakistan and into a dozen countries of the Central Asian mountains. How could the species survive in the areas beyond this small area of Pakistan? To be sure, the global conservation community was interested in funding the replication of these efforts in other locations. How would the herders of Afghanistan, India, Russia, or any of these other countries, cultural regions, and diverse communities receive this approach? Balistan was, in part, chosen because the snow leopard was the only known wild predator near the villages, making it easy to focus conservation efforts (Hussain 2000). Would the approach be different in communities where wolves were also a problem for herders? What about in areas like Mongolia with a higher prevalence of nomadic or semi-nomadic herders? What about in areas where government agencies were more involved in preservation? (Mishra et al. 2003).

In the creation of Project Snow Leopard, this small, locally focused nongovernmental organization (NGO) created a program that designed new rules for how herders interacted with endangered species in Balistan. They attained consent from local communities to implement these rules with each new member of the insurance scheme. By creating the Village Insurance Committee, they built on local capacity and reflected local norms of accountability—these committee members knew their neighbors and whether or not any retaliatory killings occurred. This NGO has harnessed the resources the global scale has to offer—funding, scientific expertise—and used it to facilitate context-specific, locally embraced interventions in environmental governance. In order to expand, it would have to address the questions raised here.

The Nature Conservancy (TNC) is the world's largest environmental nongovernmental organization. It operates in over seventy-two countries with more than three thousand eight hundred staff (over six hundred of them scientists) (Kareiva, Groves, and Marvier 2014), all working "to conserve the lands and waters on which all life depends."[2] In 2016, TNC reported revenues of $803 billion USD. While its history has not been without controversy, it has rebuilt its reputation and is now accredited by several nonprofit rating organizations. It is seen as an innovator in science, and reports numerous quantifiable results from its work. One of its hallmark methods is protecting the land through property maintenance, management, acquisition, and financing (Gunter 2004). In its history TNC has had noted success in acquiring more than one hundred million acres globally, protecting another hundred million acres of private land through conservation easements, and assisting local and national governments to manage and protect natural resources around the world. In many ways, TNC is seen as a global authority in environmental protection.

At the same time, TNC endures regular criticism over the use of this hallmark approach. In May 2002, the *Far Eastern Economic Review* printed a critical article alleging that the Indonesian Ministry of Forests had approved a private company to take over the management of Komodo National Park, the global biodiversity treasure located in Indonesia that houses the famed Komodo dragon. This company, Putri Naga Komodo, was a partnership between a Malaysian-born businessman and the U.S.-based TNC. Together, they created a twenty-five-year management plan that included an eco-tourism concession for this private company (Dhume 2002). The Nature Conservancy stressed that this nonprofit company was needed to turn the global treasure from a run-down, financially poor and mismanaged area to a world-class ecotourism destination, with profits reinvested into the park infrastructure, marketing, and management, and consequently back into the conservation of the resource (Leiman 2002). Local communities and conservationists were concerned that control over this important resource was delegated to foreign entities.

In both of these cases, nongovernmental organizations were creating the rules of resource governance on the local level. In Project Snow Leopard's case, the organization was designing and implementing species protection in Balistan. They created a program that restricted and transformed local interaction with endangered species and local communities consented to and followed these rules. The management plan of Komodo National Park created the rules for resource management of the park, as TNC had done for countless other areas throughout its history. Where this approach had worked in California, the Caribbean, and other places, and while global funders and national government agencies look to TNC as an authority in resource conservation, the communities and organizations located around Komodo National Park questioned their authority to manage it. Their consent would need to be earned, regardless of any agreements at the national or international level. Conservation is riddled with examples like these: local NGOs that are successful find difficulty when they scale up operations to other locales; global NGOs that help shape the rules of global conservation and successfully implement these rules at some locations, encounter repeated criticism and barriers in other locales. What explains these experiences? Why is it so difficult for NGOs that are seen as authorities in their field to implement projects?

This book is an effort to explain this puzzle. The study of environmental governance has often examined the effectiveness of NGOs as lobbyists or as implementers (Betsill and Corell 2008; Avant 2004; Gunter 2004 West 2006). The study of NGOs beyond the environmental field has similarly been divided into individual studies of either one NGO's intervention at the global level or another's at the local level (Okorley, Dey, and Owusu 2012; Katz 2013; Hobbes 2014). Scholars consider these questions through the lenses of management, development, international relations (IR), or environmental studies, but rarely do these fields speak to each other. This book is an effort to synthesize these disciplines, approaches, lenses, and scales to offer a detailed account and theoretical framework to explain the experience of nongovernmental organizations.

To do this, I turn to the concept of authority in environmental governance. I will detail how some nongovernmental organizations can be seen as an authority on particular causes on a global scale, but then fail to effect change for those causes in the local communities where they work. In the pages that follow, I offer a new theoretical framework based on a concept: the paradox of scale. I suggest this paradox—that what gives an NGO authority on one scale can hurt its authority on another scale—is a primary barrier to NGO effectiveness.

This chapter will introduce the paradox of scale, what it is, why NGOs are particularly susceptible to it, and how it develops for these actors. It will explore why scale is important for nongovernmental organizations as actors in governance. Next, because this paradox is a problem of NGO authority, I will briefly define and distinguish authority as a specific form of power. I will then explain how scale creates both complications and opportunities for the study of NGOs and their authority. Before detailing the plan of the book chapter by chapter, this introduction will discuss the research methods used to answer the question: why do NGO efforts to scale up their impact seem to break down their authority?

The Paradox of Scale

Why do NGOs experience difficulty in creating the changes they seek in the world? Many NGOs, like The Nature Conservancy, begin their work at the global scale, garnering and legitimating power at that scale. They influence global decision making through media campaigns and producing research, and then demonstrate their authority through global fundraising efforts that authorize them to implement those decisions at the local scale in communities where they can then gather data on local resources, institutions, or policies. Access to the local scale increases the NGO's legitimacy at the global scale as a representative of the local communities and resources, piquing the interest of funders (both governmental and private), and ultimately leading to increased financial support (Fisher 1997; Slim 2002). The multiscale dynamics are mutually reinforcing: more funding means more access, which means more legitimacy as the only global or national "experts" on the local issues, which ultimately leads to more funding to return to the local scale. NGOs can then use this expertise to gain positions of authority to implement rules locally. However, the NGO will soon discover that the capacity and accountability processes that gained it power at the larger scale are not helpful at the local scale. What's more, in order to maintain its command globally, an NGO must prioritize the capacities and accountability norms of that scale over the local scale, undermining its ability to create lasting change on the ground.

Alternatively, some NGOs, like Project Snow Leopard, begin solely as locally focused organizations. They concentrate on one geographic area or community, and tailor context-specific programs to change local behavior and create public good (Ebrahim 2010). If these organizations are successful, they gain a reputation at the local level that spreads among the global organizations working to solve that same problem. They become authorities on the issue at the local scale, which gives them opportunities to scale up by expanding to other geographic areas and by speaking about local issues to larger audiences. Through the spread of their reputation both locally and globally, Project Snow Leopard has received funding to expand into several other villages and even other countries that are snow leopard habitats. Thus, these NGOs that started out locally focused are pulled toward a transnational model.

This is how the paradox of scale works: organizations that use their global authority to gain local access will find that the capacity and accountability practices that created their legitimized power at that scale are not only inappropriate for the local scale, but are also detrimental to their work there. For example, as chapter 3 details in the experience of Conservation International in Papua New Guinea, reporting on progress in a document with a logical framework analysis and pages of accompanying text might be just what the global funder wants, but it will likely not move community members to support the organization's work. Adhering to this global norm of reporting signaled to communities and local partners that the organization did not respect their traditional forum for deliberation requiring face-to-face discussions. However, in order to maintain their legitimate power on a global scale, NGOs must systemically favor the requirements of the global scale over the local scale. This causes a paradox where the capacity and accountability practices that gained the NGO global authority and access to the local scale reduces the organization's power and legitimacy locally. This holds equally true for organizations that leverage local authority to gain global access. Organizations that begin locally, like the ones in chapters 4 and 5, are pulled into the global scale only to find that the capacity and accountability practices that helped make them successful locally and garner global attention will not help them be effective in the global arena; but building their global capacity and operating with global norms of accountability will not help them be effective on the ground. Thus, whether initially focused at the global scale or the local scale, NGOs find themselves caught in this paradox.

The Argument
Power. Legitimacy. Authority. Capacity. Accountability. The previous section employed these concepts in illustrative examples of NGOs to explain how the paradox develops for these organizations. This section will begin to connect and distinguish these concepts through the layered argument of this book. First, in order to create durable change, NGOs cannot just influence governance; they cannot just use economic incentives to coerce actors to comply with an NGO's mission: NGOs must build authority to create, implement, or enforce rules and generate consent from the governed. Second, following the generally accepted definition of "authority" as legitimated power, NGOs must both demonstrate power and legitimate

that power. While these concepts of power, legitimacy, and authority might seem like nebulous theoretical concepts, I argue that we can begin to assess them by using proxy concepts. As the methods section in this chapter and the exploration of authority in chapter 2 assert, the concept of capacity works well as a proxy of power and the concept of accountability serves well as a proxy of legitimacy. Thus, the third layer of this argument is to demonstrate how capacity and accountability can be used to assess NGO authority.

NGOs seek to make meaningful impact on fairly large social and environmental problems. They work to do no less than "to save lives, defeat poverty and achieve social justice";[3] "create a world where no child goes to bed hungry";[4] and "conserve nature and reduce the most pressing threats to the diversity of life on Earth,"[5] to name just a few goals. The problems NGOs seek to resolve are widespread: they are not confined by state boundaries. Thus, the fourth layer of this argument is that NGOs experience a "growth imperative" to expand their reach and scale up operations. As the NGOs cross boundaries to systemically address the issues of their missions, they find that the traits and processes that legitimate power to create authority in one scale will not gain it authority in another scale.[6] What's more, trying to utilize the capacities and accountability norms in the wrong scale will cause the NGO to lose authority.

The cases in this book illustrate this paradox of scale, but do not indicate that the paradox is an insurmountable obstacle to NGO authority. Each case demonstrates what I call "bridging capacity," which functions both to connect the norms of the local and global scales as well as to manage the actors on each scale so that they understand the importance of the other.

NGOs and the Paradox of Scale

Why are nongovernmental organizations susceptible to this paradox? Two particular traits make transnational NGOs[7] distinctive players in governance. First, they are private actors creating rules to produce and govern public goods and reduce public "bads." They create programs to reduce poverty, increase environmental benefits, raise the level of education of citizens, to name a few. Second, they operate on multiple scales (Demars and Dijkzeul 2015). The convergence of these two traits not only distinguishes NGOs from most other governance actors, but also makes them more vulnerable to the paradox of scale.

As nonstate actors, NGOs produce rules to govern public goods with different strategies and authority than the state. The democratic state derives much authority from its military might and election processes. NGOs, however, have no army and are not elected to participate in governance. They must build authority by other means. Recent scholarship indicates this authority can be delegated to them by the state, but more often private actors must build entrepreneurial authority—they must persuade the potential subjects with their expertise that their actions are not only logical, but also reflect the needs and desires of the governed (Green 2014). To be accepted as an appropriate actor to produce public goods as well as the processes and rules that generate these goods, NGOs must garner consent of the governed.

Where some organizations might advocate at the national or global scale, and others might implement policy locally, a growing number of NGOs do both. Some nongovernmental organizations operate on the global level to lobby governments, set policy agendas, and create implementation plans for global agreements using the stories and data from their work at the local level as evidence. Others might leverage their local experience on the global scale by informing or creating norms and policies through global media campaigns, working with states on global conventions, and offering solutions to the world's most pressing problems. These transnational NGOs work locally to create the change on the ground that supports and enforces the norms and policies created at the global level. They implement and enforce the rules created at the global scale by monitoring elections, choosing which capacities to build locally to govern, reporting on human rights violations, and creating protected areas for endangered ecosystems. They both participate in rules creation for certifications schemes and work with local producers to ensure compliance with those rules. In this way, NGOs influence the goals of policy and become authorities in its implementation.

Because NGOs are private actors pursuing public good, they must exercise authority by different means than other actors. That NGOs work on multiple scales complicates this authority because what makes an NGO powerful and legitimate changes depending upon the scale of operation (Avant, Finnemore, and Sell 2010). Thus, these two core traits of NGOs combine to create the paradox of scale: despite the need to achieve their goals on multiple scales, to achieve outcomes and change behavior based on consent rather than compliance, what makes an NGO an authority in one scale can ultimately undermine its authority in another.

Scale and the NGO Growth Imperative

The concept of scale is central to this book's analysis of NGO authority. While the idea that scale impacts an actor's effectiveness is not new (Fisher 1997), the pressure for NGOs to scale up their operations in order to create meaningful impact brings new importance to this type of analysis. There is already a robust body of literature focused on nongovernmental organizations that maintain their current size or focus—local organizations that partner or interact with global ones to achieve a purpose (Bob 2005; Keck and Sikkink 1998). What prevents an NGO from being content working on just one scale? This section examines what appears to be an NGO growth imperative within the field, pushing these organizations to work across scale.

"Scaling up" to make an intervention have more impact on more people has become a popular term since the turn of the millennium (Ford Foundation 2004). It can be as simple as creating similar projects in a few new locales, or as complex as creating a national or international network of projects, reaching millions of people (Orosz 2000). It involves "expanding, adapting and sustaining successful policies, programs or projects in different place and over time to reach a greater number of people" (Hartmann and Linn 2008).

This imperative for NGOs to grow and take their current efforts to scale is driven by several factors. First is the recognition that the scope of problems that NGOs aim to tackle is enormous—often beyond local or national boundaries—driving to scale up their programs to a commensurate size (Ford Foundation 2004; WRI 2008). The number and size of NGOs are growing (Balboa 2017), but not yet to the degree where they can create systemic change on massive problems like poverty, inequality, climate change, or biodiversity loss (Murray 2013). Both academic and practitioner literature asserts that in order to make durable and profound change, organizations must work at multiple scales (Westley et al. 2014; Eckhart-Queenan et al 2015).

Particularly in environmental conservation, scaling up operations is a reaction to the scientific understanding about landscape and ecosystem management, the impacts of and adaptation to climate change, and the chain of custody or supply for natural resources (Hardin 1968; Ostrom 1990; Wallace, Fine, and Atkinson 2010). The push to scale up operations for conservation can be seen in calls for national and regional conservation plans, as well as in the proposals and funding reports of the NGOs themselves (Diamond 2002; Kennedy et al 2016; Mazor et al 2014; Wallace, Fine, and Atkinson 2010; World Resources Institute, The World Conservation Union, and the United Nations Environment Programme 1992).

Scaling up has also been the noted reaction to the increased levels of development assistance promised by wealthy countries at the G8 summits in the early 2000s. To coordinate large levels of assistance, funders look to support bigger, broader programs instead of individual projects, which may seem like piecemeal responses in light of the massive problem. Moreover, managing a larger number of smaller projects is much more time- and resource-intensive than fewer larger projects (Hartmann and Linn 2007). The substantial growth of development assistance is mirrored by expansion of the environment sector in recent decades, from both private foundations and the Global Environment Facility (Balboa 2017). Funding from public and private sectors alike, for both development and conservation efforts, has increased the scale of these efforts.

Since scaling up involves the expansion of a successful program, it can be seen as a sign of organizational success when funders choose to invest in an intervention to bring it to scale (Ebrahim and Rangan 2014). Larger organizations want to demonstrate success by expanding impact. Smaller organizations are directed by funders to replicate their local success. This "growth imperative"for NGOs could also be seen as a spillover effect from the increased interaction and blurring lines between nonprofit and for-profit logics. In business management and economics in general, growth it not just seen as a sign of success, but an essential element of survival as well. For NGOs seeking positive evaluations from nonprofit "watchdogs" like Charity Navigator, growth is essential since it is one of seven performance metrics used to measure an NGO's impact on mission.[8] Thus, there is an increased pressure on NGOs to scale up their finances, programs, and impacts. Moreover, as these NGOs scale up, they cross national boundaries and perform different functions at different locales, which makes studying this phenomenon solely from the perspective of management or organization theory too confining. All these fields of study must be integrated with international relations to understand the problems NGOs experience when scaling up operations.

Scholars and practitioners have puzzled over this phenomenon in various fields with different ideas about its causes. Some use lenses of resource dependency theory and interdependence to demonstrate how southern NGOs have more difficulty achieving their mission because of the energy they must expend to please northern or global funders (Hudock 1999), while others go so far as to argue that transnational funding creates isomorphic forces on local actors, causing them to act more like their funders and less like their constituents (Henderson 2003). Stroup (2012) suggests that the NGO's country of origin influences how it operates on the ground, while other scholars have argued that transnational actors cannot achieve their missions on the ground because their nonlocal status relegates their interventions to technical fixes rather than the broad political change they seek (Banks, Hulme, and Edwards 2015; Bush 2015). Wong (2012) asserts that there is an appropriate division of agenda-setting function in transnational NGOs between centralized (i.e., global) and decentralized (i.e., local) units in order to achieve optimum political salience on an issue. Still others have demonstrated that when global and local actors have competing priorities for interventions, the global actor goals win regardless of the needs of the community (Dowie 2011), resulting in these interventions lacking accountability to or participation of local constituencies (Deloffre 2016). Daring practitioners have gone so far as to state that the very idea of scaling up interventions and implementing big ideas in multiple locations is inherently wrong (Hobbes 2014). While all these efforts have refined our understanding of how NGOs do or should change depending upon the scale and location of operations, this book synthesizes these multiple approaches and concepts under the causal mechanism of the paradox of scale. Since this paradox explains NGO authority, this next section will define exactly what I mean by the concepts of power and authority.

NGO Power and Authority

I have suggested that NGOs experience a growth imperative in order to address the social and environmental ills at scales that are meaningful for the broad-reaching, pervasive, and growing problems. But how do they actually accomplish these goals? How can we assess whether or not these actors are capable of fulfilling their mission? To answer these questions, I turn to the concepts of power and, more specifically, authority. These concepts will be explored in more detail in chapter 2, but in order to explain the central argument of this book, I must foreground that discussion here briefly.

Because power and authority can seem like nebulous theoretical concepts, it is important to define and distinguish them. To create the change they seek on the scales they desire, NGOs must have substantial power. Broadly defined, "power" is the ability or capacity of an actor to achieve the outcomes it desires (Giddens 1984, 257; Jinnah 2014, 43; Koppell 2010). A business exerts power when it convinces a consumer to purchase its product, or decreases its costs to augment its bottom line. A revolutionary militia exerts power when it is able to overthrow the current regime and install its own leaders and governors. An NGO exhibits power when the information it produces changes global agreements or when it implements programs that move it closer to achieving its mission. The desired outcomes for NGOs are usually articulated in the form of a mission statement and in proposals for project funding. These missions are lofty; collectively, they aim for no less than ridding the world of its ills. As NGOs take on larger roles in their issue areas and demonstrate some progress toward their missions, their power grows. But that power tends not to last forever; in fact, it often deteriorates quickly when the funding dries up. To achieve their missions in a durable way, NGOs must not just implement change in the short term. These changes must take root broadly and persist over time in order to truly make an impact.

I assert that to achieve these ambitious and difficult goals in any enduring way, NGOs must demonstrate authority (Cooley and Kohl 2006). There seems to be a consensus that "authority" is defined as legitimated power. This uncomplicated definition makes authority sound simpler than it is; it is a particularly tricky concept for NGOs. For government scholars, the concept is somewhat more straightforward. Some governments that wield legitimate authority derive that authority from the process of democracy. If government actions and policies are not in line with what its constituency wants, there are processes, such as elections, by which the constituency can make its displeasure known. In this way, the process of democracy legitimates the power of government (Beisham and Dingwerth 2008). Nongovernmental organizations are not subject to the process of democracy, so they must find other means of creating authority or legitimating power (Slim 2002; Bernstein 2011). One of this book's main contributions is detailing how NGOs do this, both theoretically and empirically. Thus, I begin with definitions. Specifically, this book works with the broadly accepted definition of "power" as the ability or capacity of an actor to achieve the outcomes it desires (Giddens 1984, 257; Jinnah 2014, 43; Koppell 2010). Authority is the legitimated power that allows an entity to create, implement, or enforce "rules, standards, guidelines, or practices that other actors adopt" (Green 2014, 6). Using this restrictive definition—that authority is not just about influencing other actors to favor NGO's missions, but about creating, implementing, or enforcing the actual rules that govern behavior—makes this explanation of NGO experience not just about their management and not just about short-term expressions of power, but about these actors' places in environmental governance and long-term, durable change.[9] For reasons outlined in the earlier section on the NGO growth imperative, these organizations seek change across scale, which necessitates the incorporation of scale in our analyses of NGO authority.

The Complications and Opportunities of Scale

The nature of nongovernmental organizations and their organizational goals makes it imperative that we study them across scale. Taking on this challenge creates some complications in how we apply concepts and in what disciplinary approaches we use. It also creates opportunities to refine broad theoretical concepts in a way can be useful for practitioners, answer some of the conundrums in international relations for private authority, and define new research agendas.

For example, the literature on NGO power is often divided by scale. International relations examines it at the global scale, focusing on NGO diplomacy, advocacy, and influence on global negotiations (Betsill and Corell 2008). The field of international development often examines NGO power at the local scale, focusing on either the NGO capacity to deliver results (Brinkerhoff and Morgan 2010), or the NGO as an instrument for community empowerment (Slim 2002; Hinton and Groves 2013). Management literature examines internal organizational aspects of power and structure, as well as how these variables impact achieving mission (Fleming and Spicer 2014). Chapter 2 will connect these literatures by laying out a theoretical framework that expands and anatomizes NGO power at each scale, and by explaining how NGOs' distinct capacities, accountabilities, and actions on one scale impact the other. I create a typology of NGO authority based on scale: raw power, which is power that has not been legitimated; local authority, which is power that has been legitimated at the local scale but not the global scale; global authority (the converse of local authority), which is power that has been legitimated on the global scale but not the local; and broad-based authority, which is power that has been legitimated on both the global and local scales. (Figure 2.1 in this book illustrates this with a more detailed discussion.) In doing so, this book acknowledges not only that NGOs as actors are far from homogeneous, but also that each individual NGO acts differently in different contexts. Thus, the analysis herein adds to the growing but nascent literature that explains how the internal management of an NGO impacts its external relationships (Wong 2012; Stroup 2012; Bush 2015).

The past decade has seen substantial advancements in our understanding of private authority, but scale complicates this by suggesting that different scales have different legitimizing requirements for authority. Green's typology includes two types of private authority. Delegated private authority reflects the traditional principal-agent relationships between a state and a nonstate actor, while entrepreneurial private authority occurs when the state does not delegate authority and actors must persuade others to adopt its rules and practices (Green 2014). But since NGOs work across scale, this private authority must be created through interaction with a multitude of actors, each with their own requirements for legitimacy. Applying Green's typology across scale, we can see authority delegated at some scales while simultaneously being entrepreneurial at others. For example, funding agreements create an extended principal-agent relationship between states, IGOs, and NGOs, where NGOs are delegated authority to implement rules on conservation by the parties to an agreement. At the local level, communities governed by traditional authorities that do not participate in global agreements must adhere to rules created by the NGOs, without their leaders having participated in any form of delegation. Or, the authority at the global level can be entrepreneurial, perhaps with funding to implement programs by a private foundation, another private actor whose authority is not derived from the state. However, local actors might have different requirements to be persuaded of the NGOs' authority. In this way, studying authority over scale expands Green's contributions to the field.

The cobweb of legitimizing norms and actors renders principal-agent theory—a bedrock theory of international relations—too constraining to explain NGO authority. Where previous work on NGO legitimacy, authority, or accountability has tried to control for this cobweb by analyzing just one relationship—NGO-State; NGO-IGO; NGO-NGO; NGO-Community— one cannot fully explain NGO authority simply from one relationship. Understanding authority across scale requires us to look beyond bilateral relationships, to focus on how the norms of legitimacy and power change from scale to scale, and how the different actors either reproduce these norms or attempt to break them. As chapter 2 will describe in detail, this book advances our understanding of how NGO authority is created, maintained, and undermined, because it offers two scale-based typologies of norms: one for capacity as a proxy for power, and one for accountability as a proxy for legitimacy.

In studying NGO authority across scale and the paradox this produces, I offer potential answers to a few dilemmas raised in international relations. First, I respond to the challenge Koppell raised in his 2010 exploration of global governance organizations. Citing several real-world examples like the existence of authoritarianism and other authorities without legitimacy, he asks how, considering our definition of "authority" as legitimated power, there still can exist "illegitimate authorities." He suggests the answer lies in specifying the sources of both legitimacy and authority. While I do not pretend to explain the existence of authoritarian governments in this book, I do unpack the idea of NGO "illegitimate authority." By explaining how environmental NGOs create authority (either starting from the global scale or the local), defining what authority looks like empirically, and detailing how they expand that authority broadly to operate in scales that have different requirements for legitimacy and different scopes of power, this book breaks new ground for the study of private authority and the role of nonstate actors in global governance.

The second dilemma of international relations is what Parks and Kramarz call the accountability paradox, which arises when an increase in accountability has not resulted in an increase in environmental gains. Both Parks and Kramarz's "accountability paradox" and Koppell's question on "illegitimate authorities" can be explained by the concepts in this book.

The paradox of scale demonstrated in these pages explains how global norms of legitimacy and accountability work to undermine NGO authority locally, rendering them impotent in the implementation of global rules and agreements, and thus in the attainment of their own missions. Through this book's examination of NGO authority over scale, we come to explain what Koppell refers to as "illegitimate authorities" with this paradox—that power can be legitimated by some but not a critical mass of significant sources; that outcomes can be achieved based on a mix of compliance and consent from other actors.

Examining NGO authority across scale brings to light the many different disciplines that inform our understanding of NGOs. My approach to this analysis is that it must be meticulously data driven for us to gain a holistic understanding of how NGOs operate. Thus I started with the empirics of these organizations' experiences and became a conceptual and theoretical opportunist to explain the phenomenon of NGOs in environmental governance. As such, this book contributes to international relations by drawing into the field concepts from management, development, and other disciplines that focus on nongovernmental organizations.

Perhaps what is driving the siloed, multidisciplinary study of NGOs is simply that they are complex actors. While the cannon of research on NGOs is growing, projects often focus in depth on one concept—either capacity, accountability, legitimacy, or authority. *The Paradox of Scale* is a synthesizing book: it illuminates the connections between these concepts for three environmental NGOs working in Papua New Guinea, the Philippines, and Palau, and demonstrates their dynamic relationships across scales. By anatomizing in thick detail these concepts, this book is an effort to explain transnational NGOs' experiences and their struggles in creating and maintaining authority when facing the paradox of scale.

A Methodology for Creating Theory on NGO Authority

The goal of this research is to help explain the experience of nongovernmental organizations as they try to create large-scale, durable change—change that I assert can only come to fruition through NGO authority. In doing this, I use NGO authority to offer an explanation for why some NGOs seem powerful and achieve so much and yet run into so much difficulty creating change on the ground. Using the theory of authority to parse out the basic elements of this paradox helps paint a clearer picture of NGOs: rather than calling them by the oxymoronic name "illegitimate authorities," we can instead determine which scale's norms they uphold and which they violate, and then map out their authority in detail. Scholarly literature on governance has examined NGO accountability, legitimacy, influence, effectiveness, and capacity, to name just a few concepts. But as yet there is little insight into how these concepts interact to explain NGO experience. Other previous work has examined NGO accountability to various actors (donors, the state, communities, other NGOs) and in multiple directions, but not on how the norms of accountability on different scales impact each other. Methodologically, the paradox of scale functions as a causal mechanism that joins these concepts, questions, and understandings to explain NGOs experience in governance.

Moreover, while examining individual relationships are important (i.e., NGO relationships with funders, the state, the community, other NGOs), this book examines not *who* is exerting the norms but *what norms* are being exerted in the field as a whole. Thus, the focus is on how the norms of global and local resource governance impact individual NGOs and their multi-actor, multiscale relationships and influences. To analyze how NGOs react to norms from multiple scales, I needed to choose NGOs that operate on multiple scales. Then, I had to understand in rich detail both the external relationships and pressures these organizations experience as well as the internal operations and decisions made in response to these external factors.

To comprehensively understand these organizations, I introduced new theory based on the paradox of scale, and identified a new method for assessing NGO authority through the proxies of capacity and accountability. Since qualitative research methods are especially suitable for discovery and theory creation, I used qualitative comparative case studies and process tracing to describe and explain the central argument of this book. While the theory presented in this book is based on empirical cases, the analytical process was typical of qualitative research in that it was iterative: alternating between data collection, analysis, and theory refinement (Checkel 2008). For example, while I had initially sought evidence of capacity and accountability in each case of transnational NGO, the typologies of these concepts based on distinct scales did not appear until I started collecting and analyzing the data. This trait of the qualitative method—that researchers must go where the data takes us—was instrumental in the creation of this new theory.

The method of process tracing was essential in this course of discovery. Process tracing is a qualitative method used to test or create theory. In its heuristic function, it "inductively uses evidence from within a case to develop hypotheses that might explain the case" (Bennett and Checkel 2008, 7) and is particularly suited to generate new variables, typologies, or hypotheses based on detailed observation of the sequence of events over time (George and Bennett 2005). Process tracing requires demonstrating both a correlation between possible causes and observed outcomes (George and Bennett 2005, 6) and a causal mechanism to connect independent and dependent variables. A causal mechanism is a "set of hypotheses that could be the explanation for some social phenomenon" (Checkel 2008, 115; Hedstrom and Swedberg 1998, 25).

The causal mechanism identified in this research is built on a suite of assertions, starting with the simple equation that power plus legitimacy equals authority. Authority is essential for NGOs to create lasting change because without it, actors merely comply with NGO actions rather than consent to them and compliance is a fleeting state. As stated earlier in this chapter, this book adheres to common practice of using proxies for its variables (Checkel 2008). Capacity is the proxy for power and accountability is the proxy for legitimacy. Thus, in order to demonstrate authority and to attain the consent of those impacted by their work, these case studies must offer evidence of both capacity and accountability (see figure 1.1).

The second assertion in the paradox of scale is that accountability and capacity manifest differently in the local and the global scale. The typologies of these concepts detailed in chapter 2 demonstrate these differences based on the empirical data. Thus, as figure 1.1 indicates, only global capacities and global accountability norms will create global authority, and only local capacities and local accountability norms will create local authority. When both global and local authority are achieved, then the NGO is said to have broad-based authority.

Next, I assert that trying to use local capacities and local accountability norms in the global scale will preclude global authority for the NGOs and vice versa. The cases also demonstrate evidence that there is pressure to prioritize global capacities and global accountabilities over local ones—a practice that attains compliance rather than consent, and precludes local

1. Basic elements of authority

Authority = legitimacy + power

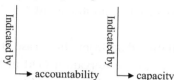

2. Authority by scale

$\text{Authority}_{(G)}$ = legitimacy + power

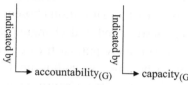

$\text{Authority}_{(L)}$ = legitimacy + power

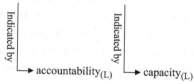

3. The paradox of scale asserts that authority problems result from adhering to the wrong norms of capacity and accountability for the scale—most frequently, when NGOs prioritize global capacity and accountability norms over local ones.

$\text{Authority}_{(G)}$ ≠ legitimacy + power

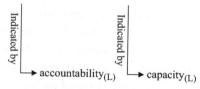

$\text{Authority}_{(L)}$ ≠ legitimacy + power

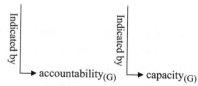

Figure 1.1
NGO authority and the paradox of scale

authority. Chapter 2 will detail both the types of evidence that might be found at both the local and global scales for accountability and capacity, as well as how an NGO can be simultaneously authoritative and ineffective.

This book draws on qualitative data from three case studies of three transnational NGOs working in the conservation field in Southeast Asia and the Pacific: Conservation International's work in Milne Bay, Papua New Guinea (PNG); the International Marinelife Alliance in the Philippines; and the Community Conservation Network (CCN) working in the Republic of Palau. At the time of selection, each organization chosen for study worked transnationally, and experienced varied and changing degrees of power and legitimate authority. More frankly put, each case study organization was brought to my attention because, depending upon who you asked, their authority ran the gamut from being a consummate authority in its field to being completely unaccountable and ineffective. This variation on the dependent variable initially drew my attention, but the variation on authority that each case demonstrated over time made them particularly helpful in overcoming selection bias (Geddes 1990; Collier, Mahoney, and Seawright 2004). Since "the strongest means of drawing inferences from case studies is the use of a combination of within-case analysis and cross-case comparisons within a single study" (George and Bennett 2005, 18), the fact that each case demonstrates multiple manifestations of authority— broad-based authority, local authority, or global authority—was particularly helpful not only in observing how organizations maneuver between these types of authority, but also in creating conceptual clarity for the paradox of scale. An important aspect of within-case analysis is that the cases come with their own built-in counterfactual. While the qualitative research here does not test causal relationships, the theory of this book was created by examining the variables that made authority (the dependent variable) different in time one, time two, and time three of each case study. Thus, we can see in the same case study the affirmative of NGO authority and its counterfactual.

These three organizations also exhibit differences and similarities that are important to explain NGO authority. As table 1.1 shows, these cases have a range of sizes, staffing levels, funding, and initial scale of focus, in addition to authority types over time. Where CI began its work in PNG with global authority, IMA and CCN started with local authority and expanded.

Table 1.1
Case selection

NGO	Location of project	Initial scale of authority	Budget (USD)*	Number of staff	Year established	Initial type of authority
Conservation International	Milne Bay, Papua New Guinea	Global	$92 million	800	1987	Delegated
International Marinelife Alliance	Manila, Philippines	Local	$1.9 million	120	1984	Entrepreneurial
Community Conservation Network	Helen Reef, Palau	Local	$800,000	12	1998	Delegated

*Budget and staff at time of case selection

There are also key differences between IMA and CCN, including size of the budget and staff, and their organizational ages. IMA's authority was initially entrepreneurial, with no source delegating authority over governance of the live reef fish trade. CI and CCN began with delegated authority from various states and local governments, but still had to legitimize their power to other actors. These differences broadened my understanding of NGO authority and the various conditions that help create and dismantle it.

The evidence for the paradox of scale was triangulated with primary and secondary sources. Primary data comes from over one hundred interviews conducted over the course of two years (2006–2008), with rich detail provided in person by sources from Port Moresby and multiple villages in Milne Bay, Papua New Guinea; from Manila and Puerto Princesa, Philippines; from Koror and Hatohobei villages in Palau; and from practitioner offices in Honolulu and Washington, DC (see Interview Sources). This work is also informed by years of internal memoranda and communications from the case study organizations, as well as the organizations' external documents (e.g., funding reports, publications) and press coverage of the cases.

The puzzle that inspires this research was drawn from NGOs in all fields. The problems outlined in this book are often seen by NGOs whose work transcends scales, or whose mission focuses on both advocacy and service delivery, and policy creation and implementation. The efforts to balance quarterly reporting to multiple funders while building meaningful relationships with village chiefs, as experienced in Milne Bay and Palau, echo the efforts of the Humanitarian Accountability Partnership International at the turn of this century (Deloffre 2016). The difficulties of "scaling up" successful programs, as the International Marinelife Alliance experienced, have plagued interventions to provide potable water, to increase educational outcomes by deworming students, and countless other initiatives that were developed for one community and quickly funded to be expanded to hundreds of other communities (Hobbes 2014). Issues of going to scale are also felt by domestic nonprofits (like City Year and Lift) as they replicate their programs in other cities and become actors on the national policy scene (Bradach 2003; Fenton 2010). The urgent pressure to have measureable results toward fulfilling an organization's mission when your mission focuses on broad, long-term change is felt in NGOs focused on woman's equality, socioeconomic development, youth empowerment, democracy, education, and just about every other social issue marginalized communities face.

The cases in this book, however, are decidedly focused on transnational nongovernmental organizations with missions concerning environmental causes and in particular conservation, thus generalizing conclusions to the broader world of nongovernmental organization actors would be premature. The typologies of capacity, accountability, and authority emerged from these particular set of data but hopefully the concepts ring true to scholars and practitioners who focus on NGOs in other fields. These concepts serve analytical purposes not only for scholarship, but also for practitioners. I offer this model so that scholars and practitioners in humanitarian relief, development, and other fields can turn this analytical framework toward their own work and assess its validity in the broader context.

Plan of the Book

While the purpose of this introduction was to briefly introduce the theoretical framework I use to explain NGO authority, chapter 2 will go into further detail to explain the cobweb of theoretical concepts in which NGOs operate. It will review the historical growth of NGOs as actors in governance, and clearly define and draw lines between and among the concepts of authority, power, influence, and legitimacy. It will explain why capacity and accountability work as proxy concepts for power and legitimacy, offering typologies for how these concepts change over scales. Building on these two typologies, chapter 2 will offer a third typology that delineates the different authority states for NGOs based on the argument that legitimizing factors for NGOs change in different scales. In doing all this, chapter 2 does the heavy theoretical lifting to back up the argument laid out in the previous pages.

Each empirical chapter of this book explores a different reaction to the paradox of scale. Chapter 3 demonstrates a classic example of how an NGO can start with global authority, build broad-based authority, and then struggle with the paradox of scale. Focusing on Conservation International's work in Milne Bay, Papua New Guinea, this case exemplifies how an actor's capacity and prowess at the global scale systematically undermines its ability to be accountable and effect change on the ground. CI demonstrated global, legitimate authority by setting the priorities for conservation research and through successful fundraising, including securing funding as the first NGO to be an executing agency of a project funded by the Global Environment Facility (GEF), an intergovernmental organization and the world's largest funder of environmental efforts. These accomplishments helped it gain access to very remote areas of coral reef, and earned CI authority over marine conservation in Milne Bay, delegated to it by the GEF member countries and the government of Papua New Guinea. As CI began its work in Milne Bay in 1997, it was careful to involve local stakeholders in the project through building local oversight boards and other processes of local engagement that mirrored the communities' norms. As a result, the NGO developed broad-based authority in the first few years of the project. Over time, however, the program began to come apart at the seams. This chapter will trace CI's efforts to exercise authority at the global and local scales from 1997 to 2005, as well as detail how the dynamics of this paradox undermined this broad-based authority through the project's inflexibly urgent deadlines, inappropriately universal reporting requirements, and global norms of management. Unable to effect lasting change on the ground in Milne Bay, Conservation International left the Milne Bay Province in 2005, five years before the project was slated to end.

While the CI case study is a classic demonstration of a globally focused NGO struggling after expanding to a new locale, the International Marinelife Alliance (IMA) story in chapter 4 explores how this paradox manifests when an organization with local authority tries to extend its operations on the global scale. IMA, which focused on combating destructive fishing practices in the Philippines, was a powerful actor, wielding entrepreneurial authority on the local stage. As it grew to become a more globally focused organization, it tried to resist the dangers in the paradox of scale. There were specific practices that helped make IMA successful at the local scale and garner attention at the global scale: long-term relationship building with fishing communities, engagement with broader stakeholder groups, and responsiveness to local needs even when they may not be directly on mission. None of these practices, however, helped IMA become effective in the global arena. Moreover, its attempts to build global capacity to operate within global norms of conservation inhibited its effectiveness on the ground. As the grip of the global scale became more powerful on the organization, the executive director's grip on the organization also became tighter, turning decision-making processes opaque and starkly delineating the differences between how IMA operated locally and how the actors at the global scale wanted it to operate. This chapter will explore this dynamic, which culminated in 2001, when the delayed release of major funding from United States Agency for International Development (USAID) intensified this local-global dilemma for IMA's leaders. They could conform to global accountability norms and lose trained staff, jeopardize their surviving staff's financial well-being, and seriously delay the program, or they could refuse these standards and use restricted funds from another program's grants to cover the salaries that were supposed to be funded by USAID. When it came to light that IMA's executive director chose the latter option, the International Marinelife Alliance was forced to close its doors.

Chapter 5 tells another story of a small, locally focused NGO that was able to maintain its broad-based authority until it endeavored to shift its focus to the global scale. Even with delegated authority from the state government, the Community Conservation Network had to legitimize its power on the local scale. Like IMA, CCN began resisting global norms that then expedited their exiting the global scale altogether. CCN began in 1998 with the goal of conserving the Helen Reef atoll contained in the Hato-hobei state of the small island Republic of Palau. It succeeded in engaging the community at both traditional and bureaucratic levels while also bringing in specific forms of global capacity, which created a reputation of broad-based authority for conservation. The organization soon began to expand to the United States (in Hawaii) and other countries. This global expansion was accompanied by calls for more global administrative capacity in Hawaii and the funders. At the same time, the organization's local authority had created an environment where local leaders demanded more control of the program, and more face-to-face interaction with CCN's leadership. CCN's funders and staff demanded more organizational structure and policy to conform with global norms of administrative capacity, the creation of which required CCN's leadership to be away from Palau and in the Honolulu office more often. Moreover, these policies and procedures created an inflexibility in CCN's modus operandi that was seen as directly conflicting with local accountability norms. Whether deliberately or unconsciously, when given the choice of continuing its modus operandi or converting to more global capacity and norms, key leadership members repeatedly chose the local scale over the global, eventually causing the dissolution of the organization but not its programs, which continue as their own local organizations to this day.

There is much to be learned from these three nongovernmental organizations' struggles with taking their operations to scale while building and maintaining broad-based authority. Each case demonstrated an increase in authority from solely the global or local level. As the organizations grew, they balanced the global and local accountability demands and exerted capacity on each level. In doing so, they demonstrated broad-based authority. Chapter 6 will explore important organizational and systemic elements that lead to this authority as well as how various actors promoted global norms that brought about the paradox of scale. By comparing the time periods when these NGOs balanced scalar demands, the time periods when this balance was consistently challenged, and the time period when authority was lost, chapter 6 will review the theory and operationalization of the paradox of scale, and how it developed over time. It will examine broad-based authority in each case and review the lessons these NGO experiences offer on how bridging capacity—and as a result broad-based authority—was built, maintained, and eroded over time. Next, in an effort to assess the robustness of the theoretical framework proposed in this book, I direct a critical eye to my argument and examine potential alternative explanations for the difficulties these NGOs experience with authority and effectiveness. This chapter also examines the implications these cases, theory, and methods might have for the study of nongovernmental organizations in international relations and across other disciplines that contribute to our understanding of these complex actors. In doing this, chapter 6 highlights new areas of research for scholars of transnational actors to further expand our understanding of the paradox of scale, and strengthen efforts to dismantle it.

At the core of this book is the idea that nongovernmental organizations are complex actors that operate within a cobweb of multiple concepts, scales, and actors. Focusing on just one concept (capacity, accountability, legitimacy, authority, or power), on one scale (the global or the local), or on one relationship (funders, the state, local communities) may illuminate one strand of that cobweb, but it will not necessarily reveal how these concepts, scales, and actors *affect each other*. By better understanding the connections between these concepts, the dynamic nature of the relationships between actors, concepts, and scales, and how NGOs are shaped by individuals, organizations, and the norms of the organizational fields, NGOs can begin to navigate the divide between scales that confounds their work and to build the broad-based authority they need to participate in governance. Equipped with this knowledge, nongovernmental organizations can begin to create durable progress toward their mission, and lasting change to solve the world's most pressing problems.

2 A Theory of NGO Authority

When tragedy occurs in some far-off place, we expect to see certain nongovernmental organizations (NGOs) respond. When issues arise and local events become global concerns, we look to certain NGOs to provide services to those locales and keep the rest of the globe informed. Is an epidemic like Ebola taking hold of a region? Doctors Without Borders (MSF) will inoculate the community and care for the ill. Did a hurricane or tsunami just ravage a coast, reducing its infrastructure to nil? The Red Cross will help affected populations survive and rebuild. A crucial election? Endangered species? Extreme poverty? Call the Carter Center, the World Wildlife Fund, and CARE (respectively).

These NGOs have become household names, even if our particular household has had no interaction with them (Jepson 2005). We know about them because we see them in the news; they sponsor 5K races; and their representatives speak as experts on news programs. Global leaders talk about them and consult with them. Celebrities and business entrepreneurs sit on their boards. And, with no one government assigned to the task and few able to quickly dispatch this high level of expertise to remote areas in need, these groups seem the best equipped to take on these issues.

Our first impulse is to call for their expertise, not wonder if their particular expertise is suitable for the job or the communities in crisis. That line of questioning comes once the complaints start trickling in. Most dramatically, we hear stories accusing relief workers in Haiti of starting cholera epidemics or making millions off the tragedy of others (Hrabe 2014); or of environmental groups around the globe employing unethical business practices or partnering with unethical businesses (Stephens and Ottaway 2003); or of the improbability that the money you donated for the 9/11 response will actually leave your home state and reach its intended recipients (Attkisson

2002). These scenarios are often invoked in discussions of NGO account-ability and effectiveness. They call into question these organizations' legiti-macy and authority. These are the cases that catch the public's imagination and ire.

Less dramatic, but perhaps more frustrating to the millions of NGO workers across the globe, are the concerns that, even after following the processes the world has set out for them, NGOs do not seem to be creat-ing the lasting change on the ground that they need to achieve their mis-sions and solve the problems they are charged with solving (McKeever and Gaddy 2016). Regardless of the $16.3 billion raised in the first three years, and the estimated nine thousand NGOs mobilized to work in Haiti since the 2010 earthquake, most of the 1.5 million displaced people are still liv-ing in tents among the rubble and cholera has reached epidemic propor-tions due to lack of clean water and sanitation (Rodgers 2013; Katz 2013; Jones 2015). In the environmental realm, "despite the large investments in the last twenty years—the thousands of projects and trained professionals and billions of dollars spent—progress in conservation on the ground has been slow and erratic" (Jepson 2005, 517). International experts in democ-racy building cannot seem to change corrupt practices of government offi-cials in Kenya, Peru, and hundreds of other countries.[1] The world's leading doctors struggle to change local burial practices to stop the spread of the Ebola virus (Maxmen 2015).

For both practitioners and scholars, this is truly puzzling. These nongov-ernmental organizations seem to wield authority in a multitude of ways. They have staff and boards composed of the world's foremost experts and billions of dollars in funding. Scholars tout NGOs as the most appropriate type of organization to tackle these issues—with the flexibility of business but the public good as their primary goal. They follow the rules of their trade and report regular progress toward their missions. Despite all this, they continue to have their authority questioned by communities, states, and even other NGOs. Despite all this, these organizations cannot seem to create lasting change on the ground.

This book offers an explanation of this puzzle through an examina-tion of NGO authority across scale. The paradox of scale is plainly put, that the capacities and norms that create an NGO's authority in one scale will not help it build or maintain authority at another. Moreover, priori-tizing the norms or capacities of one scale while working in another will actually undermine NGO authority, and reduce its effectiveness. As chapter 1 argued, this paradox is an important dilemma, because in order to address the issues detailed in their missions in any meaningful way, NGOs often scale up their operations to work in new locales, increasing the number of contexts in which they operate and thus making themselves more susceptible to this limiting dynamic.

This chapter will build the theoretical argument to explain how scaling up operations causes a breakdown of authority for NGOs in general, and conservation NGOs in particular. Before explaining the paradox of scale, I begin by briefly reviewing how the role of NGOs in governance has expanded, creating new questions about their authority to govern. Then I define and distinguish the concepts of power, legitimacy, and authority, and explain how these concepts will be demonstrated in the case studies through the use of proxy concepts. To do this, I further define and distinguish power and authority, and discuss how influence interacts with these concepts for NGOs. Next I detail the justification and process for converting power into legitimate authority. Since authority is legitimated power, the next sections will define and operationalize NGO authority through the concepts of capacity (as a proxy for power) and accountability (as a proxy for legitimacy). Because capacity, accountability, and authority change from scale to scale, this chapter offers typologies that distinguish each of these concepts by scale. These typologies give both theoretical traction to the paradox of scale as well as offer practical application of the concepts. Lest the reader lose hope for the role of NGOs in global governance, the last section of this chapter will discuss and define a potential antidote for the paradox of scale: bridging capacity. Based on the skills demonstrated by key actors in this book's case studies, the elements of bridging capacity helped balance local and global demands to resist the paradox of scale.

Governance and the Great Expanding NGO

Why do scholars, practitioners, communities, and government agencies seem to have this increased interest in NGO roles in governance? The past few decades have demonstrated a marked increase in the importance of NGOs. They have increased in number, size, funding, and global reach, all contributing to a change in their roles in governance. While the absolute size of the sector is difficult to quantify, the number of organizations has increased considerably in recent decades (Balboa 2017; Balboa and Delof-fre 2015; Jepson 2005, Kaldor, Anheier, and Glasius 2003; Anheier 2014). Almost every country has experienced a growth in its nonprofit sector in recent decades. In India alone the number of registered nonprofits has grown from 144,000 in 1970 to over 1.13 million in 2000 (Casey 2016, 22). The rise of the NGO sector is not just in quantity. On environmental, human rights and health issues, NGOs have garnered more of the public's trust than governments, corporations, and the media combined.[2] In addition to being the providers of direct public goods, NGOs are often seen as the connective tissue between national and international actors, states, and society, public and private, and conflict and cooperation (Demars and Dijkzeul 2015). Despite this, or perhaps because of it, there also seems to be a commensurate rise in questions about these actors' authority in governance from practitioners, citizens, and scholars alike.

There is a wealth of evidence that NGOs are growing in power and size, particularly in environmental governance. According to the Yearbook on International Organizations (YIO), in 2014 there were over thirty thousand international NGOs, a 20 percent increase in the past twenty years (Union of International Associations 2014). In the 1990s, membership in NGOs more than doubled in the world's middle income countries and increased by a third in both high-income and low-income countries (SustainAbility 2001). The number of NGOs with consultative status to the UN increased from forty-one in 1946 to over forty-one hundred in 2014 (Balboa and Del-offre 2015). The sector's financial weight is substantial as well. The NGO sector in New York City alone generates over $4 billion in revenue per year (Balboa, Berman, and Welton 2015). Even seventeen years ago, the global nonprofit sector was valued at more than $1 trillion in worth annually (SustainAbility 2001), indicating clearly that states are not the only actors in governance.

Looking specifically at the growth of environmental NGOs, Longhofer and Schofer (2010) demonstrated an increase since the 1970s in both domestic and internationally focused environmental NGOs in both the industrialized world (with a 300 percent increase in domestic environmental NGOs and a marked increase in international ones) and the developing world (increasing its domestic environmental NGOs and quadrupling its international ones).

Trends in funding environmentally focused NGOs are also pertinent to the argument in this book, since with these funds NGOs exercise their authority in the creation and implementation of conservation rules. The Global Environment Facility (the largest public funder of projects aimed to improve the global environment) has more than quadrupled its funding to NGOs since its inception in 1992 (from $20.94 million to $89.8 million) with the number of projects given to NGOs increasing more than fivefold (Balboa 2017). Private foundation funding in the United States to environmental NGOs increased almost four times between 1987 and 2012, reaching $1.3 billion. The majority of these grants were given to organizations in California, Washington, DC, and New York, which house the headquarters for several NGOs that work on global conservation. In addition to funding U.S.-based NGOs, these same foundations granted $125 million directly to environmental NGOs outside the United States (Balboa 2017).

The annual revenues of the three largest U.S.-based ENGOs (environmental NGOs) also rose considerably between 2004 and 2014. In just a decade, Conservation International increased its revenues from $92.2 million to $164.8 million (Conservation International 2005, 2015a); TNC increased its revenues from $865.8 million to $1.11 billion (TNC 2004, 2015); and the WWF more than doubled its revenue from $126.3 million to $266.3 million (WWF 2005, 2015). These numbers indicate that environmental NGOs are being delegated more authority (in the case of funding from the GEF [Global Environment Facility]) or are creating entrepreneurial authority (in the case of private foundation funding) in environmental governance.

Our understanding of NGOs in governance is only starting to fully map the complexity of these actors. While studies of nonprofits have tried to neatly contain these organizations in either service provider or advocacy roles, these categories blur together as organizations become hybrids in order to achieve their missions (Minkoff 2002; Anasti and Moseley 2009). They advocate to create global conventions and agreements, but then often become the implementers of those conventions and agreements. That NGOs focus on solving the social and ecological issues at both global and local scales has allowed these organizations to take on multiple roles— advocating on behalf of local communities at the global level, and implementing interventions at the local level that are mandated by the global policy arena (Balboa 2014). It is the nature of NGOs to defy the local/

global, service provider/advocacy, and public/private dichotomies (Demars and Dijkzeul 2015); this defiance of category is also what pulls these well-intending actors into the dynamics of the paradox.

NGO Authority: Justification and Assessment

As the previous section indicates, NGOs are definitely increasing their role in governance. In this book, I focus on NGO authority as a concept to explain NGO experience transnationally. Chapter 1 offered these brief definitions and distinctions for concepts of power, influence, and authority: "power" is the ability or capacity of an actor to achieve the outcomes it desires (Giddens 1984, 257; Jinnah 2014, 43; Koppell 2010); authority is the legitimated power that allows an entity to create, implement, or enforce "rules, standards, guidelines, or practices that other actors adopt" (Green 2014, 6).[3] To these definitions, I add that influence is another specific type of power that helps create authority by mobilizing power to realize an outcome (Jinnah 2014, 42). This section will more deeply explore these conceptual distinctions and then build on them to argue why NGOs must legitimate their power to create authority and not just rely on influence to create change. Next, I explore how the concepts of capacity and accountability can work as proxy concepts for legitimate power. In these sections, I propose a typology of these concepts to demonstrate how they change over scale and, thus, so do the requirements of authority.

Distinguishing Forms of NGO Power

Because the terms "power," "authority," and "influence" are related concepts, they are often invoked by scholars of governance. But different research projects define terms differently. Some might conflate or combine terms that others see the need to distinguish. The result can be confusing. How do we avoid conflating the concepts of power, authority, and influence for NGOs? The historic fuzzy boundaries of these concepts are a result of a few dynamics in academia. First, the field of international relations has only recently included nonstate actors in its power analyses. As a result of the state-centric focus on power, much of the international relations literature on NGOs focuses on influence—lobbying governments, persuading citizens and donors—rather than authority. The idea of nonstate actors as authorities has only been developed since the turn of the millennium. Second, the concepts of power, influence, and authority—as bedrock concepts of political science—have long, debated histories of definitional and causal theory, which creates confusion when applying them to these new actors. Which conceptual definition of power is most empirically accurate and theoretically rigorous to apply to NGOs? Which definitions of influence and authority are most helpful? Third, the distinction of these concepts is somewhat difficult to operationalize. How does one measure power? After all, some of these concepts refer to latent capacities. Without witnessing their attempts to exert power, or the outcomes of those efforts, how does one know power exists?

The differences between these concepts, however, are essential for this study on NGO authority. One cannot assess the durable effect of NGOs in governance unless we know whether we are examining their right to create rules or their effectiveness of lobbying other actors who make the rules. As their definitions above indicate, this is one clear difference between influence and authority.[4] To help understand the boundaries of these concepts, I raise three distinguishing measures to clarify authority and influence as two specific forms of power.

The first distinction, as I just mentioned, is between latent or potential action versus a mobilization of that potential. Power and authority (as a specific form of power) are concepts that seem more constitutive and latent where influence is the exercise of that power to realize outcomes (Jinnah 2014). As Jinnah succinctly summarizes, the concept of influence helps us understand how an actor mobilizes power to impact outcomes, where the concept of authority is more constitutive and helps us understand *why* actors are able to influence. Power helps us understand when influence matters: is influence exerted over big or small issues, over large or small swaths of the populace? Affirming our definition of "power" as the ability or capacity to achieve desired outcomes, to possess power one must possess the capacity to persuade, influence, or otherwise compel others to act. To extend this analysis, influence is about impact, power is about when impact matters, and authority is about why actors are allowed to create impact.

NGOs do influence many kinds of actors in governance. In fact, the evidence of many of the capacities in this book's cases is clear because these NGOs mobilized their capacity to effect change. However, equally important to the explanations of NGO authority are the examples where NGOs did not influence an outcome. Where the field of international relations often asks "Why and when do NGOs matter?," just as important are the instances where the NGO theoretically possessed the power or capacity but failed to make an impact. Indeed, most critical to the development of the paradox of scale are the instances where the NGO exerted power but failed to influence because it exerted the wrong kind of authority for the scale. In other words, the NGO tried to use its capacity, or power, to create an impact, or influence, but failed because it lost authority by not adhering to the norms of the scale in which it was working.

The second distinction reflects the level of routinization of power. Green's treatise on private authority has advanced our thinking by clearly defining private authority specifically as rules creation, implementation, or enforcement by nonstate actors (Green 2014). Thus, authority is a distinct form of power not just because it is legitimated but also because it focuses on the creation, implementation, and enforcement of rules that others follow because of this legitimacy. Influence may change behavior, but this behavior change may not be systematic and routinized; it can be ad hoc or opportunistic. This distinction has important implications for governance, since influence is not necessarily about rules creation, implementation, or enforcement, but can be about a single act of an individual actor. Actors may influence governance without governing themselves, but actors with authority have the right to govern and do so by creating, implementing, or enforcing rules.

The third distinction comes from Baldwin (2002) who argued that discussions on authority, or power in any form, require consideration of the scope (what parts of behavior are affected by the authority) and domain (the number of actors subject to the authority) over which it is exercised. Skepticism over whether or not NGOs have substantial power in world politics or can be considered authorities in governance can be explained by considering these parameters. I do not claim that NGOs are rule-making authorities for all environmental governance. They do not have ultimate say in what is written in multilateral environmental agreements (MEAs) around the globe. They can merely exert influence on this scope and domain. However, if we consider how these MEAs are interpreted, implemented, and enforced, we can see NGOs do wield authority in the creation of environmental programs on the ground, in locales with rich and threatened biodiversity. To explicitly connect the theory of power with the experience of NGOs and the growth imperative, this book asserts that to understand how NGO authority operates, we must examine how it changes in different scales, reflecting the parameters of scope and domain.

These distinct forms of power interact. For conservation NGOs, this interaction of power, influence, and authority over global and local scales represents the breadth of their work. At the global scale, these NGOs inform debates where they influence policymakers in the creation of the goals of global conservation agreements. They influence by using their expertise. Once those agreements are created, however, the expertise of NGOs is relied upon to interpret, implement, and enforce governance rules at specific locales. At the global level, NGOs create large-scale programs that decide how conservation is done. At the local scale, these same organizations work in resource-dependent communities to implement these programs. For example, the NGO WildAid published research on the trade of the world's most trafficked animal: pangolins. This research was used on the global scale to successfully lobby members of the Convention on International Trade in Endangered Species of Wild Fauna and Flora (CITES) to bar trade of all eight pangolin species. On the local scale, WildAid now works to raise awareness and strengthen enforcement efforts of this ban in China and Vietnam (WildAid 2016). When large global funders of conservation like the Global Environment Facility and private foundations look to NGOs to implement the agreements of global conservation, they are giving these NGOs authority to interpret the agreements for a specific locale, thus creating, implementing, and perhaps enforcing the rules of resource governance. However, delegating authority is not as simple as a state funding a program. Indeed, the phenomenon of NGOs working in different scales complicates authority because the requirements of authority change in different scales. An NGO being funded and having delegated authority by a national government does not necessarily mean local resource users will automatically consent or even comply with changes in resource rules. Applying the concepts of power, authority, and influence across scale creates complications and opportunities for more accurately understanding NGO authority.

The Stability of Legitimate Authority as a Form of Power

Why do NGOs need to legitimate their power? Before answering that specifically for NGOs, let's examine why legitimate authority is a more sta-
ble expression of power in general. In order for an actor to achieve the
outcomes it desires, it will have to mobilize its capacity and have other
actors conform to its will. There are two paths to conformity that these
others (e.g., diplomats, government representatives, community members, funders, other NGOs) can take: compliance or consent. Compliance
is achieved by coercion, force, or manipulation, based on the threat or act
of physical or psychological violence or economic sanctions (Ribot 2002;
Lukes 1974). Authority, on the other hand, achieves conformity in the form
of consent by other actors. To wield authority and achieve consent, one
must be acknowledged as being legitimate in that role, of having the right
to that power. Thus, coercion seeks compliance while legitimate authority
seeks consent (Krieger 1977).

For NGO and non-NGO alike, power demonstrated through compliance
is a fickle endeavor. It is evident when actors have a conflict of wills, usually over values or a course of action, and one wins out over the other
(Lukes 1974). Economists suggest that compliance by coercion is only sta-
ble when an optimum level of coercion is achieved. Too little coercion and
the rewards and sanctions are not powerful enough to ensure the actions
of others. Too much coercion—and in particular too many sanctions—will
make the enforcement seem capricious. After all, what's the use in comply-
ing when one can be punished even if one follows the rules of those in
power? Thus, too much coercion will not ensure compliance either. What's
more, once the optimum coercion level is attained for compliance, the
agent of power cannot waiver; a reduction in coercion is likely to precipi-
tate collapse of the relationship altogether (Harrison 2001). It is difficult to
maintain power that is rooted in anything other than legitimate authority.
This authority is durable because it is often seen as the routinization of
power (Koppell 2010).

When most people think of coercion, they imagine violence and punishment, but there is much more to the concept than that. Financial rewards
also qualify as coercion. They are often given to incentivize a certain behavior, and to further complicate matters, their absence can also qualify as a
punishment. In other words, coercion can also come in a monetary form.
Like the threat of violence, economic coercion (the carrots and sticks of

economic aid/sanctions between countries) and financial incentives on an individual basis are seen as artificial motivations since once the threat of punishment or the incentive of reward vanish, so too does the motivation to comply (Kohn 1993). Thus, for actors who take a coercive approach to power, compliance is most often fleeting.

As a correction for the fickle nature of coercion, democratic governments demonstrate both the power of their military or police and the processes of elections and policymaking that signal legitimacy. In the absence of legitimate authority, NGOs have been known to display force from time to time,[5] but more often these "illegitimate" NGOs employ economic coercion to achieve compliance toward their missions. That is, they might offer funding to make something happen in a community: build latrines, employ locals, and travel to the local capital to make the local community's needs known to a larger audience. The activities under this form of coercion may or may not directly support the NGO's mission, but all are offered to the community if its members comply with that mission. These interactions are exchange-based and, when the currency dries up, so does the compliance.

What NGOs really want is durable change. They want to "tackle the root causes of poverty and create lasting solutions";[6] or to "stop the degradation of the natural environment and to build a future in which humans live in harmony with nature."[7] They want to accomplish these missions beyond a limited financial interaction with a community. To attain durable change, NGOs need to be seen as an authority (Beisham and Dingwerth 2008), with missions and processes aligning with local norms. They must seek consent rather than compliance. In this way, legitimacy is seen as a top asset for NGOs (Jepson 2005; Cooley and Kohl 2006).

But legitimate authority is a difficult concept to evaluate for governments, much less for NGOs. How does one assess legitimate authority for nonstate actors? This question has recently received much attention in international relations (Cashore, Auld, and Newsome 2004; Green 2014; Auld 2014; Stroup and Wong 2017), where scholars have employed both qualitative and quantitative methods to explore the questions surrounding authority for nonstate actors. Adding to this work, this book asserts that the use of capacity and accountability as proxies for power and legitimacy (respectively) can help analyze the presence of authority for NGOs.

Capacity and Scale: A Framework for Assessing Power

While capacity is regularly invoked in definitions of "power," the sheer volume of implications for the word capacity can be overwhelming. This section briefly explores different disciplinary implications of "power" before offering a typology that integrates this variation. I identify three different types of capacity, which I apply in both scales to demonstrate how power will be assessed in this book's empirical chapters.

The broad definition of "capacity" sounds fairly close to the broad definition of "power": it is the ability to achieve some collective purpose (Brinkerhoff and Morgan 2010). Perhaps building on the state-centered discussion of power, recent studies of NGO diplomacy have also equated power with capacity (Baldwin 2002; Jinnah 2014; Betsill and Correll 2008). The word "capacity" has a wide range of implications across different specialties and among different populations. It can mean something different to those with different goals, such as managing a store or growing crops or completing a degree. "Capacity" can also have different implications in different scholarly specialties. For example, it usually refers to state sovereignty in international relations; in management, it refers to more concrete skills needed for an organization to function; in public policy, it refers to a middle ground of categories ranging from the broad survivability of organizations to the specific financial management of them. "Capacity" can also mean different things to people operating at different scales (Fukuda-Parr, Lopes, and Malik 2002; Steinberg 2001; Balboa 2014; Honadle 1981). Consider, for example, how the fundraising capacity differs for a nonprofit addressing issues of public health in a small town (where many individuals might be solicited for smaller donations) versus one working on the same issue at a global scale (where one bilateral institution might fund the entire organization).

Drawing on Balboa 2014, this book's theoretical framework suggests three fundamental types of capacities for achieving outcomes on any scale: political capacity, administrative capacity, and technical capacity. All three are required for any organization or group of organizations working on the same issue to function and be successful. The more capacities an actor has (whether an individual or an organization), the more power it has to affect change.

• *Political capacity* refers to relations with outside individuals and organizations and includes politics in the sense of the contestation of ideas. Within any network, various actors jockey for access, exposure, and resources. Political capacities reflect an actor's ability to interact deliberately with others and manage external relationships. It also reflects an understanding of the processes of communication, decision-making, and collaboration on a network level. In this category, actors strive to sell their ideas and norms to other actors.

• *Administrative capacity* addresses the internal management skills needed to function as an individual or organization, such as financial reporting, strategic planning, payroll and accounting, and internal communication. Actors must have these skills to fulfill the organization's strategic niche in the network.

• *Technical capacity* involves the ability of an individual, organization, or network to access information and to do the work of its mission. It is the capacity to understand whatever scientific, resource, legal, and technological factors influence an actor's ability to fulfill its mission. For a health NGO, this technical capacity includes an understanding of medicine. For a human rights organization, this might include understanding the laws that protect or violate those rights.

There is considerable overlap and interdependence between these three categories. One capacity is often directly contingent upon the other two. Understanding the legal framework of a network (i.e., political capacity) also affects an NGO's capacity to manage its finances and contracts (i.e., administrative capacity), which in turn impacts its ability to raise more funds (i.e., political and administrative capacity). An organization's reporting and evaluation capacity can also impact the level of fundraising. Without political and communication capacities, an organization cannot fully understand local resource use, a required technical capacity for conservation. The dynamic nature of these types of capacities becomes even more evident in the empirical cases of this book. Because of this interdependence, lack of any one of these types of capacity could greatly limit an NGO's ability to exert power.

These three types of NGO capacity manifest differently at the global and local scales (see table 2.1).[8] Moreover, investments in global and local NGO capacity are often mutually exclusive due to the limited resources for the NGO. Building political capacity to influence the creation of global agreements will not likely help an NGO influence a local chief's agreement with provincial government agencies. The technical capacity to contain a

Table 2.1
Norms of capacity types over scales

Capacity		Global scale	Local scale
Capacity	Political	• Fundraising from bilaterals, foundations, multilaterals • Global media networks • International and intergovernmental legal processes for conflict resolution • Ethical debates on global conservation, development, human rights • International treaties and conventions • Foreign aid processes • UN languages	• Understanding of local views on partnership, accountability, leadership, and legitimacy • Partnering with local groups and organizations • Facility with local conflict resolution processes • Ability to work with, within, or alongside local governance and tenure processes (chiefdoms, clans, etc.) • Local languages • Communication processes and venues • Local history with other cultures, and NGOs
	Administrative	• Vision, mission and strategy of global organizations • Reporting requirements and processes • Contractual norms and Memoranda of Understanding • Internal capacity building to adapt to global changes in professional norms • Global accounting norms and laws • Leadership and governance approaches	• Local view of obligation/contracts • Internal capacity building, culturally appropriate employment practices, and professional development • Audience analysis capability to create appropriate reporting requirements • Domestic accounting practices and tax laws • Local approaches to work, management, and professionalism
	Technical	• Globally accepted approaches to the issue, including Western science • International policy processes and mandates • Global norms of practice for the field • Global development norms and best practices	• Local status of the issue (e.g., resource status, resource use) • Ability to acquire local data on the issue (e.g., monitoring) • Cultural ideas about nature, philanthropy, leadership, human rights, government, public health, and business practices

disease in a local village will be very different from the technical capacity to track and reduce the disease's movement globally (Balboa and Deloffre 2015). Operations and management norms are distinct at every local scale, and how an organization operates in those localities will likely be very different from how it operates at its global headquarters. Because of the importance of scope (i.e., which part of the actor's behavior one wants to impact), domain (i.e., how many actors will be impacted), and scale (i.e., whether the actors to be impacted are local or global) on the exercise of power, this book uses a typology of capacity that recognizes and builds on these differences. By specifying how capacity changes by scale, this typology connects the ideas of power as a resource (or capacity) and power as a relationship (with each relationship having different requirements).

The relationship between the local and global scale is important for an NGO to exercise authority and achieve its mission. The ideas and interventions created at the global level are implemented at the local level—in households, villages, and towns. The local scale is where bottom-up approaches meet top-down policies, the results of which offer incredible variety depending upon the capacity of the NGO. It is at this level that NGOs with global implementation authority have had the most difficulty. Household-name organizations like Doctors Without Borders and other humanitarian NGOs experience "significant failures in contingency planning, ... in site planning, in information sharing and in redirecting programs to respond to new needs" in refugee crises in Sudan, the Democratic Republic of the Congo, and Jordan (Healy and Tiller 2014). Education NGOs aim to reduce inequality of opportunity in poor countries, but often find their programs reproducing these very disparities through elite capture of their services (Yershova, DaJaeghere, and Mestenhauser 2000). Conversely, local or national NGOs working successfully to provide childcare and protection in Indonesia, Ghana, and Mexico were skeptical of creating partnerships with global NGOs. As the international NGO EveryChild found out when discussing organizational structure with local partners, "international NGOs poach staff, dominate forums, and take all the credit for work created, designed and delivered" by these smaller, in-country NGOs (Feuchtuang 2014). All this indicates a troubled relationship between global and local capacities.

This book asserts that the pull toward the global scale of capacity is more powerful than the pull toward developing local capacity. The global scale, where these NGOs often demonstrate the most capacity, reflects the norms from the nations and even localities that dominate the policy arena. As one moves from the global to the local, the norms diversify to reflect the heterogeneity of multiple countries and localities. More details about the scales begin to emerge upon their empirical application. While funding sources are prevalent at the global scale, they are less available domestically (Ron, Pandya, and Crow 2016). Concepts like partnership, obligation, leadership, nature, philanthropy, communication, work, exchange, and business can be interpreted differently at each scale. Because of these differing interpretations, the same organization needs to adjust its operations in different contexts. This homogeneous nature of the global scale—with one overriding set of definitions and interpretations—is part of what makes prioritizing it attractive; it is easier to build one set of capacities than multiple sets for each locale.

It is important to note that over time the norms on each scale change, altering the definitions of certain capacities and reprioritizing them. These changes in norms demand different technical, administrative, and political capacities. For example, the diffusion of for-profit business management practices in nonprofit management changed the required administrative capacities for NGOs, which is reflected in the growing percentage of ENGO boardmembers that work in the private sector. The current chief executive officers of The Nature Conservancy and WWF-US are not scientists but rather leaders in finance and business (Hance 2016). Another example of changing norms is "Western science." Placing this concept at the global scale does not mean this research is promoting it as a global norm or that it is a permanent global technical capacity. Rather, current power structures and epistemological hierarchies that rank it as a global capacity may change as norms change (Elgert 2011). Both scales are subject to a dynamic interaction of competing norms, which over time will change the focus of capacity at each scale. As actors work to diffuse norms of accounting, conservation, fundraising, language, and other subjects, they create normative priorities for specific kinds of capacity as demonstrated by the increased numbers of MBA-degree holders in conservation management positions, and the prevalence of social networking positions in environmental NGOs. Through the diffusion of these capacity norms, the scales interact and begin to reflect one another.

Sources of NGO Legitimacy

The typology presented in the previous section suggests how one might assess power for NGOs. Returning to our definition of "authority" as legitimated power, how do we know when that power has been legitimated? Legitimacy has been a popular concept in the study of global environmental governance as of late, and with good reason. As the traditional ways we once thought about governance shift—as environmental issues cross state boundaries and the lines between public and private and nonprofit and for-profit organizations blur—it makes sense that scholars and practitioners ask why actors obey other actors.

Like many concepts in international relations, legitimacy has only recently been applied to nonstate actors. Also, as is the case with so many concepts in IR, scholars have had to search beyond our current literature for a definition that fits the empirical phenomenon of NGOs. As the types of actors in global governance diversify, so too do the strategies for legitimizing their power. Nonstate market-driven institutions or certification schemes create and manage their legitimacy through interactions with the market (Cashore 2002). Intergovernmental organizations derive their legitimacy from an extended principal-agent relationship with the state and the legal delegation of authority. But NGO authority has its own complexities; it cannot be derived from the democratic, legal, or market bases of legitimacy. Moreover, since NGOs must derive their legitimacy from multiple other actors in different contexts, NGOs can simultaneously attain entrepreneurial or delegated authority while also having their authority questioned by other legitimizing actors.

In order to resolve this problem, this book, like the work of so much scholarship on governance, will look to the sociological definition of "legitimacy" (Bernstein 2011; Cashore 2002; Koppell 2010; Green 2014). This definition acknowledges multiple and diverse audiences of an actor while identifying the relevant political communities (Bernstein 2011). According to this definition, legitimacy occurs when "the actions of an entity are desirable, proper, or appropriate within some socially constructed system of norms, values, beliefs and definitions" (Suchman 1995, 574). It can come through deliberate normative approval of an actor's outcomes, processes, or personal charisma or through subconscious absence of any other legitimate alternatives. Remembering our definition of "authority" as legitimated power, this understanding of legitimacy suggests that an actor wields authority when others deem its actions desirable, proper, or appropriate due to either a normative approval of the outcome, the process, or the individual, or a failure to perceive any other alternatives (Suchman 1995). But how does an NGO make certain that its actions meet this approval? The next section suggests that in adhering to norms of accountability, NGOs ensure that their actions are indeed desirable, proper, or appropriate to other actors.

Accountability and Scale: A Framework for Assessing Legitimacy

I am not alone in linking the concept of accountability to legitimacy, as much of the literature on NGO legitimacy consistently links the ideas together. Some NGO scholars suggest that the concept of accountability arose as a reaction to questioning NGO legitimacy (Slim 2002). Others state that if civil society organizations are legitimate actors in global governance, then they need to be more accountable (Scholte 2004). NGO practitioners often invoke accountability as a means for an actor or an action to become legitimate (Kovach et al. 2003). This book uses accountability an indicator for NGOs' legitimacy in their new and expanding roles in governance. Accountability is broadly understood as the organization's "answerability," although to whom, for what, and how an NGO answers is unique for each organization.[9] As the social distance between actors in governance increases and the "closeness" once experienced between actors is diminished, the idea of accountability as an institutional element becomes more common (Gray, Bebbington, and Collison 2006). If legitimacy applies when an actor operates within a socially constructed system of norms, values, beliefs, and definitions, then accountability is the way one assures compliance to that system (Balboa 2015; Slim 2002). Where accountability is actor-centered and focuses on a particular relationship, legitimacy is more a quality of social or political order, based on a multitude of these accountability relationships (Risse 2005). From the vantage point of the power wielder, accountability can be viewed as a means to turn its power into legitimate authority; that is, to maintain the current power relationship based on consent rather than fickle compliance. At the same time, from the vantage point of those demanding accountability, it can be viewed as a means to ensure that others' power is used in a way that reflects the accountability agent's needs and desires; that is, as a tool to curb power. For both the powerful and the weak, therefore, accountability is an instrument for legitimating power (Balboa 2015).

An organization that adeptly answers the calls for accountability on a global scale may not be able to answer local calls for accountability in the same way. While most scholars and practitioners recognize that accountability relationships differ depending upon both the object and agent of accountability, there are some characteristics of accountability at the global and local scales that seem consistent.[10] I assert that these consistent traits are actually norms, derived empirically from the case studies and from the literature on NGO accountability. Through the delineation of these norms, I suggest that for an NGO to legitimate its power on the global or local scale, it must adhere to the accountability norms of that scale.

Accountability at the Global Scale

Accountability at the global scale is used by NGOs to gain legitimacy and thus sustain power by converting it to authority. Drawing on the NGO accountability "myopias" defined by Ebrahim (2005a) and expanded by DeMars (2015), I identify three NGO accountability norms at the global scale. While the details of NGO accountability may change from relationship to relationship, as noted in table 2.2, global accountability norms demand

(1) quantifiable, short-term reporting on work, with an emphasis on quick deadlines;
(2) a focus on the technical aspect of accountability (which does not allow for meaningful participation that might change the trajectory of the NGOs' work ex ante); and
(3) a primary focus on the demands of actors who have enough power in the relationship to make demands.

Adhering to these norms helps the NGO gain legitimacy at the global scale, giving it more funding, more exposure, and more power to operate around the globe.

The first global accountability norm involves an emphasis on short-term goals and evaluations, with quantifiable results rather than long-term social change (Ebrahim 2005a; Elbers and Arts 2011; Gourevitch and Lake 2012). Funders are increasingly introducing the process of outcome measurement to their grantees in a variety of NGOs (including grassroots organizing, social services, and neighborhood development) in hopes of improving effectiveness of those organizations (Benjamin 2008). Multiple studies from the dataset of the Transnational NGO Initiative also confirm this norm. Of the 152 NGOs included in the study, most executive directors saw organizational effectiveness as synonymous with outcome accountability—which is usually defined as "measurable progress towards specific outcomes" (Mitchell 2012, 333). While these efforts often track measurable results of their work, this emphasis tends to bring an air of financial accountability. Sixty-four percent of these same NGO leaders referred to their "accountability" in terms of financial management (Schmitz, Raggo, and Bruno-van Vijfeijken 2012) and another form of effectiveness as "overhead minimization" (Mitchell 2012). This quantified focus may be in part due to the length of grants given by funders. In a 2014 survey, the Grantmakers for Effective Organizations report that 58 percent of their funders gave multiyear grants at least sometimes and only 10 percent gave them always or almost always (McCray 2014). Even still, these multiyear grants often operate on short, two- to five-year timelines, giving grant makers control over NGO programming, and making NGOs liable for the objectives promised to funders. With grants to be renewed or initiated every few years, short-term quantifiable results remain the global accountability norm.

Second, accountability for NGOs on the global scale is fixated on technical approaches to political problems. Ebrahim (2005a) indicates that participatory processes are more about the demonstration of participation

Table 2.2
Accountability norms across scales

	Global scale	Local scale
Accountability norms	(1) quantifiable, short-term reporting with an emphasis on quick deadlines; (2) a focus on the technical aspect of accountability rather than political or ex ante accountability; and (3) a primary focus on the demands of actors who have enough power in the relationship to make demands.	(1) context-specific and flexible responses to local demands; (2) the development of long-term relationships; (3) a focus on the demands of a broad definition of "stakeholders"; (4) an emphasis on political changes to the operations, managem ent, and even the mission of the intervention; and (5) added focus on accountability of ex ante interactions.

than about sharing procedural power: "technical" participation in lieu of participation that changes the power dynamic of the network. This emphasis of technical support over political change undermines an NGO's ability to question the underlying causes of the problems their missions aspire to tackle, thus muting the increasing number and ubiquity of NGOs in governance (Banks, Hulme, and Edwards 2015). By focusing on service delivery and democracy promotion, these actors actually take attention away from the broader structural issues that cause the social ills they seek to address. This "taming" of the nonprofit sector (Bush 2015)—which results in what Stroup and Wong refer to as "vanilla victories" (2017)—is inexorably linked to the first global accountability norm, since technical changes are much easier to quantify and report on the short term than political and structural changes. It is a reasonably straightforward endeavor to report how many citizens were registered to vote or how many poor were given shelter. It is harder to demonstrate how the power structure in a given area is shifting to address inequalities of opportunity that, despite these numbers, lead to the same actors being voted into office, or the increasing chasm of realities between the poor and the rich. Some have even argued that addressing these root-level issues might lead to the shrinking of funding sources available for such NGO programs, since many of those sources (i.e., philanthropic foundations created by leaders of industry) were created as a positive externality of such inequality. After an inquiry about the future of civil society funded by the Carnegie UK Trust, chair Geoff Mulgan stated, "It's an irony that growing inequality could mean more money for philanthropy" (Mulgan 2007).

Third, global accountability norms also tend to focus on engaging the obvious and mutually recognized stakeholders in a network (DeMars 2015). This norm maintains the bias toward the squeakiest wheel or the most powerful actors in the network (Jepson 2005). Just as Benjamin (2008) discusses funders' emphasis on outcomes measurement, Jepson links the efforts of the accountability structures that focus on quantifiable outputs to NGOs "tactically or unwittingly gear(ing) their accountability structures to suit powerful stakeholders (donors, governmental partners) whilst ignoring their accountability to stakeholders, such as memberships, who lack the desire or capacity to press their claims" (Jepson 2005, 521). These two accounts focus on accountability toward the most demanding actors, alluding to a hierarchy of actors to whom an NGO might be accountable.

Lowest on this list of actors are those who perhaps do not even register as stakeholders in the NGO mission, like the community members who do not attend project meetings out of protest or apathy. DeMars suggests "following the partners" to find the actors at different layers of politics in activist networks. Partners of partners of NGOs may have broader influence on the actors and, thus, must be considered in accountability regimes. I add to this admonition a concern about the norms of being a stakeholder altogether. While at the global scale, norms of stakeholder accountability might count silence as apathy and thus, the least in the accountability hierarchy; at other scales silence is considered a strong opposition. However, local agents invoke the concept of accountability in very different—and often contradictory—forms than the global accountability norms.

Accountability at the Local Scale

Accountability at the local level is invoked as responsiveness to community needs, and is used by agents to limit the power of NGOs. While each community will have its different definitions and implementations of accountability, there are a few characteristics that emerge universally as accountability norms at the local scale. In order for an NGO to legitimate its power at the local scale, it must adhere to five norms. These local accountability norms require:

(1) context-specific and flexible responses to local demands;
(2) the development of long-term relationships;
(3) a focus on a broad definition of stakeholders (i.e., "hidden stakeholders");
(4) emphasis not just on technical fixes to the intervention but also political changes to the operations, management, and even mission of the intervention; and
5) added focus on the accountability of ex ante interactions.

With regard to the first norm, because local communities are remarkably diverse, requiring different administrative, political, and technical capacities on the NGOs operations, accountability expectations must be context specific. Some communities will require an NGO to be transparent by giving regular reports to their leadership in oral format. Others might require a written report. Still others will be more focused on the process of accountability—that NGOs follow the processes of decision-making and deliberation that their community usually follow. In Ghana, local actors working with Action Aid, Ghana, and Catholic Action for Street Children, suggested that attending Durbars (week-long traditional meetings that are held every two years) is important for informing beneficiaries, sponsors, staff, and other stakeholders of the organizations' activities and progress (Okorley, Dey, and Owusu 2012). In other local communities such as in South Sudan, the difference between the NGO norms of direct, honest feedback and the local norms of saving face may require more circuitous or subtle forms of feedback (Beattie 2012). Accountability will mean different things to different communities and NGOs must be able to accommodate that.

Second, local accountability must be flexible while fostering longer-term relationships (Stern 2008). Timelines for getting work done will differ by locale, as will the histories that these communities have with the policy issue, making long-term procedural accountability a priority over short-term accomplishments. While many NGOs may have a well-practiced procedure for their work, each location will take a different amount of time on each step, displaying varying types and degrees of capacity at the local scale. In many cases, local accountability norms will require "ongoing processes rather than … formal tools and mechanisms as with the case of (global accountability norms)" (Oxfam-Monash Partnership, n.d., 3). The Tearfund's efforts to increase their accountability to beneficiaries in South Sudan indicated that the biggest impact came when the NGO's staff had established long-term relationships with the community (Beattie 2012). Through extended engagement with community members, the organization received frank and detailed feedback that resulted in significant modifications making their nutrition programs more effective (53). In other cases, even if the short, three-to-four-year funding timeline was long enough to establish these relationships with local communities, they are often cut short by the funder with little or no explanation, leaving local organization staff and community members confused and often calloused toward global partners (Barber and Bowie 2008; Balboa 2014).

Moreover, since these local communities are the ones that will be most impacted by the policies and programs NGOs seek to implement, their members will likely have an acute interest in the programs that will impact their lives. While the expertise of the global NGO might give the actor enough authority that the communities will not question its approach or goals, the NGO must take an interest in the needs, desires, and procedures of the local community in order for the relationship to convert from mere compliance into full, long-term consent and social transformation.

Thus, the third local accountability norm takes form: NGOs must make efforts to include all stakeholders, including the "invisible" or nonvocal stakeholders. When these efforts are not successful, on the one hand, we begin to see discussion of concepts like "elite capture" within a project—where local elites disproportionately benefit from the NGO intervention, often causing NGO programs to exacerbate existing inequality rather than diminish it. On the other hand, adhering to this norm can make all the difference in the world: in 250 projects in Indonesia, community-driven development has been demonstrated as an antidote to elite capture (Fritzen 2007).

Fourth, as the focus of NGO programs' impact, local communities are compelled to press NGOs to question not only their strategies, but also the assumptions upon which these strategies are built. Thus, local accountability norms incorporate a true organizational learning approach[11]—one that goes beyond creating strategic and technical approaches to stakeholder demands to genuinely collaborate with local actors, even if such collaboration may require rethinking the assumptions the organization holds dear. This requires our fifth norm, an ex ante approach to accountability—one that does not merely account for actions after the fact, but incorporates local ideas into the very planning of projects. An AIDS medical relief NGO's local director in Malawi was frustrated by the lack of ex ante accountability when the project's "final contract differed from the proposal submitted by the local institution and was offered with a 'take-it-or-leave-it' attitude. No negotiations were allowed" (Barber and Bowie 2008, 753). This lack of flexibility or interest in incorporating local input or expertise in the project planning phase is a clear failure to follow these local accountability norms.

Due to the tensions raised here, it's not surprising many organizations find maneuvering between these global and local norms difficult. A common critique of locally focused NGOs is that they are more accountable to their global partners than to their local constituencies (Igoe and Kelsall 2005). Some organizations resort to misrepresenting their programs to global funders in order to maintain funding while understanding that these global accountability norms do not reflect the contextual complexity of the local programs (Burger and Owens 2008). Other research demonstrates how global support goes not to the neediest local advocacy groups but rather to those savviest about global accountability norms (Bob 2005).

Being accountable at both the global and local scales is difficult, and the more an NGO invests in and adheres to global accountability norms, the less it is able to invest in and adhere to local accountability norms (Andrews 2014).

Connecting Accountability and Capacity for NGOs

While the preceding sections detail typologies of accountability and capacity to help understand how NGOs build authority, how do these concepts interact with each other? The relationship between authority, accountability, and capacity is clear, if not perfect. Capacity for nongovernmental organizations is a proxy for power. It is context specific and aimed at achieving outcomes. Without capacity, there would be no power (and, as a result, no authority, since authority is a type of power). Accountability is the primary means by which an NGO converts its power into legitimate authority. An organization cannot be fully accountable without the capacity to fulfill the promises of its relationships. Similarly, an NGO can demonstrate the capacity to achieve short-term results toward its goal, but without accountable relationships these achievements are not sustainable (Balboa 2017). Sometimes accountability, capacity, and authority can be at odds with each other. One fear voiced by NGO chief executive officers is that by being accountable and disclosing any weakness—particularly in project delivery—NGOs could jeopardize funding and thus their capacity to achieve their mission (Jepson 2005). In another strain of conflict, an actor can lack authority if it adheres to all the accountability norms of that scale, but is unable to demonstrate power to achieve results. This is what Koppell (2005) calls "multiple accountabilities disorder." It occurs when an actor's efforts to be accountable drain resources from the organization, rendering it paralyzed and therefore unable to implement its programs. These relationships will be illuminated more clearly in this book's discussion of the empirical case studies that demonstrate the paradox of scale.

Though previous typologies in international relations approach authority in a slightly different manner than I do, these typologies support the idea of capacity and accountability as operationalized elements of the concept and are not contradictory to the definitions used in this book. Jinnah (2014) suggests that authority for treaty secretariats can be derived from delegation, morality, expertise, institutional memory, and social networks. This list can be divided easily into concepts of capacity and accountability.

"Expertise," defined as technical knowledge or training, along with institutional memory, or collective experience in rules and practices, are concepts that reflect an ability or capacity of an organization. Delegation, the principal-agent relationship with the state and how that is implemented; morality, based on claims of representation and similar value interests; and social networks, or the lateral relationships with other nondelegating actors, must all be supported by upholding accountability norms with those actors.

This book talks about both accountability and capacity in terms of norms, and the prioritization of certain global norms are the reasons why NGO efforts at the local scale are often undermined. The typologies I've introduced on accountability and capacity are normative, in that they reflect the standards of appropriate behavior in each scale (Finnemore and Sikkink 1998). For both concepts, the global scale norms are reinforced both by how they are promoted and by the way in which breaking them generates disapproval. If an NGO demonstrates the types of political, administrative, and technical capacities that are valued at the global scale, the NGO is seen as powerful in that scale. If an actor adheres to the norms of global accountability, it is seen as legitimate in that scale. Attempts at breaking these norms will result in disapproval and perhaps scorn.

In the local scale, these norms emerged from stories and cases—both previously published and in the case studies of this book. For capacity, an organization is seen as more powerful when it adheres to the norms of local capacity, as seen in cases where the NGO is able to work within indigenous social structures, and maneuver through local government regulations. For accountability, the norms are a reflection both of NGOs that are seen as legitimate and the practices that result in NGOs being called "unaccountable" by local actors. They are called unaccountable when they do not adhere to the norms or try to use global accountability norms at the local scale. Thus, a central contribution of this book is this typology and a clear description of both capacity and accountability norms on the local scale.

Understanding Power, Legitimacy, and Authority across Scales

If, as this book and others have argued, the meaning of legitimacy is context specific (Hudson 2001; Bernstein 2011), then it follows that each NGO must contend with the need for legitimacies at both the local and global scales. In other words, gaining authority at the global scale does not mean an NGO can claim authority in the many local arenas in which it operates. Similarly, having more authority on the local scale does not mean the NGO is necessarily legitimate at the global scale. As the case studies in this book will show, the paradox of scale indicates that NGOs are pressured to prioritize the global norms that create global authority over the local norms. This prioritization is demonstrated in the instances where NGOs follow global norms in the local scale, resulting in loss of authority. Figure 2.1 demonstrates how these differences might play out for NGOs.

In the bottom-left quadrant, power has not been legitimated in either the global or the local scale. An NGO's raw power may be legitimized by some actors but not a critical mass of them. When Muhamad Yunus first introduced the Grameen Bank to the development field, microfinance was seen as an unreliable and ineffective tool, or a band aid that would not address systemic roots of poverty. Some believed that Grameen was

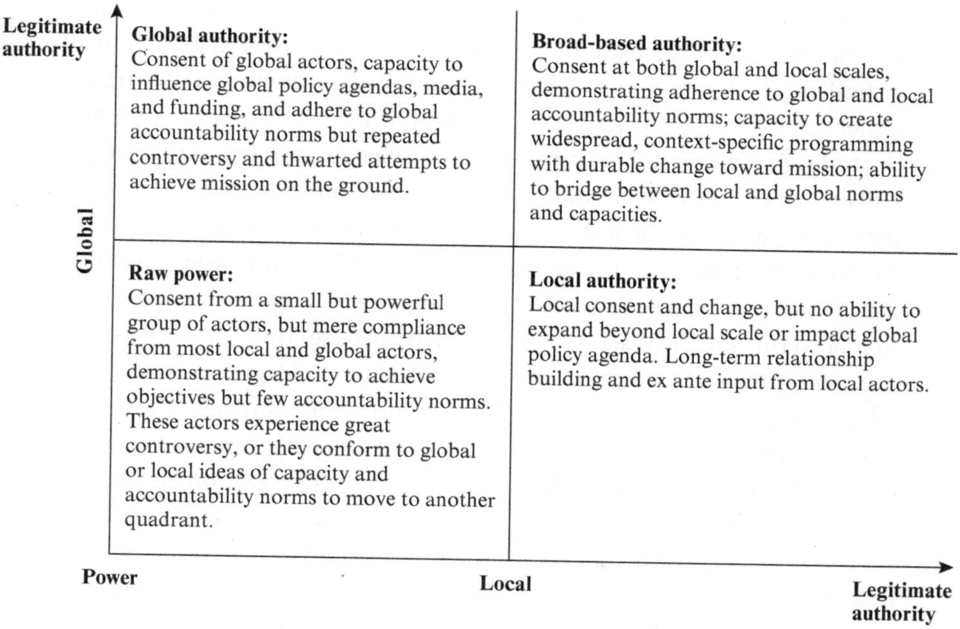

Legitimate authority ↑ **Global**

Global authority:
Consent of global actors, capacity to influence global policy agendas, media, and funding, and adhere to global accountability norms but repeated controversy and thwarted attempts to achieve mission on the ground.

Broad-based authority:
Consent at both global and local scales, demonstrating adherence to global and local accountability norms; capacity to create widespread, context-specific programming with durable change toward mission; ability to bridge between local and global norms and capacities.

Raw power:
Consent from a small but powerful group of actors, but mere compliance from most local and global actors, demonstrating capacity to achieve objectives but few accountability norms. These actors experience great controversy, or they conform to global or local ideas of capacity and accountability norms to move to another quadrant.

Local authority:
Local consent and change, but no ability to expand beyond local scale or impact global policy agenda. Long-term relationship building and ex ante input from local actors.

Power **Local** **Legitimate authority** →

Figure 2.1
Power versus authority on local and global scales

trying to take over the roles and responsibility of the government (Johnson 1999; Bornstein 2011). At the local scale, some religious organizations had to overcome suspicions that it would "encourage anti-religious behaviors" (Syed 2005, 44), like requiring religious women to leave their homes and interact with unrelated men (Syed 2005). The organization continued to operate, striving to address these concerns, and increased local and global buy-in for its work.

Policy entrepreneurs often start in this lower-left quadrant. As Green states, these entrepreneurs must "devise potential ways to govern and then peddle their ideas to those who might comprise the governed" (Green 2014, 35). This occurs even if some actors legitimate the NGO power but others do not: perhaps one generous funder endorses the NGO's efforts while others do not; or one powerful local official gives it access while other local actors do not see the mission or intervention as being in line with their values or goals.

When an NGO begins the work of achieving its mission by exercising raw power, it must increase the buy-in for this mission or approach by a critical mass of actors in order to gain authority—moving in the figure either up (for the global scale) or to the right (for the local scale) or toward the top-right quadrant if the organization manages to demonstrate capacity and accountability at both scales. If the organization does not legitimize its power into authority, it will enjoy short-term success. Without authority, the NGO must seek compliance from actors rather than consent, making use of force or coercive measures. By wielding the force of funding, of access to a powerful subset of actors, or of Western science, these actors can display power through coercion without a critical level of legitimacy.

Seemingly powerful NGOs may lack authority for many reasons. In the global arena, the actor can demonstrate some capacity, but perhaps seriously lacks the ability to report to funders. A new operator on the global scale, for instance, might not yet be aware of or able to answer all calls for accountability in this sphere. NGOs with raw power may be embroiled in some controversy with a stakeholder, or are not seen by their peers as following the processes of their trade. The New Life Children's Refuge—an organization formed by a U.S. Baptist church—demonstrated this raw power in Haiti, where eight of its members were put in jail facing charges of kidnapping thirty-three Haitian children and transporting them to an orphanage in the Dominican Republic (Lacey 2010; Balboa 2015). This group followed neither the global norms of adoption agencies, nor the local norms or processes of transporting children across national boundaries, but was able to fundraise quickly from its home church, travel to Haiti, and collect and transport dozens of children to the border. The raw power New Life Children's Refuge exerted momentarily toward achieving its mission was thwarted and scorned by the Haitian government, the global adoption and development communities, and global media, discrediting the organization.

As the actor converts its power into authority, it moves upward and toward the right in figure 2.1. If it gains legitimacy in the global sphere but not the local, giving it global authority, it will encounter numerous hurdles before it can achieve its mission on the local scale. In this scenario, the actor has the consent of global actors since it favors the global accountability norms and capacities, but it still must seek compliance of local actors. These NGOs with global authority might have a series of short programs at multiple local scales, but they will not display much long-term success.

This is a common manifestation of the paradox and is exemplified in chapter 3 through the exploration of Conservation International's efforts in Milne Bay, Papua New Guinea. In this case, Conservation International (CI) had received criticism that previous projects demonstrated its global authority but were lacking in local authority. By basing the project plan for Milne Bay on the lessons learned from these criticisms, the organization moved toward more broad-based authority. However, as chapter 3 details, multiple pressures and shortcomings at the individual, organizational, and field level undermined the efforts at building local authority, pushing the organization back into the top-left quadrant.

Actors with only local authority will experience local consent, but no ability to expand beyond that local scale. The NGO may reach out to global actors for funding support or media coverage, but the actor's inability to manage those relationships makes any progress in the global realm short-term and hard-won. Importantly, the more these NGOs with local authority try to engage on the global scale, the more they feel the pressure to prioritize the global over the local, and to become the obverse: an NGO with global authority. Chapters 4 and 5 demonstrate this scenario with case studies in the Philippines and the Republic of Palau. What made global actors in these cases take notice of these NGOs—their long-term relationships with communities, and tailored and context-specific interventions, to name a few traits—did not help the actors live up to the global norms of quantifiable results on short timelines.

The top-right quadrant of this figure is the optimum state of any actor operating at both scales. With appropriate capacity and accountability in both the global and local arenas, actors with broad-based authority demonstrate a successful conversion of power to legitimate authority. These actors achieve what they desire with the consent of a critical mass of stakeholders at both scales. Because of this broad-based authority, they will achieve durable progress toward mission.

I argue that an actor's ability to manage and build its capacity and accountability relationships can move that actor from a state of being less legitimate to more legitimate; from raw power to broad-based authority. What's more, the case studies in this book demonstrate that an actor can move from broad-based authority to any of the other states rather quickly as well. The difficulty in moving toward attaining authority is in the context-specific nature of capacity and accountability. What works on a larger scale will not work at the local scale and vice versa, and the pressure to prioritize global legitimate authority makes broad-based authority challenging.

Bridging Power and Authority across Scales

Given the context-specific nature of building NGO authority, and the different, often competing demands from the local and global scales, how can an organization build and maintain broad-based authority? How can they stay in that upper-right quadrant of that two-by-two matrix?

These differences in capacity and accountability norms starkly delineate the global and local scales where NGOs operate. Nongovernmental organizations with global authority possess a wealth of capacity at the global scale. They are expert fundraisers, media facilitators, international negotiators; they have professionally designed and implemented organizations; and they have a preponderance of scientific knowledge. They also have a strong sense of what the global agents of accountability require and are able to answer these calls effectively. While domestic and local governments may have domestic or local capacities, their lack of global capacity makes their profile relatively lower than the NGOs, which reduces their funding and, therefore, their capacity.

Operating at this expert level at the global scale enables the NGO to access remote locations in pursuit of its mission. For conservation NGOs, having the capacity and accountability relationships at the global scale helps them obtain global authority which brings in more funding. All this helps them obtain unique access to assess the state of remote natural resources and how local resource-dependent communities interact with those resources. As the only global actor with access to local resources, their global authority grows their funding to create scaled-up conservation projects and access more local resource data. However, because the initial source of power often comes from the global scale, NGOs become more like the global actors than the societies they mean to represent (Kamat 2003; Gray, Bebbington, and Collison 2006), causing them to prioritize the global accountability norms and capacities over the local (Pallas 2010; Pallas, Gethings, and Harris 2015).

While most stories of powerful NGOs begin at the global scale, the obverse of this also holds true. NGOs can begin their work focusing locally, demonstrating all the capacity and accountability relationships that the local scale requires. For their success, these organizations then get pulled by global actors to scale up their operations. Their local authority gets recognized with the opportunity to replicate their successes globally. However, once these organizations secure footholds at both scales, they find that the accountability relationships and capacity that garnered recognition at the global scale are not enough to help them wield authority there. The transnational nature of these NGOs comes with a perceived ultimatum: local or global. For example, how can NGOs give local partners the direct feedback and criticism that is valued at the global scale while allowing these partners to "save face"—a value that requires more circuitous feedback, takes more time to give, and runs the risk of being misconstrued? The capacity and accountability norms that made them successful at the local scale will not help them operate at the global scale; the norms of the global scale will not help them achieve lasting change on the ground. Thus, even NGOs that have obtained local authority become subject to the paradox of scale.

However, while having broad-based authority is difficult, this book asserts that it is not impossible. Indeed, the NGO that demonstrates broad-based authority—balances its interscalar capacity and accountability relationships to overcome this paradox—exhibits the most durable power an NGO can hope for: the ability to affect lasting change toward achieving its mission. On the global scale, the NGO with broad-based authority can raise enormous amounts of funding to implement its programs. It can have its finger on the pulse of the latest scientific, legal, and technological advances in its field. It can consolidate administrative costs by having many organizational functions centralized. At the same time, the NGO can tailor its interventions to reflect local context, it can engage local communities in meaningful ways, and it can do all this in true partnership with local institutions, resulting in genuine and profound organizational learning. The Locally Managed Marine Area (LMMA) Network is a network of practitioners from a range of organizations including small, community-based organizations to branches of large NGOs (like the Wildlife Conservation Society, WWF, TNC, CI) and universities, created to improve local livelihoods and resource management by facilitating access to experiences elsewhere and bringing in nonlocal advisors for capacity building, strategic issues, and research methods. As an example of how NGOs might sustain broad-based authority and bridge local-to-local and local-to-global differences, the network engages multiple participants, while demonstrating quantifiable progress toward its vision of "vibrant, resilient, and empowered communities who inherit and maintain healthy, well-managed, and sustainable marine resources and ecosystems."[12] Indeed, garnering legitimate authority on both the local and the global scale is a powerful achievement.

These cases indicate the key to achieving this broad-based authority is a specific type of capacity: bridging capacity. As the methods section in chapter 1 explains, each of the cases in this book involved a range of authority types over time. Before each NGO experienced the loss of authority, they did, for a time, successfully achieve broad-based authority. Their stories—how they built, maintained, and lost authority over time—help delineate three features of bridging capacity. Chapters 3, 4, and 5 will detail this in each case study, raising new questions of research for our understanding of NGOs and environmental governance.

These cases suggest that bridging capacity is comprised of three essential pillars: (1) in-depth intercultural and cross-cultural (ICCC) understanding; (2) commitment and discipline to act as intermediary; and (3) enough power in the organization to influence or change how work is done (Balboa

2014). Cross-cultural understanding implies some comparing and understanding of the similarities and differences between cultures. Intercultural understanding signals knowing how to connect two or more cultures. Together, these traits combine knowledge of different cultural practices, worldviews, accountability norms, and capacity requirements with awareness of one's own cultural practices and assumptions, and skills to communicate and work across cultures.

While ICCC understanding is key to bridging capacity, it is inadequate without the other two pillars; an individual who has cross-cultural and intercultural understanding can do nothing to help an organization achieve its mission without both the commitment and power to make changes within the organization. An actor with ICCC understanding can quickly lose commitment and discipline to act as a bridge if his or her actions are perceived as counter to global accountability norms, causing others to undermine or even punish bridging endeavors. An NGO may have individuals who demonstrate ICCC understanding, but if they are less powerful than other actors in the organization, the changes they seek do not take place. For example, anthropologists often take on the responsibility of translating "the actions and beliefs of one set of actors for another" (West 2005), but have limited effect in changing operations within a conservation project (West 2006). Conversely, an actor can have both the desire to act as an intermediary and the power to influence his or her organization. However, without in-depth ICCC insight, his or her actions can be useless or even harmful to both networks' actors and the NGO's individual mission. As this book explores in several case studies, while local staff (or expatriates who had lived locally for decades) can demonstrate ICCC understanding, their bridging capacity will be rendered impotent if they do not have the organizational sway of those in charge.

In other words, all three traits must be present for bridging capacity to have effect. When bridging capacity is securely in place, an NGO can convert power into broad-based legitimate authority across scales and create durable change on multiple scales toward achieving its mission. Each empirical chapter and the conclusion in chapter 6 will detail how bridging capacity is both created and undermined in the three case studies.

This theory to understand NGO authority was not deductively created. In exploring the rich details of this book's case studies, the concepts of the paradox of scale, the typology of authority across scales, the operationalization of authority through the proxies of capacity and accountability, and the potential mechanism for maintaining broad-based authority—bridging capacity—emerged. The three chapters that follow trace these concepts over the lifetime of three projects. The case of Conservation International in chapter 3 demonstrates a typical example of how broad-based authority is undermined by the paradox of scale for NGOs that begin their efforts with global authority.

3 Conservation International in Milne Bay: The Paradox of Scale for Global NGOs

Conservation International (CI) is one of the world's largest conservation nongovernmental organizations (Chapin 2004; Dowie 2011). With an annual budget of more than $164.8 million USD, more than one thousand global staff in over thirty countries, and upward of 375 global partners (Conservation International 2015a), CI has worked since 1987 to create and implement rules for the use and governance of natural resources. It influences global debates and sets agendas both as participant in multiple global environmental agreements (like the United Nations Framework Convention on Climate Change, the Convention on Biodiversity, and the Convention on International Trade in Endangered Species of Wild Fauna and Flora, to name a few) and as a source for scientific research that informs these agreements. It was the first nonprofit accredited as a GEF agency,[1] which means it can directly access and distribute funds from the GEF (Global Environment Facility), the largest environmental funder in the world, to assist national governments around the globe to incorporate environmental concerns into their policy agenda. CI collaborates with major corporations to green their production, and produces prize-winning documentaries on resource use (Conservation International 2013a). It is a household name among NGOs and a global authority in conservation.

Its mission is to empower "societies to responsibly and sustainably care for nature, our global biodiversity, for the well-being of humanity (Conservation International 2010)." Like most transnational NGOs, CI experiences success on the global level, but its global mission can only be achieved through concrete local changes. Without changes in local behavior, the societies the organization seeks to empower could not sustain resource use or global biodiversity. Indeed, if "possession is nine-tenths of the law," then the involvement of local resource owners in global conservation is the key to sustainability for the planet.

CI's global reach has not been without controversy. From the fields of Latin America to its own Washington, DC–area offices, there have been concerns about how the organization interacts with local communities. In the November 2004 issue of *World Watch Magazine*, Mac Chapin's article "A Challenge to Conservationists" (Chapin 2004) accused the "big three" environmental nongovernmental organizations—Conservation International, the World Wildlife Fund, and The Nature Conservancy—of neglecting the local and indigenous communities whose land they see as paramount to conserve. Chapin's paper traced the exponential financial and political growth of these large conservation organizations and proffered that with its recent growth, the conservation field has either abandoned its efforts at participatory conservation or has used certain participatory practices as window dressing for otherwise top-down conservation projects. Criticisms of their lack of sensitivity toward community needs have festered in Guatemala (Grandia 2004), Guyana (Siegel 2003), Mexico, Surinam, Panama, Philippines, Columbia, West Papua, and Aceh (Choudry 2003), each citing different ways in which the organization has ignored local demands, including its lack of social scientists on staff (Grandia 2004; Chapin 2004).

In light of all this scrutiny, CI has worked deliberately to attain local authority by achieving its mission while correcting for these past criticisms. It has an indigenous advisory group for its board, indigenous representation on its board of directors, a vice president for social policy and practice, and an executive director of CI's Indigenous and Traditional Peoples Program, which has recently started an Indigenous Leaders Conservation Fellowship to help traditional leaders create strategies to combat climate change. CI has published guidelines on what free, prior, and informed consent of indigenous peoples should look like in multiple contexts. With a large proportion of its staff from local communities or with social science expertise, CI has taken steps to ensure that interventions are appropriate and supported by local communities.

Since authority is legitimized power—operationalized in this book as accountability and capacity—and since accountability and capacity change depending upon the scale and context, this chapter will begin its analysis of the paradox of scale by describing the global authority CI attained to become a local implementer of conservation projects. The organization might have been delegated authority at the global scale, but it then had to legitimize its power in other ways at the local scale (Pandya 2006). Because of all these efforts to transform global authority into broad-based author-ity (valuing the context of its work, and incorporating local communities into its organizational structure and decision-making), Conservation Inter-national's work in Milne Bay is a very instructive case for well-intended NGOs still struggling with scaling up their efforts by expanding programs to new locales. Its experience as an actor simultaneously in global conser-vation and on a local scale in Milne Bay is a telling example of how an NGO's global capacities and accountability relationships create access to the local level, where these global norms and abilities are unhelpful and often a harmful substitute for context-specific approaches. This chapter will trace the organization's rise as a global authority, its efforts to broaden its authority by incorporating learning from past critiques in the design and beginning stages of its work in Milne Bay, and its subsequent reversion to a state of global authority. As figure 3.1 indicates, this chapter will detail these changes that took place in a span of just over a decade,[2] with evi-dence and competing pressures originating from individuals' actions and organizational policy that reflected and enforced field-based norms. The original processes of balancing the global and local scales through Village Engagement Teams and multiscale oversight were undermined by pressure to adhere to global norms of accountability, legitimacy, and capacity in hiring project leaders with global management expertise and prioritizing short-term, quantifiable results. In this case, the global norms of account-ability and capacity were unsuccessfully applied on the local scale to create authority, developing a clear illustration of the paradox of scale.

The Milne Bay Community-Based Coastal and Marine Conservation Project

Papua New Guinea's Milne Bay Province is part of the "coral triangle"—a biologically rich marine area extending between Indonesia, the Solomon Islands, and the Philippines (Government of Papua New Guinea 2002). Of the nineteen provinces in PNG, Milne Bay is the largest maritime prov-ince (Conservation International 2003) and contains the country's largest complex of coral reef—32 percent of the country's total reef area (Kassem

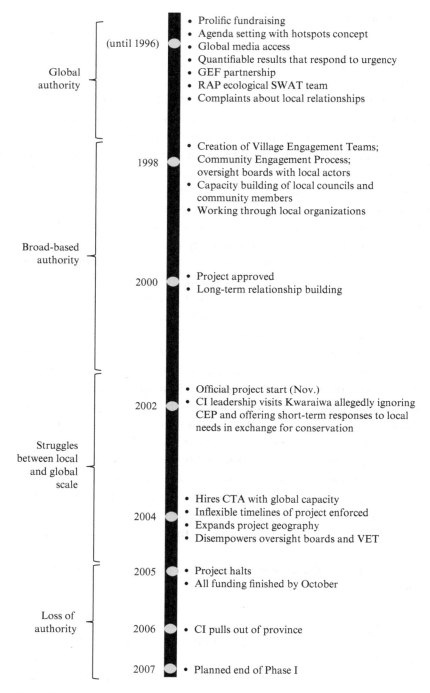

Global authority

(until 1996)
- Prolific fundraising
- Agenda setting with hotspots concept
- Global media access
- Quantifiable results that respond to urgency
- GEF partnership
- RAP ecological SWAT team
- Complaints about local relationships

Broad-based authority

1998
- Creation of Village Engagement Teams; Community Engagement Process; oversight boards with local actors
- Capacity building of local councils and community members
- Working through local organizations

2000
- Project approved
- Long-term relationship building

Struggles between local and global scale

2002
- Official project start (Nov.)
- CI leadership visits Kwaraiwa allegedly ignoring CEP and offering short-term responses to local needs in exchange for conservation

2004
- Hires CTA with global capacity
- Inflexible timelines of project enforced
- Expands project geography
- Disempowers oversight boards and VET

Loss of authority

2005
- Project halts
- All funding finished by October

2006
- CI pulls out of province

2007
- Planned end of Phase I

Figure 3.1
Conservation International: how the paradox of scale developed in Milne Bay

and Madeja 2014; Seeto 2001). Overharvesting of resources and destructive fishing practices are the main threats to the province's reefs (Milne Bay Community-Based Coastal and Marine Conservation Project 2005; Conservation International, n.d.; Government of Papua New Guinea, n.d.).

Milne Bay communities are concerned about the recent efforts to conserve their marine resources. As one of Papua New Guinea's least populated provinces, Milne Bay's small population seems to have a lesser impact on the reef resources compared to neighboring provinces (Werner and Allen 1998; Government of Papua New Guinea 2002; Bailasi 2005; Seligmann 2005; Conservation International, n.d.). However, these communities' dependence on the reefs for livelihood is still high,[3] and they are concerned about maintaining traditional rights over marine resources while continuing to benefit from them economically (Werner and Allen 1998). Conservation efforts are often met with the suspicion that foreigners intend to exploit resources for their own wealth, rather than conserve them.[4]

The initial plan of the Milne Bay Community-Based Coastal and Marine Conservation Project (known in this chapter as "the Milne Bay project" or simply "the project") consulted with a wide range of actors, including government, private sector, and community members within Papua New Guinea and in Milne Bay specifically (Baines, Duguman, and Johnston 2006). Each actor had its own priorities for the project—increasing tourism, building government capacity, or encouraging socioeconomic development for the province to name a few—but CI's ultimate objective was to implement a system of community-managed marine protected areas that would conserve important ecosystems, preserve biodiversity, and protect marine resources in order to achieve sustainable development and livelihood benefits for vulnerable small island communities (Milne Bay Community-Based Coastal Marine Project 2001; Milne Bay Community-Based Coastal Marine Project 2005). With elements of both conservation and development, this project can be categorized as an "integrated conservation and development project" (Conservation International 2003).

In the five years of phase one, several community-managed marine protected areas were to be created within one of three zones. This pilot phase involved building the administrative, technical, and political capacity of local actors in both the public and private sectors to take over the project in phase two,[5] and expand the project to other zones.[6] By planning to turn the project over to local actors in phase two, CI demonstrated potential in upholding local accountability norms that move the local actors' input beyond the mere consultancy and into broader control of the program. These local accountability norms were balanced with global accountability norms, since each phase was approximately five years long (e.g., short term) and key milestones were required (e.g., quantifiable results) to be met in order for CI to secure phase two funding for expansion to more zones (Government of Papua New Guinea 2002).

The project achieved many global markers of success. It was one the largest employers in the province and in the country for conservation (People Against Foreign NGO Neocolonialism 2003).[7] Its staff had been recognized with an international award.[8] Many staff and community members thought that work was progressing along an appropriate timeline,[9] and eleven communities had expressed interest in creating a marine protected area in their waters, with six communities already advanced to candidacy.[10]

Regardless of these achievements, the project was brought to a halt in October 2005, when it was discovered that the project leaders had spent all five years of funding nearly two years before the end of phase one (Baines, Duguman, and Johnston 2006). What was originally scheduled as a late mid-term evaluation became the project's final evaluation. Both the Milne Bay governor and CI sought to continue the project with other funding, but neither actor could agree on who would have control of the funds. Depending upon the source, CI was either "chased" out of the province by the governor because of project mismanagement or chose to withdraw in the absence of appropriate government capacity (Alotau Environment Ltd. 2006a,b).[11] Regardless, the missions of both the project and CI were not accomplished. Events leading up to the project's demise illuminate how a seemingly powerful transnational NGO can succumb to the paradox of scale.

When Global Authority Creates a Local Niche: Conservation International in Milne Bay

Throughout over thirty years of existence, Conservation International has gained considerable delegated and entrepreneurial authority on the global scale. This section will detail how CI legitimized its power on the global scale through consistent demonstrations of its global capacity and its ability to adhere to global accountability norms. As stated in this chapter's introduction, it operated successful fundraising campaigns raising close to $165 million in revenue in 2014 alone. The organization has influenced the creation of rules for global markets by taking various levels of leadership roles in the efforts to certify sustainable products, including aquarium fish, biofuels, nuts, coffee, forest products, soy products, seafood, and tourism ventures. CI has also collaborated with corporations like Walmart and Starbucks to "green" their product lines and processes, making them more sustainable (Argenti 2004; Gunther 2006). The organization maintains several hundred partnerships with local and global organizations every year. It has also demonstrated administrative capacity to adhere to global accountability norms of global conservation through multiple annual reports, impact reports, and globally approved measures of conservation success. These efforts at creating the rules for certifying sustainable products and implementing conservation projects worldwide has afforded the organization entrepreneurial authority in the global conservation field.

Perhaps the most impressive illustration of CI's ability to use its technical and political capacity to shape the rules of conservation at the global scale is its focus on "biodiversity hotspots." Conservation International has used the concept of hotspots for prioritizing its work since the early 1990s (Gunter 2004). Two publications helped the concept gain traction in the global biodiversity conservation arena. In 1999, Russell Mittermeier, Norman Myers, Cristina Mittermeier, and Gil Robles published *Hotspots: Earth's Biologically Richest and Most Endangered Terrestrial Ecoregions* (Mittermeier et al. 1999) through Conservation International's press. The next year, Norman Myers was the lead author for "Biodiversity Hotspots for Conservation Priorities" (coauthored with several CI employees) (Myers et al. 2000), published in the highly ranked journal *Nature*. These publications define biodiversity hotspots as "areas featuring exceptional concentrations of endemic species and experiencing exceptional loss of habitat" (Myers et al. 2000, 853). The article then uses quantitative and qualitative methods to define twenty-five priority hotspots for biodiversity conservation.

CI is not the only organization that has built its research and conservation strategy around the concept. A sizable amount of funding has been directed toward research and conservation of these hotspots. As an indicator of how these works have shaped normative discourse, the 2000 *Nature* article has been cited by scholarly articles an impressive 10,679 times in the past sixteen years (Clarivate Analytics 2018);[12] the book was cited 896 times by scholarly and other sources (Google Scholar 2018).[13] Moreover, the concept of hotspots has been referred to in publications and reports by multiple national governments and global environmental organizations, including as a method for setting global conservation priorities. National reports to the Convention on Biological Diversity and the Convention on International Trade in Endangered Species of Wild Fauna and Flora (CITES) use their hotspot designation as justification for becoming a conservation priority (Subregional Steering Committee: CITES/MIKE–South Asia 2004; Towns 2007; Ministry of Environment and Forests, Government of India 2009). Documents from the World Bank, especially the Global Environment Facility, use hotspots to prioritize biodiversity evaluations and funding (Risby 2008; Risby 2009; World Bank 2010). The World Conservation Union's Red List of Threatened Species (which informs decision-making on CITES) also uses the term (Cuttelod et al. 2008), as does the Liaison Group of the Biodiversity-related Conventions (a group that seeks to coordinate cooperation in the implementation of six biodiversity-related conventions)[14] to discuss its fund priority-setting (Liaison Group of the Biodiversity-related Conventions 2009). Thus we see that CI's expertise in the creation, use, and promotion of the hotspot concept has not only changed normative discourse on conservation, but it has also been adopted by the very institutions that create conservation rules and regulations across the globe.

CI leverages its global capacities and adheres to global accountability norms to gain access to local communities through its Rapid Assessment Program. CI's founding Chief Executive Officer Peter Seligmann describes the program: "RAP expert scientists act as an ecological SWAT team to accurately assess the biodiversity and health of an ecosystem in a fraction of the time it would normally take" (Conservation International 2015b). These rapid assessments are snapshots of the resource, gathered by state-of-the-art scientific methods. While most also look at social aspects of resource use, the majority of these reports focus on the technical scientific status of the resource. In just the first twenty years of the program, CI conducted eighty rapid assessment expeditions, and in the process discovered more than thirteen hundred new species, informing both indigenous land tenure bids and strategy for extractive industries, and training students from local communities on scientific methods (Rapid Assessment Program (Conservation International) and Alonso 2011). In this way, CI follows a typical path of a transnational NGO, utilizing its global power through technical (scientific expertise), political (to raise funds for these expeditions and disseminate the results), and administrative capacities (to assemble teams of globally known experts) to access the local scale where conservation efforts must be implemented to achieve its mission.

With its ability to answer demands and maneuver through global political, technical, and administrative complexities, it is no wonder CI has grown to be a powerful NGO in the global scale of the conservation field. Its experience is a clear demonstration of how global authority can create access to local communities to gather data on their resources. With incredible amounts of funding for its work and impressive capacity to shape both scientific research agendas and political conservation agendas, the NGO is seen as an authority to design and implement local conservation efforts around the globe. Their Rapid Assessment Program's access to the local scale increases the NGO's expertise and thus power in the global scale as a representative of the local communities and resources, piquing the interest of the funding community, and ultimately leading to increased financial support to implement conservation programs. These local-global dynamics are mutually reinforcing: more funding means more access, increasing the NGO's capacity as the only global "expert" on the local scale and, ultimately, bringing the NGO more funding to return to the local scale.

CI began its efforts in Melanesia in 1991 (Conservation International, n.d.). In 1996, it started working as a small team in Milne Bay Province after identifying it as a top conservation priority and consulting with the provincial government on how best to build a partnership for marine conservation (Milne Bay Community-Based Coastal and Marine Conservation Project 2001). In 1997, CI performed a rapid assessment of the province's marine resources, assessing fifty-three sites in twenty-two days (Werner and Allen 1998), with a second rapid assessment in 2000. The 1997 report demonstrated the wealth of biodiversity in the province, and flagged some primary threats to that biodiversity. That same year, the United Nations Development Programme (UNDP) chose marine conservation as its priority for work in Papua New Guinea (Milne Bay Community-Based Coastal and Marine Conservation Project 2001). CI worked with the UNDP and the local government to create the Milne Bay Community-Based Coastal and Marine Conservation Project with plans that addressed global conservation goals while responding to the needs of the communities in which it worked.

Since CI was the only transnational environmental NGO working in Milne Bay, it uniquely held the power to mold global thinking about how conservation should be done there. It was the only global "expert" on Milne Bay coastal resources, and its unique ability to access local information about a resource gave it an apparent legitimacy to speak on behalf of a resource most global actors had never encountered.[15] Those local actors who live with the resource do not have access to the global decision-making or opinion-making fora. CI's unique role connecting the local and the global scales issues also gave CI the opportunity to fund its work in Milne Bay on a large scale.

In 1998, based on the findings of the assessments, CI, UNDP, and Milne Bay Provincial Government drafted the proposal for the Milne Bay Community Based Coastal and Marine Project. In 1999, the governor of Milne Bay Province expressed his support of the proposal along with CI and UNDP, and the final proposal was submitted to the Global Environment Facility, the UNDP's funding mechanism. The GEF approved the proposal in 2000, and CI opened an office in Alotau, Milne Bay, in 1999–2000 (Van Helden 2004). CI then performed another biological survey of the marine resources (Milne Bay Community-Based Coastal and Marine Conservation Project 2001). The project itself began in November 2002 (Baines, Duguman, and Johnston 2006) after funds were released (Van Helden 2004; Callister 2006a,b).

This CI-GEF relationship is indicative of the transnational—and thus interscalar—nature of NGOs. The GEF funding process is a complicated one, requiring evidence of multiple types of global capacity and the ability to adhere to the GEF's accountability guidelines. Typically, this involves a United Nations agency to be the implementing agency (in this case, the United Nations Development Programme) and a local government agency to execute the grant. Since the GEF/UNDP initial assessments indicated the government agencies in Papua New Guinea lacked the capacity to execute the project, CI was named the executing agent of the project. No other global actor had the local access or expertise. No local actor had the global political or technical capacity. CI was the only organization positioned to implement the project. Thus, CI became the first NGO ever to be the executing agency of a GEF grant, a clear example of the organization's political prowess and global authority.[16]

The negotiation of the details of the Milne Bay Project was drawn out and contentious.[17] As a large bureaucracy, the GEF imposed long waits throughout the process (i.e., eighteen months to complete an agreement, another eighteen months to wait for the first payment). With a budget of nearly $7 million dollars (Government of Papua New Guinea, n.d.),[18] the Milne Bay Project was one of the largest marine conservation projects to date (Kula 2002; Kinch 2003) and therefore had many bureaucratic requirements. CI had its own administrative processes that worked in addition to—and sometimes contrary to—the GEF's requirements. Negotiations took place on multiple issues, including CI's overhead rates. The GEF was concerned about the administrative capacity of the CI office in Papua New Guinea to achieve the objectives of the grant and required a capacity assessment of the NGO. This capacity assessment flagged key administrative areas in the local offices that needed improvement. CI headquarters in Washington, DC, and its Papua New Guinea national field offices in Port Moresby drew up plans to address these shortcomings to satisfy the GEF's concerns—bridging the gap between the CI PNG staff's and the GEF's capacity and expectations for accountability—and included them in the proposal. CI's ability to navigate these demands for the opportunity to execute the grant demonstrates its ability to fulfill global accountability norms of technical, quantitative, short-term expectations of the stakeholder who held the most power at this time: their funder. CI staff state that they could only survive the drawn-out negotiation process because of CI's ability to raise funds from other sources,[19] an indication of global political capacity. CI's power to endure delays in funding by raising funds from other sources juxtaposed with the other two cases in this book (which experienced similar funding delays but without other funding sources) reflects an important contradiction at the global scale about NGO capacity: that NGOs must be able to diversify their funding sources and accrue unrestricted funds for rainy days, even when they are praised for being lean financially (Mitchell 2015).

Building Broad-Based Authority for CI with the Milne Bay Project

The CI experience illustrates how an NGO's global capacity and accountability not only give it access to local communities and resources, but also push the NGO to prioritize the global over the local. While all CI's activities described in the preceding section indicate CI's authority on the global scale, this section will explore how balancing that global authority with capacity and accountability at the local scale helped the organization experience broad-based authority. While it was delegated authority to implement conservation projects by the GEF and other funders including the Government of Papua New Guinea, it had to deliberately work to attain authority at the local level, as well as balance the demands and competing norms of the global and local scales through exertion of bridging capacity. Even with a few incidents where global norms and capacity were favored over local ones, CI maintained broad-based authority roughly from the planning, data gathering, and community awareness phases of the project in 1998 until the official start of the program in 2002. During the planning phase of the project, the organization started the process of building relationships with communities, seeking local input into the project plans ex ante, and identifying potential stakeholders in the province. Once the project officially began, however, a series of events and decisions revealed the systemic prioritization of global capacities and accountability norms over local ones, delegitimizing the project at the local scale, and destabilizing this broad-based authority. This systemic prioritization came from multiple actors—funders, intergovernmental organizations (IGOs), NGO leadership, project leadership, and even local actors—demonstrating that developing the paradox of scale is not merely about one relationship, but about the norms of the field.

The change in project leadership is important to mention for both the analysis of local authority and the timelines of the project. The planning stages of the project saw a series of interim project leaders who were primarily people with global expertise in conservation but also years of experience living and working in Papua New Guinea either as an expatriate or a citizen. While these people demonstrated the intercultural and cross-cultural understanding, they still struggled with the other two pillars of bridging capacity: having enough power within the organization to change operations or the desire to act as a bridge. Under this group of leaders the project plans incorporated many instruments of local accountability norms, including Village Engagement Teams, the oversight boards, and the timelines to turn over the project to local leaders. Each of these leaders, however, left for other projects (perhaps a sign of lack of desire to act as a bridge). After eighteen months of searching, the project hired Peter MacKay as the permanent chief technical advisor (CTA), or project leader, and the project began in full force in 2002. MacKay was not as familiar with PNG's culture but had demonstrated the ability to meet global accountability norms in projects in other transnational contexts. Throughout this chapter, this analysis will examine both how the global and local norms were distinct, as well as how prioritizing global norms was exacerbated by the prolonged search for a leader.

As table 3.1 lists briefly and the following sections will explore in detail, to balance the global authority I have described, CI acted deliberately to answer calls for environmental NGOs to incorporate the communities whose members depend upon these resources for life and livelihood in the work of conservation (Grandia 2004; Khare and Bray 2004). The project

Table 3.1
Evidence of broad-based authority in Milne Bay

	Accountability (as an indicator of legitimacy)	Capacity (as an indicator of power)	Bridging capacity
Local	• VETs were local actors who built relationships with communities • CEP guided appropriate interaction with communities • Provincial and National Steering Committees with local members • Participatory evaluation and monitoring processes	• Worked in partnership with local organizations, churches, and provincial government (P) • Assessed conservation ideas and priorities originating from communities (T) • Largest staff of a conservation project in PNG that hired many local actors (A)	• Project designers with ample experience in MB and global conservation • Project plan that incorporated multiple points of local accountability and global accountability • Steering committees with global and local expertise
Global	• Quarterly reporting with quantifiable results • Tripartite reporting requirements to UNDP, CI, and the provincial government • Complex and incompatible accounting systems	• Successful fundraising program (P) • Created hotspots concept and rapid appraisal protocol (T) • Global media campaigns (P) • Managed an organization with more than 1,000 global staff in over 30 countries with hundreds of partners (A)	

P = political capacity; A = administrative capacity; T = technical capacity planning team (including Jeff Kinch, a lead project designer and an anthropologist), spent much time and energy in the proposal phase learning from past projects in Papua New Guinea, assessing not only the biological resources of the area (Seeto 2001), but also the cultures, resource use (Mitchell et al. 2001), area stakeholders (Kinch 2001a, 2001b), and needs of various communities within Milne Bay. His team designed the Village Engagement Teams whose job was to introduce the project to the communities and assess the communities' priorities (Kinch 2001a, 2001b).[20] The processes of drafting the background documents and the project plan (known as the *Project Document*) were long, but both the processes and the resulting documents encouraged an approach to the project that reflect both global and local accountability norms—communication and conflict resolution strategies, long-term capacity building, creating local oversight boards, working through local institutions, and the coupling of Western science with local ecological knowledge (Kinch 2001a, 2001b).

Village Engagement Teams and the Community Engagement Process

The Village Engagement Teams and the Community Engagement Process were a major part of how the project goals were to be accomplished. The teams and process also had great potential for bridging local and global demands and capacities for the project. However, any local authority these teams built for the organization initially began to erode four years after local staff was hired.

The project planning team incorporated learning from a previous conservation project in Papua New Guinea that found itself embroiled in the paradox of scale. The Bismarck-Ramu Group was also an integrated conservation and development project funded by the GEF (Callister 2006a) that used participatory rural appraisal methods to determine the wants and needs of the communities with which its staff worked. After the first phase of this project, however, the Bismarck-Ramu Group refused further funding from the GEF (in the amount of $23 million dollars [Callister 2006a] and began its own work, with different timelines, goals, and methods [Callister 2006a]). Concurring with this book's definition of local accountability norms, the staff preferred a smaller, personal approach to conservation that builds trust and allows the communities to determine the project goals and outcomes.[21] In their theory of change, daily relationship building and mutual respect bring about conservation and development, and the large sums of money and large scales of work that epitomize the GEF's mission and modus operandi got in the way of those actions (Van Helden 2004; Callister 2006a). Thus, as this pioneering conservation project started to break down after a massive infusion of funds to scale up activities, its staff recoiled and disengaged from the global scale.

The Milne Bay Project embraced many lessons from the Bismarck-Ramu Group with the goal of bridging the local and global divides. For the first several years, the project concentrated on the Community Engagement Process,[22] hiring villagers from nearby communities as Village Engagement Team members and performing several in-depth "patrols" of communities. The very first step in this process was "Making contact and establishing trust" (Pontiu, n.d., 5). Hiring villagers from nearby communities to become engagement team members was essential to establishing this trust, since they were seen as outsiders but could still communicate and understand the communities. These teams walked the line between raising awareness for conservation projects without being "preachy"[23] and focused on listening to the communities and bringing their desires back to the project staff (Kinch 2003). This process helped identify priorities for the communities—including nonconservation priorities.[24] In the community of Nuakata, for instance, the first priority was easier transport to the mainland.[25]

Their programs were aimed primarily at social activities, including education and awareness campaigns, promoting understanding of the concept of biodiversity conservation; increasing individual, community, and institutional capacity for resource management; and promoting community development along with conservation (Bailasi 2005). The project emphasized stakeholder participation via a cyclic process of disseminating conservation information, allowing time for communities to absorb the information, and then attempting to capture the communities' responses to the information (Kula 2002). Ward Development Plans would be based then on these priorities. This type of engagement took time, and a willingness to adjust the project plan to fit the needs and desires of each community.

The Village Engagement Teams were essential to the process of site selection for marine protected areas, since they had the most interaction with the communities. These sites were to be chosen both for biodiversity value and the expression of local interest; site selection was to be dependent on community interest. In theory, if the communities did not want the engagement team to return to their village, they would not return.[26] Three years into the project, eleven communities had expressed interest in creating a marine protected area and six had advanced to candidacy.[27]

The Village Engagement Teams seemed to epitomize CI's efforts to establish a bridge to the local scale of community conservation and resource use. However, a visit by CI leadership and funders to Milne Bay in late 2002 revealed how an organization can disempower and deprioritize local authority. The CI Melanesian Program had carefully written visitor protocols for interaction with villagers that included avoiding displays of wealth, consulting local staff on the types of questions and discussions to be raised, and using local facilities and expertise as much as possible (Melanesia Centre for Biodiversity Conservation 2001). While the details of this global-local interaction are contested, multiple reports allege that CI leadership from Washington, DC, told the village councilor in the community of Kwaraiwa to prepare a list of community needs that CI would deliver (Callister 2006a; Dowie 2008). This exchange typified an approach to conservation local staff took great pains to avoid: the "cargo for nature" approach to conservation.[28] In this context,[29] "cargo" translates into rural communities viewing conservation agencies as a source of material goods rather than long-term, engaged partners (Beehler and Kula, n.d.).[30] After witnessing the expensive boats, diving equipment, and nice hotels used by CI on this trip, project staff worried that requesting such a list would undo the self-reliance approach that was called for in the original *Project Document*, replacing the consent they sought from these communities with a form of economic coercion, and jeopardizing any potential durable conservation that could come of it (Callister 2006a). The approach outlined in the Community Engagement Process sought longer-term self-reliant options for resource-dependent communities and balanced the long-term demands of the communities with the urgent mission of CI. This alleged offer to provide resources to the community reflected short-term thinking that might convince the community members to work with CI, but only in terms of seeking payment for their actions rather than seeking longer-term resource-use alternatives. The short-term, quantifiable, technical approaches to accountability and conservation of resources (e.g., global accountability norms) were prioritized over the long-term, political changes required for sustainability of resource-dependent communities (e.g., local accountability norms),[31] demonstrating how the urgency of the missions of NGOs can contribute to NGOs deprioritizing local account-ability norms.

The Village Engagement Teams achieved some gains in the objective of creating marine protected areas,[32] even if they were not empowered as agents of bridging capacity by other project staff and leadership. While most project staff and volunteers could not function in a village without these teams for local linguistic and political reasons,[33] the team members themselves did not have the capacity or authority to manage disputes with these communities, which were resolved by either the project's leader Peter MacKay or the second in command Bena Seta.[34] In CI publications, the head of the Village Engagement Teams criticized the project: "CI staff need to know the community better before they enter the communities. She stressed that the Project must also analyze the VET's patrol feedback reports before engaging in communities" (Bailasi 2005). These teams offered the Milne Bay Project a brief era of bridging local and global capacities and accountability norms, before prioritizing the global norms of urgency and quantifiable results over the long-term political change the engagement teams were designed to engender.

Oversight

Project oversight is another area that reflects both CI's efforts at creating broad-based authority and its reversion to global authority over time. Project planning documents called for in-depth community engagement; they created a National Steering Committee that was to be the highest authority for decisions and oversight on project activities (Government of Papua New Guinea 2002); and they even created a monitoring and evaluation schedule that would ensure funder oversight of the project. The National Steering Committee membership represented multiple spheres of expertise—local and international staff of competing NGOs, community members, government officials—led by government officials to oversee the project. These oversight committees could theoretically act as bridges to connect the global and local conservation worlds by assuring that the project obtained its goals while respecting local tradition. Moreover, these committees were meant to build their own bridging capacity through exposure to any politi-cal conflict, technical miscommunication, or administrative difficulty they would be required to resolve (Milne Bay Community-Based Coastal and Marine Conservation Project 2001; Government of Papua New Guinea 2002).

The National Steering Committee had decision-making power and an advisory function over the project and was chaired by the Secretary of the Department of National Planning and Rural Development. Meetings were to take place at least biannually with more as needed in order to advise project management, review project progress, approve the work plan, and monitor expenditures. The project leader, once hired, was to report directly to this committee (Government of Papua New Guinea 2002). A provincial steering committee was not in the initial *Project Document* but was eventually formed to perform the same functions on a more local level. Both of these committees indicate an interest in incorporating local and global perspectives into project planning and oversight, increasing broad-based authority of the project.

The *Project Document* also included a fairly detailed process of monitoring and evaluation. Logical frameworks were to be used both as a reporting and a management tool (Milne Bay Community-Based Coastal and Marine Conservation Project 2001). Participatory approaches to monitoring and evaluation were to be used whenever possible (Kinch 2001), including in the creation of terminology and indicators for the project, an adaptive management cycle for institutional learning, timetables for reporting and evaluation, and roles and responsibilities for each activity. Reporting was to play an important role in this process. A tripartite review by the government, UNDP, and CI was required once per year to determine the progress of the project and make improvements (Government of Papua New Guinea, n.d.). The project was also subject to quarterly operational reports, and mid-term and final independent evaluations (Government of Papua New Guinea 2002).

These plans seemed to embrace the bridging functions NGOs need to overcome the paradox of scale, connecting the global and local scales in efforts to shape the project as it progressed. However, while they incorporated local actors in oversight functions, the processes also incorporated short-term, quantifiable measures that did not necessarily allow for change in the project trajectory. Reflecting these global accountability norms made the oversight and reporting functions difficult and often disempowered local actor participation. While concerns about the infrequent interaction between these committees and project staff were raised throughout the first years of the project, members of the National Steering Committee cite the meeting to approve MacKay's *Inception Report* in 2004 (the first tranche of reporting on project implementation) as the clearest example of their disempowerment. In that meeting, members felt that MacKay as project leader did not allow discussion to take place.[35] According to those who disagreed with elements of the report, they were "made aware that their opinions were not welcome."[36] Committee members had very little interaction with CI and relied on MacKay to organize the meetings (and he did organize the meetings when they took place, despite the fact that the project documents indicate this was the committee chair's responsibility).[37] When CI did supply reports or proposed programmatic changes to the committee, they were given to the steering committee in long, poorly organized documents (e.g., one was 137 pages long), making it less likely that these busy people would be able to fully digest the content (Baines, Duguman, and Johnston 2006). Government officials felt uninformed because project staff sent them technical reports on the project "on disk and small print" that seemed officious, instead of briefing them in person on the details of the project.[38] Some members report never hearing about the *management* of the project, just the project plans.[39] Notes from the National Steering Committee meetings were rarely circulated to the public,[40] and committee members were often seen as "managed" by MacKay, instead of the other way around.[41] The National Steering Committee met only two to four times in three and a half years (Baines, Duguman, and Johnston 2006).[42] Moreover, even if there was clear and consistent evidence in the reports that the current activities were failing to meet their objectives, the committee could not alter project objectives or outputs—only project activities and/or implementation arrangements. Changes to GEF-funded activity required the consent of the GEF/UNDP executive coordinator or his representative (Government of Papua New Guinea 2002). Thus, like the global accountability norms proposed in chapter 2, even under the best scenario, these committees' input was end-of-pipe and technocratic, with no ex ante ability to change the direction of the project.

The Provincial Steering Committee was also seen as a body that was undermined by administration.[43] This committee was created by Bena Seta (the project's second in command and former provincial government official) after the project began[44] and was meant to be populated by provincial leaders, and led by the Milne Bay provincial administrator.[45] In the beginning the administrator did chair the committee, but after the provincial election (which replaced the administrator), the former administrator kept attending.[46] The new provincial administrator did not organize meetings;

he relied on MacKay to brief the group and call meetings, but because hiring MacKay took so long, there was no project leader in the beginning of the project and the board was not briefed properly. While the Provincial Steering Committee was more active than its national counterpart, they were similar bodies in that neither had true oversight power over the project.

Reporting lines and requirements were convoluted and complex, and driven by global norms of quantitative, short-term reporting to the actors with the most power. CI was obligated to provide UNDP quarterly operational and financial reports, combined annual project reports and project implementation reviews, and certified annual financial statements. However, because of the complicated reporting structure, the protracted search for a new project leader, and the few reporting demands by the funders, very little reporting was ever done. There were no status reports for the first seven months of the project and only two project status reports in the life of the entire project. Almost half of the quarterly progress reports were never filed and there was no annual report for UNDP and no complete physical inventory of the project. The Milne Bay Project office was required to report its finances to the Port Moresby CI office, which would in turn report to CI in Washington, DC, which would then report to funders. However, the Milne Bay office would also report directly to UNDP.[47] Not only were there multiple reporting centers, but there were multiple accounting procedures required by the two major players in this project: CI and UNDP. Their accounting systems were not compatible with each other, often making reporting a double task (Callister 2006a).[48] These complexities were raised by MacKay in the inception workshop, but were never fully addressed (Callister 2006a) and often caused conflict between the CI offices in Washington, DC, and Milne Bay.[49] Accounting also required training for Milne Bay staff, which occurred outside of Papua New Guinea. There were changes in accounting software and frequent changes in accounting staff in Alotau[50]—four financial managers in fewer than thirty months (Baines, Duguman, and Johnston 2006).[51]

The issue of oversight brings to light many local demands of the project. Local board members wanted to have a say in the project direction, they wanted to be informed regularly of project activities in face-to-face meetings, and they wanted some of the wealth of the project to stay in the communities, not just with CI.[52] In short, they wanted to have authority on parts of the project and required standard local accountability norms by the project staff. Without the ability of project staff and leadership to understand the local accountability norms of personal, individual, oral communication both to convey information and as a form of respect, and without the steering committee's understanding of how to best invoke the members' oversight power, these committees were rendered useless as local accountability mechanisms.[53] Having context-specific accountability norms could have empowered the steering committees, giving them oversight power that went beyond technocratic suggestions toward root changes in operations, and making the project's interventions more locally focused and sustainable. Instead, these committees were disempowered and resources that could have been focused on their engagement were diverted to reporting to funders. CI's investment in their global communication capacity (manifested in written technical reports that are revered in the global scale) was prioritized over the local approach, marginalizing any local input and driving the organization from plans that created broad-based authority to implementation that favored global authority.

"Options"

A fitting example of how both the Village Engagement Teams and the oversight boards were well intended but eventually disempowered instruments of local accountability norms was the idea of sustainable livelihood "options." In many ways, the engagement team acted to adhere to local accountability demands by building long-term relationships and demonstrating project flexibility to local demands. As an integrated conservation and development project, staff interactions with communities both discussed the benefits of conservation in and of itself, but also helped to determine sustainable livelihood "options" that would support the communities as they reduced their reliance on the reef. Although the engagement teams conducted several meetings and formal surveys to determine what the communities wanted and needed, many of these options did not come from the communities' ideas of how they would develop themselves. Staff were concerned that it was an expert-driven process rather than a community-driven one (Callister 2006b). In addition, the word "options" itself was problematic, since community members eventually equated the term with the concept of a promise, instead of *potential* programming. Creating an options document is best practice in the global realm of technical conservation and development. The options documents for the Nuakata and

Netuli island areas listed yam and taro cultivation, diversifying household gardens, and training in new fishing methods as possible development projects (Milne Bay Community-Based Coastal and Marine Conservation Project 2005; Baines, Duguman, and Johnston 2006). Sources often asked me to have CI come back to their communities and "do the options" like they said they would do, indicating that while the vocabulary of global conservation had entered the communities, the concept had not.[54] When CI pulled out of the province, these options represented broken promises of the project, making the engagement teams seem disingenuous and local oversight impotent.

Other Examples of the Paradox

There were other examples of how the paradox of scale operated in this project's short history. One indicator of overlooked local accountability norms was the lack of interest in socializing with community members. While project leadership understood that the Napatana Lodge, a local restaurant and inn, was "where perceptions get made"[55] and feedback could be solicited for the project's work, they discouraged staff from frequenting this popular bar. Regardless of CI staff's absence, the discussions at Napatana, owned and operated by a prominent and opinionated expatriate, formed public opinion on the project. By not participating, CI project staff lost any input into these opinions, and any ability to respond to them or incorporate them into the project. More importantly for local accountability norms, they lost an opportunity to build long-term relationships and consent among the community.

The differences in accountability norms were evident in the agreements CI created with many groups including resource-dependent communities and local organizations. These agreements are best characterized not as contracts, but as memoranda of understanding (MOUs) (Niesten, n.d.). CI staff engaged local actors in many discussions about what the MOUs entailed and great ceremony was associated with their eventual signing.[56] But the administrative and political ideas behind these instruments confused the communities and staffers. One former CI partner stated: "(CI) stressed that it's not a legally binding document. If one partner is not happy they can pull out with thirty days' notice. If it's not legal, then why do we need it? It just raises expectations. (The locals) have their ways of agreement. Why not just follow that?"[57] Communities in Milne Bay operate more on trust than on legalities. These MOUs were seen as a personal promise between the local groups and CI. This exit clause also puzzled the expatriate partners of CI, who saw CI's breaking of the agreements when it exited Milne Bay as undermining CI's own espoused values of respect and integrity.[58] Additionally, when CI pulled out of the MOUs commitments, local organizations were not paid the funding they expected for services they had prepared to deliver (Baines, Duguman, and Johnston 2006). These legal instruments represent different cultural understandings of both the political realm (e.g., communications, partnerships, ethics) and the technical realm (e.g., legal frameworks) of this project, as well as the formality of accountability mechanisms on the global and local scale.

The issue of project financial overhead brings to light how the paradox of scale is reinforced by funders. When community members did not see an influx of cash into their villages, they had very specific ideas about where the project money was being spent. As one local business owner put it, "From the local perspective, seeing an NGO with flashy cars and knowing how much money (they raised), where were these millions being spent?"[59] Those who are not intimate with the administrative and political details of global fundraising might erroneously assume that funds spent on overhead should rather be spent on the project. As a CI staff member in Washington, DC, explained, "most people hate the idea of overhead. It's just a simple factor of life–the lights, the building, ... if your institution (infrastructure) doesn't exist then you can't get a grant, but the person who gets the grant usually doesn't care about the institution (infrastructure)."[60] Moreover, CI did not determine how much of its funding goes to overhead: strict rules and analysis generated annually by the U.S. Agency for International Development's Negotiated Indirect Cost Agreement dictate how much of CI (and any U.S.-based NGO that does business with the U.S. government) funding can go toward overhead and how much must go toward the project.[61]

The issue of high overhead costs brings to light the political and administrative needs of building bridges to educate the local scale on global funding norms. First, these perceptions indicate that not enough was done to give locals an accurate description of the project's financial obligations at the global scale. Second, in order for CI to receive such funding for its conservation work, it must show global, political, and administration capacity and spend funds on strategically located offices in Washington, DC, and on relatively expensive offices in Milne Bay that have the global communication capacity (i.e., Internet and phone technologies) expected of a transnational NGO. Without this global political prowess, CI would not have had access to evaluate the resources in Milne Bay or solicit funding for their conservation. While local staff and communities may criticize CI for its global political capacity, without this capacity there would be no project. Overhead is an NGO necessity that needs to be clearly communicated across scales, and an example of the importance of global norms and capacity to local interventions.

How Global Norms Undermined CI's Broad-Based Authority in Milne Bay

NGOs seek broad-based authority so they can operate at both the global scale where the many rules of conservation are created and the local scale to implement those rules. As the theoretical framework in this book asserts, authority is legitimated power. However, since power and legitimacy (and their proxies of capacity and accountability) are context-specific, so too is authority. In order to maintain both local and global authority through context-specific capacity and accountability norms, NGOs must also demonstrate bridging capacity to meaningfully connect and translate between scales. Individuals with bridging capacity—who have the intercultural and cross-cultural understanding, the power to make decisions within the organization, and the dedication to connect this global-local divide—are few. Even where they do exist, they can easily be disempowered by institutional forces that are blind to both the need for a conduit between scales and to the dominance of the global scale in project choices. When asked, long before the demise of the project, if this was a typical initiative for the organization, CI senior staff in Washington, DC, said, "it is typical in that it is context sensitive. It's not one-size fits all conservation.[62]" How then, with staff and leaders espousing the importance of context, was CI unable to maintain the balance of local and global demands? The first step for NGOs to enable bridging capacity and maintain broad-based authority is to acknowledge the role of norms and the prioritization of global norms that lead to this paradox. Table 3.2 summarizes the systematic replacement of local accountability norms and capacities with global ones in the Milne Bay project. The remainder of this chapter will examine how the change in bridging capacity enabled these changes and the development of the paradox of scale.

Table 3.2

The struggle between global norms and local norms in Milne Bay

Local norms and capacities ...	... replaced by or competing with global norms and capacities
Village Engagement Teams created long-term relationships and discussions on MPA creation (A)	Project area expanded to new areas with little VET engagement or input; MOUs between actors were dissolved (A&P)
VETs worked to resolve issues with leadership and communities (P&AC)	Project leadership assumed problem-resolution function (top-down) (P&AC)
Open-door communication policy between leadership and staff (A&PC)	Top-down, opaque decision-making (A&PC)
Community Engagement Process emphasized self-reliance of communities, no demonstrations of wealth, among other rules of engagement (A&PC)	Requested a list of needs from a community that was perceived as part of an exchange (A&PC)
Five years of pilot phase (A)	Shortened schedule (after delays) with expanded reach for phase one, and accelerated spending
Steering committee to combine local and global oversight (A)	Steering committee informed of changes without discussion (A)
Leadership with intercultural and cross-cultural understanding and power to make decisions in the organization (B)	Leadership with global capacity and some markers of interest in being a bridge, but no context-specific experience (B)
Hiring local staff in Milne Bay office (AC)	Need to train local staff in complex accounting and difficult reporting standards (leading to turnover of staff) (AC)
Relationships with fishers to discuss status of resources (TC)	Expensive equipment and bathymetric surveys (TC)

A = accountability norms; PC = political capacity; AC = administrative capacity; TC = technical capacity; B = bridging capacity

The initial project planning team demonstrated great potential as an agent of bridging capacity. It consisted of a Milne Bay government official, and two CI employees: one a national of Papua New Guinea and the other an Australian anthropologist with family ties to PNG who resided in Milne Bay. The anthropologist eventually became the temporary project leader. This group had experience in both the global scale of conservation and the local scale of Milne Bay, and created the project's initial plan with the bridging mechanisms of Village Engagement Teams, and the National and Provincial Steering Committees. Thus, they possessed cross-cultural understanding and were willing to serve as a bridge between Milne Bay and Washington, DC. Their effectiveness in ushering in the mechanisms described above indicated that they initially had power within the project to make project-based decisions for the organization. However, when two of these individuals left the project (the acting project leader and a PNG national), it lost the critical mass of bridging agents needed to maintain broad-based authority.

The search for the new project leader or "Chief Technical Advisor" demonstrated one way the organization reflected the conservation field in which it operates by favoring global capacity over local. Bena Seta, a local government official from the project planning team, was hired as the project's second in charge with the unwritten expectation that once he acquired sufficient capacity, he might lead the project in its second phase.[63] However, according to staff members, Seta was not yet qualified for the top leadership position because the position required conservation experience in multiple locales and a doctorate degree.[64] The ideal candidate would have both experience working in the region and managing a large integrated conservation project. There was no such person willing to take the position in Milne Bay, so those staffing the project were forced to look abroad. Finding a person who fit this description and was also willing to move to a remote location was difficult; the search took eighteen months. In the end, CI favored the global norms of capacity for a project leader over local capacity, and hired Peter MacKay, who had no experience working in Papua New Guinea but had a PhD and recent experience with marine protected areas in Australia (technical capacity), and management experience on a large-scale project in Yemen (potential to bridge to some local communities). Hiring a person with this experience is not out of the ordinary in transnational conservation (or other transnational NGO projects). Like many leaders of conservation or development projects around the globe, this person would have to balance the large number of local staff working on the project (including the project's second in command) with the bureaucratic requirements of major funder (GEF/UNDP). As with many transnational efforts, finding someone with demonstrated global and local capacity (even if the locality is different from the project) would seem a good fit.

The change in project leader marked a difference of approach for the project: disempowering bridges and prioritizing the global accountability norms of quantifiable performance measures on short timelines, and answerable to the most powerful actors with local actors left with very little oversight authority. Instead of demonstrating the give and take of long-term relationships, any potential for learning between the project leader and the second in command was seen as unidirectional. In community members' and former employees' minds, MacKay was there to demonstrate to the local leaders the global approaches to project management (as some informants called it the "top-down way"[65]) without having to learn local approaches himself. After CI left Milne Bay in 2006, local staff complained about not having any input into either the day-to-day workings or the overall approach of the project. While this research cannot speak to MacKay's desire to bridge scales, the above does indicate that he had little cultural understanding of the local context and that the second in command had both limited understanding of the global norms of the field and limited power to make decisions.

The global norms of urgency and quantifiable deliverables supplanted any long-term relationship building, context specificity, and flexibility that the project had previously prioritized. This prioritization of global norms was evident in three changes that eventually led to the project's early closure: (1) accelerated spending causing the project to run out of funds one year earlier than budgeted; (2) the expanded scope of the project that did not allow for longer-term trust building, for an already overburdened staff; and (3) unidirectional, "forceful" communication between project and the staff leadership (under the pressure of these timelines and performance measures), which eventually led to the staff's disgruntled discussions with project evaluators, demonizing MacKay, and making recovery of the project impossible without major reorganization.

While the project itself had a longer timeline than many GEF projects, five years was still a tight timeline for phase one activities, considering the scale of the area. Upon hiring MacKay, the five-year time horizon for phase one did not change. That is, while almost two years of productivity were lost while searching for a permanent project leader, all the deliverables for the project were still due in November 2007. Both CI and UNDP stressed to MacKay that "implementation had to be accelerated or 'funds might be lost'" (Baines, Duguman, and Johnston 2006, iii). This compression of the project from five to three years created a "tremendous pressure to spend" (Baines, Duguman, and Johnston 2006) and an incredible pressure to see project results.[66] With the new project *Inception Report*—which detailed *how* the project should operate—the three zones of the project were expanded and to them a fourth was added,[67] increasing the reach of the project (Baines, Duguman, and Johnston 2006). While the Village Engagement Teams supported some changes in the project (the inclusion of projects concerning women and youth, for example), they were less enthusiastic about the geographic expansion. As stated in the previous section of this chapter, the National Steering Committee was given little notice and no authority over this decision.

Project spending also accelerated, but the rate of acceleration was not well calculated, and by October 2005 the entirety of the project funding was spent. According to the final evaluation, approximately 58 percent of the total budget was spent in one year (Baines, Duguman, and Johnston 2006). When it was discovered the project had no funds to finish the last year of phase one, UNDP called for an independent audit. What should have been a late mid-term evaluation of the project turned into its final evaluation.

Almost overshadowing the overspending of project funds, this evaluation brought to light considerable shortcomings of the project management, as well as considerable complaints from the community members and staff about the project and its leadership. Before the project's acceleration, conflict resolution and problem solving were a team efforts. After, any problems the Village Engagement Teams encountered in the field were resolved by MacKay or Seta. Before, the data the engagement teams collected was incorporated into the plans of the project. But participation takes time, a resource this project was running out of. Former staff reported that the open-door policy for approaching project leadership was reversed, engendering shouting matches instead.

The Milne Bay Project had several actors and mechanisms to bridge the local and global arenas CI inhabited. Other employees, former employees, and conservation experts from Papua New Guinea were prevalent in the project's National and Provincial Steering Committees. The Village Engagement Teams acted as conduits between communities and the project. Some staff and leadership in Conservation International's Washington, DC, office had extensive experience and publication records indicating their cultural understanding of conservation in Papua New Guinea. CI's vice president for Melanesia and the PNG country director even coauthored an article in 2005 that highlighted among a list of potential pitfalls for projects in Melanesia the inflexibility of funders and timelines of projects (Beehler and Kula, n.d.). The efforts at scaling up their activities and impact undermined the authority of these actors to make decisions for the project.

Some analyses of this project lay responsibility for the Milne Bay Project's failure squarely on the shoulders of CI's leadership or specifically MacKay as the permanent project leader (Baines, Duguman, and Johnston 2006; Dowie 2008). While it would be convenient to impugn specific actors, even former CI partners in Milne Bay say "Don't blame everything on Peter [MacKay]. He had some wrong approaches but there were other things going on."[68] Indeed, other things were going on. As this book demonstrates, the organizational and field-level pressures to conform to global norms of capacity and accountability created a difficult situation for the Milne Bay Project's leaders. Both Kinch (as the interim leader) and MacKay (as the permanent leader) experienced this pressure. While Kinch at first demonstrated ICCC (intercultural and cross-cultural) capacity, he experienced pressure to conform to global norms during the Kwaiwaira field trip. After he resigned, MacKay also felt the pressures but perhaps was less equipped to resist them, due to a lack of ICCC capacity.

This is precisely how the paradox of scale undermines potential bridges and stymies the efforts of the most powerful NGOs to maintain broad-based authority. Using their global capacities as expert fundraisers, media facilitators, international negotiators, and scientists, they create policy niches for themselves in some local scale. While they may not initially have the capacity at this local scale to affect lasting change, if they do acquire it through hiring local staff or partnering, they still lack the bridging capacity to effectively reconcile local and global accountability norms. *Even if they have access to local capacity and potential agents of bridging capacity, their investment in creating and promoting the norms of the global scale—the same prioritizing of paths that bring them funding and access to remote resources—undercuts their power to make decisions as true bridges.* These norms favor global approaches to political, administrative, and technical ways of doing business and being accountable and undermine bridging capacity by devaluing intercultural and cross-cultural understanding, deincentivizing actors' desires to be agents of bridging capacity, and disempowering their abilities to make decisions based on the ICCC understanding. The more NGOs invest in creating global norms that do not allow for flexibility and context specificity, the less effective any potential bridges will be, thus ensuring NGO failure on the ground. CI leadership repeatedly demonstrated this paradox dynamic, prioritizing the global capacities of Western science, project management, monitoring and evaluation, and communication styles, resulting in CI leaving the province and the communities in which it worked for several years.

Elements of CI's experience in Milne Bay are not idiosyncratic to this case study, or even to the conservation field. The struggle between meaningful participation and the urgency of mission is a common one for development, human rights, and other transnational nongovernmental organizations. Many NGOs feel the need to report measureable results to funders, when incremental change is difficult or uninteresting to measure. NGO professionals are often called to work in different and new locales, to bring their "global" expertise to unfamiliar communities. The case study of Conservation International's work in Milne Bay, Papua New Guinea, serves to highlight how a powerful environmental nongovernmental organization that works toward balancing the local and global demands to create broad-based authority can still falter within the dynamics of the paradox of scale.

4 The International Marinelife Alliance in the Philippines: The Paradox of Scale for an Expanding Local NGO

The destructive fishing techniques used in the live reef fish trade first drew international attention in the mid-1980s. In order to catch and sell the fish alive for aquarium hobbyists or restaurants, fishers were first stunning the fish with a solution of diluted sodium cyanide. Focusing on the Philippines as the center of the trade, one organization, the International Marinelife Alliance (IMA), was created specifically to stop these problematic fishing techniques and make the trade more sustainable. IMA began with one individual, Steve Robinson, who entered a community of fish collectors, gained their trust over time, and learned about the fishing practices for the trade. While he was interested in the global supply chain of live fish, his actions were locally based. Demonstrating local accountability norms, he focused on the actors in the product chain who had the least political leverage, took time to understand their context and needs, and amplified capacities local fishers already possessed. Through his detailed publications on the issue and potential solutions to it, Robinson motivated others to action at a national and then regional scale, eventually cofounding the International Marinelife Alliance. Like many NGOs, IMA was started through the time, energy, and finances of a small group of dedicated individuals. Because it was small and scrappy, the organization was able to ignore most of the global-scale demands for many years, instead focusing on the local scale capacities, and contexts. Over the course of fewer than twenty years, this NGO became a local authority in the fight against destructive fishing practices throughout the Philippines.

Whereas the CI case in chapter 3 established how NGOs with global authority are pulled into the paradox of scale as they try to expand their operations to new locales, the story of the International Marinelife Alliance demonstrates how an NGO that begins at the local scale is also susceptible to these destructive dynamics. Without having been delegated authority by any state, IMA began its operations as many NGOs do—with raw power that had yet to be legitimated on any scale. After using this capacity to expose the issue of destructive fishing to the world, IMA established its local authority by building long-term relationships with fishers, fish traders, and the communities that depend on the fish trade. It worked with communities to demonstrate how changing their fishing practices could both be more sustainable for the resource and also create a better product to sell. In part by listening to the communities' demands for alternative livelihoods, and focusing on hidden stakeholders such as school children, IMA was able to legitimize its work by adhering to the local accountability norms.

All these activities demonstrated IMA's authority in resource governance. In its programs to change the way fishers caught fish, the organization implemented new rules for resource use. In its efforts to test fish for the use of cyanide, it enforced these new rules. It was able to scale up its efforts throughout the Philippines, but encountered the dynamics of the paradox when it entered the global scale. This local authority pulled IMA into the global spotlight for conservation—a spotlight accompanied by demands to prioritize global capacity and norms over local ones.

This expansion began as IMA grew to respond to more fishing communities within the Philippines and, eventually, in other countries. Its local authority on the trade gave it access that enabled IMA to influence the international conservation field. Its funding base expanded to include more funders with varying reporting and programmatic requirements. It started working with other NGOs, collaborating on publications and outreach with the World Resources Institute, and on programs with The Nature Conservancy, ReefCheck, and the Community Conservation Investment Forum.[1] IMA also placed its leadership on the board of the Marine Aquarium Council. Moreover, many government agencies took an interest in IMA's work—from the Philippine agencies to other countries in the region that participate in the trade, the U.S. Agency for International Development (USAID), and the U.S. Coral Reef Task Force.

As the organization expanded, it acquired several staff members whose various backgrounds and conservation experience in the global, national, and local scales poised them to act as bridges to connect and negotiate between local and global scales. These individuals worked to move the organization from a local authority to a broad-based authority by strategically planning IMA's expansion, creating a diverse board of directors, and working in partnerships with multiple organizations. Although the staff members had both the intercultural understanding and the desire to serve as bridges between the organization's operational scales, they did not possess enough power to quickly change how the NGO operated. While IMA's president was resistant to many of these changes, a funding issue brought into quick relief the differences between the global and local scales and the priorities the organization held constant.

For years, the International Marinelife Alliance danced between global and local scales. However, the tragic events of September 11, 2001 changed the conservation and philanthropic world considerably, marking the beginning of the end for the nongovernmental organization. In the aftermath of 9/11, one of IMA's major supporters had difficulty releasing money to its grant recipients. Usually a timely disburser of funds, the U.S. Agency for International Development (USAID) delayed its release of approximately $500,000 USD to IMA by almost a year. To cope with this unexpected shortfall, the organization reduced its budget, but also "diverted" otherwise restricted funds—monies raised by a separate organization that was managed by IMA—to continue its conservation efforts. Under the same circumstances of delayed funding, Conservation International (see chapter 3) was able to use its global capacity to raise unrestricted funding to continue its work. IMA did not have these capacities at the same level as CI. While IMA made some efforts to conform to the global norms of accounting, project management, and conservation in general, it did not have the capacity to do so long term, especially without the funding, support, and trust of its funders and partners. The organization was caught in the paradox of scale with pressure to prioritize the global accountability norms over the local. In 2003, after an exodus of unpaid staff and discontinued relations with funders, IMA was no longer able to continue its operations.

As figure 4.1 indicates, IMA's story can be divided into three eras: (1) the beginning (from 1984 to 1992), when IMA's founders moved from raw power to local authority by establishing locally appropriate accountability relationships; (2) Philippine success and broad-based authority (1992–1998), when the organization found continued success with its local

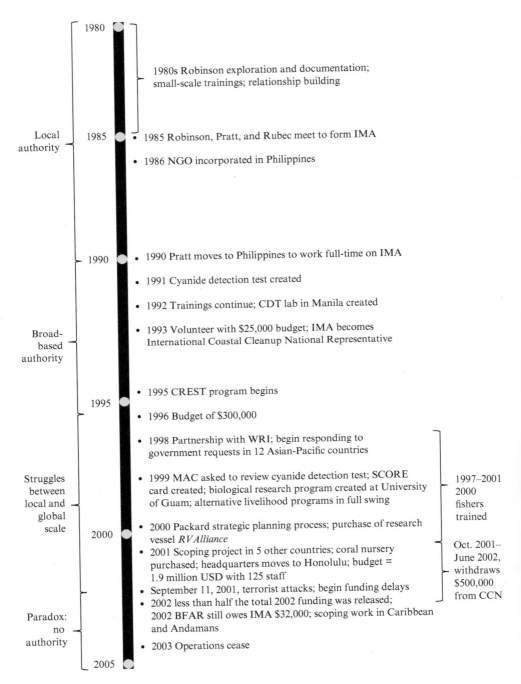

Figure 4.1
International Marinelife Alliance: How the paradox of scale developed over time

approach to conservation throughout the Philippines and complemented this approach with some global capacities and accountabilities; and (3) global expansion and denouement (1998–2003) when IMA's local success on the live reef fish trade created global demand for its work, which was accompanied by pressure to prioritize global capacities and accountability norms over the local scale. In IMA's case, the organization's leadership saw this pressure as a direct threat to what had given the organization authority in the local scale. Without empowered bridges to negotiate between local and global norms, IMA was unable to maintain both its global and local authority. Instead of giving in to the pressure, IMA's leadership chose to rebel against it, making administrative and political choices that, while perhaps acceptable at the local scale, delegitimized the organization at the global scale. Through a series of choices that rebelled against global norms, IMA eventually lost both local and global authority and was unable to continue its organizational existence.

This chapter will begin by briefly reviewing the resources and livelihood issues that brought IMA to the Philippines. Next it will turn to each of these organizational eras to explore how the NGO moved between the states of raw power, local authority, and broad-based authority, only to lose all authority and power within twenty years of its founding. This chapter will illustrate how IMA's status as a local authority on the destructive fish trade drew the organization to expand its work into other local scales as well as to operate on the global scale. After tracing how the organization was pulled into the global scale, the chapter will discuss how the pressures to build global authority threatened to undermine IMA's already established authority. It will also trace in a series of events how IMA's president resisted the pull to prioritize global norms as the organization scaled up its operations, and how this resistance eroded its broad-based authority over time. With several actors poised to act as bridges between the local and global scales, IMA's story is a clear example of how an organization might build local and global authority by demonstrating scale-appropriate capacity and accountability, but without empowering bridges to connect and negotiate between these scales, the organization's broad-based authority is precarious at best. This case also demonstrates how as an organization grows and expands to new scales, these bridges become even more important for maintaining broad-based authority and avoiding the destructive dynamics of the paradox of scale.

The Live Reef Fish Trade and the International Marinelife Alliance

The destructive practices of the live reef fish trade were first created in the 1960s and present a unique threat to the world's coral reefs. The annual global trade for this sector is considerably more humble than other natural resource industries: the ornamental fish trade totals an estimated $28 million to $46 million USD per year (Balboa 2003; Wood 2001) and the live reef food-fish trade produces anywhere from $800 million to $1 billion USD per year (Padilla et al. 2004). Despite these numbers, the trade has a disproportionate impact on coral reef ecosystems, and the reefs of the 'coral triangle' in particular (Kassem and Madeja 2014). Live reef fish are sent for final sale in the U.S and Western Europe for the ornamental fish trade and Southern China and neighboring countries for the live food fish trade. Since they are caught, shipped, and sold all while alive, there are limited techniques fish collectors can use to harvest them. Chemicals like sodium cyanide are squirted on the reef to stun fish and make them easier to capture alive. These chemicals also destroy the coral upon which the fish depend and create human risks for the fishers who handle them (Cervino et al. 2003; Barber and Pratt 1997b). Located in the center of this coral triangle, the Philippines' coral and fish species outnumber or rival any other country in the world (Burke, Selig, and Spalding 2002; Burke et al. 2001). In the Philippines, where 90 percent of the people depend directly on marine products and their high nutritive value (International Marinelife Alliance 2001a), the destructive manner in which these live reef fish are caught can have a devastating effect on the local economy and health of Philippine villages (Barber and Pratt 1997b).

In the early 1980s, ornamental fish trader and hobbyist Steve Robinson backpacked around the world, working as a fish collector as he traveled to fund his trip. He went to Bolinao, Pangasinan, in the Philippines to confirm rumors that fishers there used sodium cyanide to catch fish. The village fish collectors were secretive about their fishing methods, but after months of living there, Robinson gained the trust of a prominent villager who pressured the younger fishers to bring him on a fishing expedition. This was the first time that Robinson witnessed cyanide fishing and the first documentation of cyanide fishing as a common fishing technique in the Philippines (Baquero 1999). His article in a U.S.-based aquarium magazine (complete with photos) marked the beginning of the conservation movement to eliminate destructive fishing in the ornamental fish trade.[2] Subsequent articles also demonstrated how, with the proper training and equipment, these cyanide fishermen could be successful barrier-net fishers, like their counterparts in Mexico and Australia (Rubec 1997).[3] This small-scale, person-to-person training of fishers focused on the capacity fishers already possessed and augmented it with the use of barrier nets. Reflecting local accountability norms, these trainings were context specific and were built on relationships with local actors.

Robinson's articles piqued the interest of U.S.-based veterinarian Vaughan Pratt and academic Peter Rubec, who invited Robinson to Massachusetts so they could learn more. In 1985, within a few weeks of meeting, Robinson, Rubec, and Pratt had drafted the mission statement and articles of incorporation of the International Marinelife Alliance[4]—a small, scrappy organization focused on barrier-net training for local fishers and protection of reef habitats.[5]

During the first few years, IMA was able to balance local and global norms and capacities, since there was little interaction on the global scale. Robinson resumed his role as a bridge between scales, returning to the Philippines to train fish collectors, frame and publicize the issue, and consult with the national government on how best to combat destructive fishing throughout the Philippines. Rubec and Pratt remained in Massachusetts long enough to raise funds for programming and raise awareness on the global scale. IMA registered as an NGO in the Philippines in 1986 and in Canada (now called Ocean Voice International) in 1987 (Rubec 1997), but with little activity outside the Philippines. In the beginning, Robinson's trainings were the only interaction with the fishing communities since he had developed a relationship with them and bringing in others to train might change the organization's dynamic with the fishers. Robinson understood how to effectively work with them: "In working with fisherman, you have to create something worth stealing. A trick in collecting, a technique, better netting material, better handling of fishes with superior, immediate and obvious results, something. Otherwise, you'll be trying to change people for someone else's agenda and that's a far more difficult sale." IMA made significant progress in the 1980s, gaining government support in promoting mesh barrier nets, creating a community-based net training program, and demonstrating that barrier-net collecting was a viable alternative to destructive fishing methods (Rubec 1997).

Building Local Authority for the International Marinelife Alliance

How did IMA change from a few individuals exposing the destructive fishing techniques of fishers to a nationwide organization that engendered the trust of local fishers? How did it convert its raw power into local authority? Three programs demonstrate how local accountability norms—flexible, responsive programs; long-term relationships with communities including untraditional stakeholders; and incorporating community needs into the NGO program, no matter how removed from the reef—legitimized IMA to local communities. The 1990s marked an expansion of IMA's program throughout the Philippines.[6] In 1990, Pratt moved from the United States to Manila permanently and started working for the NGO full time as its president. In these early years, IMA focused on exposing and combating the problem of cyanide fishing in the live reef fish trade through its publications[7] (International Marinelife Alliance 2000) and training fishers on less destructive methods. Through 1996, the organization's work in the Philippines consisted primarily of these fisher trainings, cyanide testing and enforcement, and education and awareness building.[8] Later in the 1990s, IMA ventured into alternative livelihood programs for fishing communities, indicating an attempt to respond to fishing communities' demands. Between 1992 and 2001, IMA solidified its programming and then worked to expand its focus beyond the Philippine borders.

In keeping with this book's definition of local accountability norms, the organization offered context-specific, flexible responses based on the long-term relationships it developed with a broad array of stakeholders within fishing communities. Stemming from a belief that "community is not just the guy with the squirt bottle, it's the families, (and) schools,"[9] IMA focused much of its programmatic attention on broader education and awareness campaigns directed at schoolchildren, other community members, tourists, hobbyists, industry, and local and global policy players. It also focused some of its energy and resources on alternative livelihood programs for fishing communities. All of this was a purposeful attempt to be responsive and context specific. As one former staff member mentioned "Filipinos have had thirty years of community organizing and frankly, these communities see it coming and they think 'Oh boy, here comes another community organizer' and they were tired and embarrassed by telling people about their families, their sewage, their income, all that, because they never saw any benefit [from telling]. So at least when IMA came in, we actually taught people how to fish and [earn] income and [we] gave books to schools."[10] The organization worked diligently to create change that the fishing communities would appreciate.

Trainings and Relationship Building

As the organization grew, training continued to be an important part of IMA programming. They hired local fishers to train their communities both because it was effective and to reflect an ethic of hiring local people.[11] The organization also created illustrated instruction manuals on sustainable fishing techniques (Ansula and Evilio 1998).[12] Fishers were trained not only in barrier-net fishing (for the ornamental trade) and hook-and-line fishing (for the live food fish trade) techniques, but also in fish handling, marketing, and how to add value to their product (International Marinelife Alliance 1999b). Ferdinand Cruz, a former fish exporter in the Philippines, served as director of trainings. Because of his professional experience, he understood the trade intimately and served as a signal that sustainably harvested fish would be in demand, should the fishers change their methods. In demonstrating that the organization was not just thinking of habitat conservation without also taking into consideration the livelihood of fishing communities, these trainings continued the relationship-building process that local accountability norms promoted. Other nonlocal staff would "mingle with [the fishers], spend[ing] lots of time so after a week or so they start[ed] to see [the nonlocal staff] as someone they wanted to talk to."[13] While earlier documentation on the number of trained fishers is unavailable, IMA estimates that in later years (1997–2001) the organization trained fifteen hundred fishers on barrier-net fishing and five hundred in the use of hook-and-line capture technique, with only 30 percent reverting to destructive fishing methods (Rubec et al. 2001).

Education and Awareness

In the mid-1990s, IMA also developed an education and awareness program called Coral Reef Education for Students and Teachers (CREST), with manuals and kits for the Philippine school systems (created in collaboration with the Palawan State College) (Romero et al. 1996).[14] These manuals contained twenty-one lesson plans for teachers from grade school to high school level, including hands-on activities, science experiments, and comprehension questions. The teachers appreciated CREST, with lessons teaching environmental awareness using coral reefs—the communities' closest and most important natural resource—as a focus.[15] For this program, IMA acquired its own printing press, hired twenty-five educational staff, worked in 1,800 schools, produced thousands of books per month, and trained fifth- and sixth-grade teachers in Palawan, Cebu, and other provinces using IMA's curriculum.[16]

As a bonus to this program, IMA created a Quiz Bowl competition based on the curriculum. Top performers in each province were brought to Manila by IMA to compete in a national competition where the winner received a cash prize, a personal computer, and a computer for their school (all donated by Metro Manila businesses).[17] Through CREST, IMA hoped to instill a love of nature and academic excellence in students. Additionally, the organization wanted to expose students to the city of Manila (a place many fishing community members could not otherwise visit) and a life and livelihood not dependent upon fishing. In the long run, fewer fishers meant less pressure on the reef.

The education program illustrates how IMA did not conform to global accountability norms. CREST was a response to a local need for capacity building, working through local teachers (who appreciated having lesson plans drawn up for them), and focusing on fishing communities. It was not a response to a national request for educational programming and, in fact, it was created and disseminated throughout the Philippines without first consulting the Department of Education, Culture, and Sports. IMA's leaders saw creating the CREST program in partnership with the bureaucracy of the Philippine government as a sure-fire way either to delay its implementation or permanently mire it in a bureaucratic mess. Instead, the organization planned to create a successful program first, impress the other actors with its successes, and then partner with these organizations to continue the work. IMA invited the minister of education to confer the student awards for its first national Quiz Bowl competition, associating the Ministry with the program once it was deemed a success to garner future government support for the program. Without having to wade through bureaucratic processes, IMA created a successful program, responding to local needs and capitalizing on local capacity. A sign of CREST's success was that, at one point, it became part of the regular curriculum in schools all across the Philippines. Teachers in at least one province are still using the manuals, even years after the program ended (International Marinelife Alliance 2003).[18]

Alternative Livelihoods and the Microenterprise Support Program

IMA's alternative livelihood program was less successful in responding to local demands while avoiding bureaucratic red tape.[19] While the organization worked "to help conserve marine biodiversity, protect marine environments and promote the sustainable use of marine resources for the benefit of local people" (International Marinelife Alliance 1999a), it did not lose sight of community needs. Fishing communities needed income. They needed a livelihood and for generations they had depended on fishing for this. Part of the organization's plan to reduce the pressure on reef resources was to take fishers out of the fish trade and find alternative work for them.

One such project was the Coral Reef Rehabilitation Program in Cebu, a southern Philippine province. By creating certified farmed corals, IMA hoped the Filipino fisherfolk would corner the market for corals in the ornamental trade, make a decent living, remove the need for wild harvest, and even contribute to the rehabilitation of reefs by transplanting farmed coral. IMA acquired a farm that employed 25 families, contained 275 coral nursery units built by members of the local fisherfolk organization, and rehabilitated two reef sites with farmed coral (International Marinelife Alliance 2006b).

However, IMA did all of this regardless of the Philippine government's ban on trading coral—wild or farmed. Much like its approach to the education program, IMA tried to build entrepreneurial authority by demonstrating success in responding to local needs before incorporating national political actors in its work. Despite the government ban, IMA took the risk that it could convince legislators that corals could be farmed sustainably. This time, the risk did not pay off: the Philippine government refused to lift the ban. Ultimately, the farm could never sell its product. At last report, the corals were too large for the market and the farm ownership was transferred to the community.

Building Broad-Based Authority from Local Authority

Having established IMA's local authority, this chapter now turns to examine how IMA incorporated the global scale to create broad-based authority for its work (see table 4.1). During these early stages, IMA's only global activities focused on demonstrating global capacity at the local scale: defining the destructive fishing issue for tourists in the Philippines, convening the local branch of the International Coastal Cleanup, and bringing global scientific capacity to the local issue of cyanide fishing through the establishment of a cyanide detection test. It did not necessarily work to integrate global and local norms; instead, it primarily demonstrated global capacity to local actors. IMA had already established the problem of

Table 4.1

Evidence of IMA's broad-based authority

	Accountability (as an indicator of legitimacy)	Capacity (as an indicator of power)	Bridging capacity
Local	• Responded to needs of communities with education and alternative livelihood programs • Built relationships with fishing communities • Saw businesses and children as stakeholders • Took input from communities for its social enterprise programs	• Small-scale trainings that built on local capacity (TC&PC) • Worked with educators to create a context-specific education program; avoided bureaucratic delays (TC&AC&PC) • Hired local administrative staff and trainers (PC&TC)	• Founders had experience living in multiple countries • New staff had experience working in multiple countries and in global fora • While staff created pressure to balance demands, only leaders had power, indicating a weaker bridging capacity
Global	• Success measured in number of fishers trained and number of fish tested • In phase two of work (expansion) IMA had a prepackaged solution to governments, not necessarily tailored to the context	• Brought global organizations, press, and events to PI—Coastal Cleanup, WRI, CNN (PC&AC) • Cyanide tests, standard operating procedure, and labs created (TC) • Global fundraising (PC)	

PC = political capacity; AC = administrative capacity; TC = technical capacity destructive fishing for the Bureau of Fisheries and Aquatic Resources (BFAR) of the Philippines—and to some extent Robinson's articles educated both the aquarium hobbyists and the general public. For Filipino public awareness, IMA became the national representative for the International Coastal Cleanup in 1993 (International Marinelife Alliance 2001a).[20] This involved organizing a national day of community clean-up events throughout the country on an annual basis. It was the perfect event for an organization that worked so hard at building long-term relationships with community members since it focused on cleaning up their communities and bringing people together to volunteer. During IMA's work on the coastal clean-up, the Philippines reported a record number of participants for the international event.[21]

The International Marinelife Alliance also worked with scuba diving operators to raise the awareness of their local and foreign tourists. They created the Status of the Coral Reef (SCORE) card program (International Marinelife Alliance 1999). This program distributed photo cards to help divers identify reef species encountered on their dives. Since the Philippines is a top destination for scuba divers, this was a small but strategic effort to build global awareness of the live reef fish trade and destructive fishing to a specific audience, which was also motivated to protect the resource for ecotourism. With these cards, divers helped keep track of biodiversity in the Philippines, bringing a quantitative reporting process to local reef health discussions.

The Cyanide Detection Test (CDT) and Laboratories

A central element to IMA's work to deter destructive fishing techniques clearly demonstrated both global capacity and accountability norms, but also a failure to live up to those norms in the long term. The cyanide detection test (CDT) was created in 1991 to offer scientific proof of cyanide fishing in order to raise awareness of the problem, enforce the regulations against the use of cyanide, and monitor the success of IMA's programs to make the trade more sustainable.[22] While the trainings were aimed at implementing sustainable harvest methods by helping fishers learn new techniques, the cyanide tests were meant to deter them from using destructive fishing methods by enforcing sustainable fishing practices. The test procedure was created by Dr. R. Sundararajan and approved by the American Society of Testing Materials (a standard-setting body) (Holthus 1999; International

Marinelife Alliance 1999c).[23] The final test procedure was adapted so that cyanide could be detected by testing a liquid created by emulsifying fish (Department of Agriculture—Fisheries Sector Program Philippines, n.d.).[24] Following the recommendations of the standard-setting body, IMA created the standard operating procedures and determined the equipment needed to create a cyanide detection laboratory (International Marinelife Alliance 1999c).

The test's success was immediate and widespread. Pratt demonstrated the test for the Philippine Bureau of Fisheries and Aquatic Resources in 1991, and together IMA and the bureau established the first cyanide detection laboratory in Quezon City (Metro Manila) the next year (Pratt 2004; Rubec 1997). During IMA's heyday, there were six labs throughout the country.[25] In 1997, there were fifty cases in the Philippine courts based on positive cyanide test results.[26] Between 1992 and 1997, these six labs tested over seven thousand fish and invertebrates for cyanide (Rubec 1997). That number spiked in the late 1990s, with an additional 25,000 marine fish being tested by 2001 (Rubec et al. 2001). The labs were a central part of the enforcing of regulations against cyanide fishing; courts used test results as evidence to prosecute offenders (Philippine Headline News Online 1998).[27] While there is still some conflict over whether or not any fishers ever went to jail based on CDT data,[28] many businesses lost money since their live cargo died while investigations based on the test results took place.[29] In the late 1990s, word of IMA's success with the cyanide detection test spread and the organization received requests to build the capacity of local governments to establish similar laboratories in Indonesia, Vietnam, Sabah, Malaysia and the Marshall Islands, and other Asia-Pacific countries (Pratt 2004).

The development and implementation of this scientific test required global technical, administrative, and political capacities. This process also reflected global norms of accountability by giving immediate, quantitative data on both the number of cyanide-caught fish and the success of IMA's interventions to reduce this number (International Marinelife Alliance 2001a). The International Marinelife Alliance's records showed that the number of fish testing positive with cyanide was reduced from over 80 percent in 1993, to 47 percent in 1996, and 20 percent in 1998 (Rubec et al. 2001).[30] While IMA's fisher training, education, and alternative livelihood programs upheld local accountability norms by being context specific, built on long-term relationships with a broad array of stakeholders who could influence programming ex ante, the cyanide detection test program focused on global accountability and capacity norms by offering technical, ex post, and end-of-pipe deterrents to destructive fishing.

These initial stages of the cyanide detection labs demonstrate IMA's global capacity. In later years, however, the test became a symbol of how IMA did not uphold global conservation norms of scientific method, peer review, and partnerships. Around 1998, the success of IMA drew attention to the organization and the destructive fishing issue from other NGOs, bilateral agencies, governments in need, and new funders. Much of this attention was welcomed—it took the form of more funding, requests for help from governments, and more publicity. In this way, the attention garnered more global authority for the NGO. Other parts of this attention were less welcome, and led to questions about the validity and importance of the cyanide detection tests,[31] among other issues.

In 1999, the Marine Aquarium Council—an organization created for the certification of sustainably harvested aquarium fish—was asked to perform a peer review of the cyanide detection test (Holthus 1999). This external scientific review suggested—with much repudiation from IMA (International Marinelife Alliance 1999c)—that the test was neither appropriate nor accurate for the purposes of determining cyanide use in the live reef fish trade (Holthus 1999).[32] The process of developing and disseminating the test is central to the controversy. First, some claim that IMA worked with chemists to create the test and the standard operating procedure without input from any other conservation organization (Holthus 1999). While IMA offered evidence that contests this assertion (International Marinelife Alliance 1999c), the opacity of the process demonstrates a lack of adherence to global accountability norms. Next, with little or no oversight, IMA created the labs for cyanide testing throughout the Philippines and implemented an enforcement procedure for collecting and assessing fish catch. IMA then successfully managed the cyanide detection testing labs—with little to no outside input—from 1992 to 1998.

The debate is telling about how IMA's attempts to operate at a global scale and build broad-based authority fell short. With just a few activities at the global scale, the organization felt the pull to prioritize the global norms and capacities—the transparency and responsiveness of scientific peer review, working in partnership with other globally oriented organizations—over the local capacities and norms that drew it global attention in the first place (e.g., effectiveness with local authorities, achieving results with few bureaucratic delays).[33] As an organization that valued long-term relationship building with local communities as part of its approach to mission, IMA staff saw the dispute as partially personal; that questioning the test was in part questioning the ethics and legitimacy of IMA itself as well as its employees, especially Pratt and Rubec.[34] The leadership seemed genuinely flummoxed: IMA's work to define the problem of destructive fishing and create effective interventions drew global attention, but the same methods and approach that afforded that success and attention were now under scrutiny. The organization found itself caught in the dynamics of the paradox of scale.

Global Partnerships to Build Global Authority

While the trainings created a growing supply of sustainably harvested fish, IMA's programs would only have impact if there was demand for this product. The organization worked on every step of the supply chain to increase supply and demand of sustainably harvested fish, including with the Manila-based Philippine Tropical Fish Exporters Association.[35] But IMA also needed to create bigger demand with the end consumers in the United States, Europe, and Southern China. The cause needed a global campaign. In 1998 IMA addressed this need by opening an office in Hong Kong to monitor imports for the food fish trade,[36] and forging partnerships with globally oriented organizations to create a broader impact on the trade.

With limited political capacity to bring the issue to the global stage, IMA partnered with the World Resources Institute (WRI), an environmental think tank based in Washington, DC. Through this partnership, IMA began working on a global level—documenting cyanide use for the United States Coral Reef Task Force and other important players in the global environmental forum and telling its story through CNN and BBC film productions.[37] As the partners wrote in the foreword of IMA's strategic plan, "Throughout this process, WRI has drawn on its own particular institutional strengths—policy and strategic analysis, NGO capacity-building, and community outreach—to assist IMA in its transformation from a small national NGO to an organization poised to play a central role in marine conservation across Southeast Asia and the Pacific" (International Marinelife Alliance 2001a, iv). Experienced in global environmental fora, WRI Senior Associate

Dr. Charles Barber connected IMA to the global media, policy fora, and funders, as well as to other NGOs working in the region. Mirroring the local process of creating long-term relationships, the personal friendship between Barber and Pratt was immediate and deep, making this partnership IMA's most productive one. Eventually, Barber left the World Resources Institute to become a vice president of the International Marinelife Alliance for what became the last year of its existence.

Local Authority Leads to Global Expansion

The year 1998 marked the beginning of a rapid expansion into the global scale for the International Marinelife Alliance. With little funding and recognition on the global scale, IMA managed to create an extensive program in the Philippines built on long-term relationships with fishing communities, with quantifiable results measured by the cyanide detection test labs. At the beginning of 1998, it was a scrappy, Philippine-based and Philippine-focused organization (International Marinelife Alliance 2001a).[38] By the end of that year, IMA's programs were established in six other countries (see figure 4.1). IMA grew from a volunteer organization with a budget of $25,000 USD (in 1993),[39] to a budget of $300,000 USD (in 1996), and close to $1 million USD in 1997 (International Marinelife Alliance 2001a). In 2001, IMA's budget grew to $1.9 million USD as its success at the local level pulled it to work globally (International Marinelife Alliance 2001b). While the majority of its funding came from USAID, the Packard Foundation, and the MacArthur Foundation, IMA's budget was filled through grants from a dozen other sources (International Marinelife Alliance 2001b), all wanting to invest in what seemed like a guaranteed success.

In 1998 IMA sent staff to the Marshall Islands, Solomon Islands, Papua New Guinea, Kiribati, the Carolines and the Marianas, Indonesia, and Hong Kong on the request of their governments to create baseline status reports on the trade (International Marinelife Alliance 1999b). From those reports, IMA launched a regional program in partnership with WRI that established field programs in Indonesia, Fiji, Hong Kong, the Marshall Islands, Vanuatu, and Vietnam (International Marinelife Alliance 2001a). IMA also established scoping projects in Australia, Palau, Christmas Island, and Papua New Guinea (International Marinelife Alliance 2001a). An integrative Biological Research Program was created with the University of Guam Marine Laboratory in 1999. This expansion marked a transition for the organization—from the entrepreneurial authority it established in the Philippines to authority that was delegated from the governments of the countries requesting IMA's assistance. In 2001, IMA headquarters moved to Honolulu to be more centrally located for the Pacific regional program (International Marinelife Alliance 2001a). In 2002, IMA scoped potential work in the Caribbean and the Andaman Islands. It was no longer the small Philippine NGO it had been for the first decade or so of its existence. It was now operating on the global scale.

There were markers of the organization's attempts to reconcile its global expansion with the local focus that made it successful in the first place. Wherever it opened an office, IMA tried to hire local staff and local fishers for its trainings. As part of the IMA expansion, the NGO purchased a 110-foot pelagic fishing ship in Palau in 2000 (International Marinelife Alliance 2002a). Named the *RV* (Research Vessel) *Alliance*, IMA planned to move this ship to the Philippines where it would be refit with sophisticated biological and bathometric equipment for use as a roving laboratory. IMA saw this as its strategy to access and document resources in remote atolls—a unique approach since no other NGO had such a research vessel to build local capacity for scientific research throughout the region (International Marinelife Alliance 2002a, 2002d). In addition to research, this ship could be used as a source of income by serving non-IMA researchers and ecotourists (International Marinelife Alliance 2002b, 2002d).

IMA's staff expanded to respond to its growing geographic and programmatic focus. From 85 staff in 1997 (Rubec 1997) to an estimated 125 in 2001,[40] the expansion of staff made it difficult to ensure that each staff member subscribed to the organizational focus on the local scale. Indeed, many of these new staff members were recruited for their global scientific, political, and strategic capacities, reflecting the organization's changing scale. While these new staff members all seemed to understand the importance of local norms and capacities, they were advocates for rethinking and restructuring IMA, building global capacities through creation of strategic plans, organization-wide policies and procedures, board development, and other areas.

The growth of the program and funding created a snowball effect: the bigger the program, the more funding IMA needed; the more funding it received, the more requests it received to expand. In 2001 the MacArthur Foundation and the Packard Foundation granted hundreds of thousands of dollars to the organization ($900,000 USD and $811,680 USD, respectively) (International Marinelife Alliance 2002c, 2002e). The U.S. Agency for International Development's (USAID) Philippine Mission was already a funder of IMA in a limited scale and a new USAID initiative—its East Asian Pacific Environmental Initiative—had accepted their multimillion-dollar multiyear proposal. These funds were instrumental to IMA's expansion, moving from an annual budget of about one hundred thousand dollars to over a million dollars. However, for many reasons often beyond IMA's control, much of the funding promised to the growing organization was never disbursed, leaving IMA in a difficult situation. The following sections will detail the complex dynamics of this growth and the choices that Pratt, as IMA president, made to prioritize local norms over global ones in an act of rebellion against the paradox created by this growth.

The Demands of Becoming a Global Organization

An indicator of the global administrative and political capacity needed to operate at this new global scale, the NGO applied for a grant from the Organizational Effectiveness and Philanthropy Program from the David and Lucile Packard Foundation in 2000 to facilitate a strategic planning process that would highlight IMA's strengths and needs as a growing conservation entity (Parks 2001). This process brought key staff together to refocus IMA's vision, mission, objectives, and management structure to meet its new demands and interests, as well as articulate the organization's institutional values. The results of the meeting were circulated in an elegant, peer-reviewed report highlighting IMA's successful past and entailing both substantive and administrative changes to take place. The process that produced that report, however, was less elegant. While strategic planning processes often mark new beginnings in organizations, in hindsight, IMA former staff see this as the beginning of the end of the organization[41] since it not only exacerbated any management difficulties IMA had, it also forced the organization to change the approach that was instrumental to its past success.

A major constraint on IMA's ability to reorganize was its decision-making structure. IMA's centralized decision-making[42]—typical of a smaller, start-up NGO—was difficult to replace with policy and bureaucracy as the organization grew. All funding went through the headquarters office in Honolulu. Field offices would receive deposits for their activities on a monthly basis.[43]

Tied to these funds, administrative and programmatic decision-making also passed through the central office and one individual in particular: IMA President Vaughan Pratt. Staff had discretion over some issues, but anything Pratt saw as important—from political to administrative issues—he would decide.[44]

Part of IMA's success was based on its lean and scrappy approach to problem-solving. Pratt's and others' frustration with bureaucracy and politics ensured that when IMA identified a problem, the leadership mobilized to solve it immediately, rather than engaging in prolonged strategizing about a solution. Pratt was concerned that staff would spend time and energy in these long meetings only to arrive at the same solutions he could create instantly. Moreover, former IMA staff lamented: "We sit around talking for eight months and then the problem has gotten worse."[45] Pratt's approach to problem-solving was successful on fisher training, educational programs, and the creation of the cyanide detection test and labs. Changing this process was seen as a threat to that success.

Once IMA started expanding its programs regionally and its partnerships to the global scale, this approach was neither sustainable nor a reflection of global organizational capacity or norms. While communications between Pratt and the IMA staff were frequent,[46] they were often not productive. Big decisions would take longer to make, and field staff were often left in limbo while Pratt deliberated or had to focus on other issues. Multiple staff noted Pratt's temper as both a response to this increased responsibility, and a roadblock to honest discussion and feedback.[47] In this way, the IMA case seems to parallel CI's work in Milne Bay. Centralized decision-making by a strong personality was not suitable to achieve local results for a global NGO in Milne Bay, but in a small, Philippines-based organization it seemed to get the job done. Now that IMA had grown beyond a small, Philippine-based organization, this structure became a hindrance to its progress.

In keeping with the organizational ethos that scoffed at long meetings, Pratt reduced the number of meetings in IMA's Packard-funded Organizational Effectiveness Grant strategic planning process and requested that the first five-day meeting in Kota Kinabalu be compressed to three days. Pratt and the facilitator compromised on four days, but the days were so jam-packed that the exhausted participants could not finish the work, prompting a second meeting in Honolulu months later to finish the plan.[48] While this marked a compromise between global norms of strategic planning and IMA's modus operandi of avoiding delays, this disjointed process took more time combined than the original meeting would have due to the loss of continuity and the costs of preparing and executing two meetings instead of one.[49]

The retreat reflected on more than the organization's mission and vision; it also recommended management changes. IMA was to reduce its staff in the Philippines and move its headquarters to Honolulu to be more centralized for travel to its new programs in the Pacific. This was a difficult task since the Philippines program employed more than a hundred Filipinos (Parks 2001) to whom organizational leadership was very loyal. In addition, IMA established official offices in the countries of its field programs and an overarching scientific research program. The strategic plan required IMA to create financial processes and policies that would streamline the international operation and allow the headquarters to monitor financial activity with less effort (International Marinelife Alliance 2001a). Most controversially, the group decided that IMA needed to hire a new chief financial officer and create a new board of directors and that unlike the current situation, none of these actors could be related.[50] Prior to the strategic planning process, the chief financial officer of IMA was the wife of the president and the board of directors was made up of relatives and IMA staff.[51] These arrangements were no longer acceptable by global nonprofit norms or the norms subscribed to by IMA employees.[52]

This strategic planning process was so instrumental in gaining authority in the global scale that IMA began to house another organization, both physically and administratively in 2001: the Community Conservation Network.[53] Since CCN was a smaller organization, its funders required its finances to be managed by a better-known and more management-capable organization. Because IMA was undergoing a strategic planning process and had partnered with globally authoritative organizations like WRI, it was seen as having global capacity, too. CCN rented offices from IMA and, while their organization would remain a separate entity, their funds were included in IMA's accounting procedures. Thus, IMA in theory lent CCN much needed infrastructure for an NGO start-up. The actual relationship was problematic, however, and as the next section will detail, played a large role in IMA's failed rebellion against the global scale.

While the strategic planning provided a detailed map—financial policies, a legitimate board of directors, management processes—to take IMA from a smaller Philippines-focused nonprofit to a global conservation entity, it was never implemented.[54] There were overt disputes between the Pratts and the other staff about replacing Dali Pratt as chief financial officer, since her dismissal was seen as a personal slight that disrespected her skills and loyalty to the organization. Dali Pratt was not the only IMA staff member unhappy about the changes in organization. Other senior staff were quite territorial about their areas of expertise and the lines of authority and responsibility within the organization. Whereas before, senior staff all reported to the president, the new bureaucratic processes created new levels of management, making senior staff feel less powerful and prompting them to complain about the changes. Given this internal turmoil, it is not surprising that IMA was not able to balance the accountability demands about to be foisted upon it.

The Ultimatum of the Paradox of Scale

As the previous sections indicate, there were several points of friction between global and local norms and capacities within IMA's story: flexible and responsive program decision-making with fishers versus singular focus on cyanide detection and enforcement in new locales; autonomy of leaders to react to needs versus strict hierarchy and procedures for work that tied the hands of many founding leaders; creating a solution and then finding supporters versus beginning with national and global partnerships and the long interactive processes they require (see table 4.2). This constant friction between how the organization historically created its success and how global actors wanted it to operate wore on IMA's daily operations and ability to achieve its mission. This section will trace the funding and management problems that marked the end of the organization and highlight the struggles with the paradox of scale and IMA leadership's attempts to rebel against them.

With its application to the USAID's East Asian Pacific Environmental Initiative, IMA created the Indo-Pacific Destructive Fishing Reform Initiative in partnership with the World Resources Institute (International Marinelife Alliance 1999b). This comprehensive, region-wide program included cyanide testing, fisher training, working with governments to create appropriate policy for the trade, media campaigns, and support for the Marine

Table 4.2

The struggle between global and local norms and capacities for IMA

Local norms and capacities ...	... replaced by or competing with global norms and capacities
Flexibility in program to respond to local needs and contingencies (A)	Standardized program with little flexibility on how it was implemented (A&TC)
Avoided bureaucratic delays by acting entrepreneurially (PC&A)	Many bureaucratic delays in order to follow protocol (AC&PC)
Programs that implemented new fishing techniques, enforced the ban of cyanide use by testing fish, but also focused on educating youth, alternative livelihoods, as suggested by community (A&TC&PC)	Standardized program that focused on the cyanide detection test and training fishers (TC&A)
Long-term relationships with local employees in the Philippines (A)	Reduced PI staff, and suggested putting project on hold (A&AC)
Quick decision-making on program (AC)	Longer, more complicated decision-making (AC)

A = accountability norms; PC = political capacity; AC = administrative capacity; TC = technical capacity; B = bridging capacity

Aquarium Council's efforts to certify sustainably harvested fish. All of this was to occur over three years in more than a dozen countries, in partnership with multiple local and transnational NGOs, with a total budget of $3,758,000 USD. It was ambitious and bold, building on the reputation the organization had for effectiveness on a small budget. The proposal was compellingly written; it included evaluation measures and procedures and a list of exemplary staff that offered both local and global capacity on the issue (International Marinelife Alliance 1999b). When the proposal was accepted for funding, it marked the organization's deliberate entry into the global scale.

A few months after receiving notice that their USAID East Asian Pacific Environmental Initiative proposal was accepted, the terrorist attacks of September 11, 2001 occurred. While tragic in their own right, these events were also tragic for nonprofits working on issues other than national security, relief efforts, or outside of the Middle East, because it seemed much funding was redirected to these areas. IMA's leadership felt the repercussions of these events in a profound way, as it resulted in increased pressure to comply with global norms (which required global capacity the organization was still in the process of building), and to prioritize the demands of the global scale over the local norms and capacity upon which the organization had built its reputation.

The process for finalizing USAID contracts requires the U.S. Congress to approve any allocations of funds. Caught in the alarm that 9/11 created for homeland security, Congress delayed discussion of any other aid.[55] In the case of IMA, the first trench of $500,000 USD—26 percent of IMA's total budget—was delayed for almost a year[56] (International Marinelife Alliance 2002c, 2002e). On a weekly basis, IMA staff members contacted their USAID grant officers to see when the money would be released, but the story remained the same: "the money will be released whenever Congress releases it." By September 2002, IMA had received less than half of the total 2002 funding from USAID (International Marinelife Alliance 2002c).

USAID was not the only organization that withheld funds from IMA. Per an IMA internal memo dated October 2002, the Bureau of Fisheries and Aquatic Resources of the Philippines also allegedly owed the organization $32,000 USD[57] as its final installment for the cyanide detection testing labs (International Marinelife Alliance 2002c, 2002e). There are conflicting stories regarding why these funds were never disbursed. IMA claims it filed all the necessary paperwork to receive the final installment while the bureau's representatives simply state that their criteria for funds disbursement were not met. Regardless, the last installment was never sent.

With all of its potential funding tied up, IMA's leadership had a decision to make. While the money was in limbo, the problem of destructive fishing was not going away, and the loyal staff who worked hard to stop destructive fishing needed to be paid. In the IMA president's eyes, the threat was growing and the solution on hold. If they waited for their funding to address the issue, would the problem have become insurmountable? If, as they were advised, they laid off much of their staff until the funding came through, would IMA's staff—the people in whom IMA had invested time, money, and expertise—return to IMA? If not, would the organization have to start over by training new staff? What would happen to the long-term relationships the organization was building with its staff and, through its staff, with fishing communities? The process of scaling up operations seemed to create an ultimatum: follow the global processes and norms of the most powerful actors (i.e., the funders) by suspending activity; or maintain the approach that brought the organization success for decades by continuing the long-term relationships with communities and local staff, avoiding bureaucratic delays, and addressing conservation issues quickly. IMA's president made the decision to keep the program moving—albeit, on a more limited scale—despite the delays in funding. In keeping with IMA's modus operandi, he chose to affect change rather than deliberate over it. To do this, however, IMA had to "borrow" restricted funding to pay salaries. Between October 2001 and June 2002, IMA implemented three dozen withdrawals, diverting over $500,000 USD from the Community Conservation Network (the organization housed within IMA because of IMA's alleged global administrative capacity). IMA periodically reimbursed the diverted funds, but over $160,000 USD remained outstanding at the time of discovery.[58]

Other "borrowed" funding to keep the organization operating came from the ship, the RV *Alliance*. The purchase and refitting of the ship were financed by a low-interest loan from a private donor based out of the Caribbean,[59] which gave IMA some financial flexibility for finishing the refitting. During these difficult times, however, the ship became an albatross to IMA. With the USAID funds tied up in Congress, the funds for refurbishing the ship were spent on staff salaries. When the loan was called in (at a rate of $9,976 USD per month for twenty-two months [International Marinelife Alliance 2002c]), IMA had neither a working ship nor the funds to repay. IMA staff wrote proposals to funders to help get the ship in working order and out of dry dock (International Marinelife Alliance 2002b), but their efforts were not successful. The individual who loaned IMA the funding was understandably upset, since he had neither a working ship he could sell, nor an organization with any income to recuperate his costs. The last known status of the ship was that a majority share was being sold for a token price to a private company that would then refurbish the boat, but also have the majority say in its purpose.[60]

Even with all of IMA's creative accounting, many former staff members still report not having been paid. At one point, several former staff members recall being owed ten to sixteen months' worth of paychecks—some totaling in the tens of thousands of U.S. dollars.[61] Offices had to shut down because their rent stopped being paid from IMA's central offices, at times leaving the local office managers personally indebted to their landlords. Taxes and retirement funds were taken out of staff paychecks, but never paid to the necessary government offices, leaving staff members with a trail

of unknown debt and bad credit. When staff members called IMA's Honolulu office to ask about their money, they were told "it's coming; there are
things we need to do but it's coming."[62] Only a few staff members actually
knew IMA's full financial picture. In the meantime, the NGO's president
mortgaged his home and took out personal loans from family members to
keep the organization afloat.[63]

When staff members of the Community Conservation Network discovered and disclosed to their funders that their funds were being used by
IMA for purposes other than those agreed upon, funders started exerting
control over IMA, which was also their grantee. The organization had been
focused on keeping afloat and maintaining its local relationships, but it
needed to balance the demands of its funders, too. The Packard Foundation, whose funds were diverted without authorization, referred the matter
to their general counsel who strongly cautioned the organization's leaders
that—even with IMA committing to create a new board and policies for
financial and other administrative matters[64]—the NGO's deeper systemic
issues might preclude the foundation from further funding the organization. Even with the money repaid to CCN with interest "(the Packard
Foundation) cannot say now that IMA is regarded by the Foundation in
the same way as other current or prospective grantees. Getting to that
point will require time, many direct conversations, and, most importantly,
evidence of very fundamental changes in IMA's staff and the way it does
business."[65] Other major funders required documentation of changes and
resolutions to this issue before releasing their funds to IMA.[66] This, in addition to the canceled BFAR funds and the delayed USAID funds, signaled
the end for International Marinelife Alliance. IMA's funding situation
turned desperate. Both its global and local reputations were irreversibly
tarnished. The global demands would not be subordinated to IMA's priority focus on local demands. The details are still disputed, but it seems as
though everyone in the IMA sacrificed and suffered in the last few years
of the organization.[67] Sometime within the period of late 2002 and early
2003, IMA closed its doors.

How Weak Bridging Capacity Undermined Broad-Based Authority in IMA

Like so many successful transnational nongovernmental organizations, the
International Marinelife Alliance experienced a long period of time when

it was able to balance the local and global scales to achieve change. Even with its prioritizing the local scale over the global scale, the organization demonstrated some global capacity and norms. It was able to inform the global trade through the articles Robinson, Pratt, Rubec, and others wrote, through bringing global scientific processes and capacity to create the cyanide detection test and instituting the cyanide detection labs. It brought the global spotlight to the Philippines and the fish trade through the International Coastal Cleanup, the SCORE card, and the success of its programs to transform the trade. This limited amount of global-scale activity was manageable for the organization. Once the scope of its work expanded regionally and globally, the few bridges that existed in the organization were no longer able to support the growing demands.

First and foremost, Dali and Vaughan Pratt, the founding couple of IMA, represented potential bridging capacity. A Filipino-American couple who had both lived and worked in the Philippines and the United States, they were well skilled in local capacity in the Philippines and had worked in a dominant culture of the global scale: the United States. As leaders of the organization, they possessed the power to create changes in the organization. As mentioned previously, Vaughan Pratt was a dynamic leader and made most decisions for the organization. The crucial bridging element they did not exhibit, however, was the desire to make these changes. When pressed to make organizational changes, former staff state that the Pratts stalled or became defensive.[68] When challenged on the cyanide detection labs, they would not entertain the idea that another way of enforcement was possible. Moreover, when faced with an ultimatum of global norms of operation versus the locally focused approach that had made them successful and respected within both fishing communities and the global scale, they chose to rebel against the global norms and prioritize their local relationships. They refused to give in to the pressures to conform to global norms and felt the repercussions dearly.

Charles Barber, who started as IMA's partner in the World Resources Institute and became IMA's vice president at the time of expansion, worked to bridge the divide between local and global scales. His primary function was to build IMA's global political capacity. He acted as their representative in Washington, DC, on policy issues and in fundraising, and made several contacts with global media, bringing CNN and the BBC to fishing communities to cover the story of destructive fishing and the International

Marinelife Alliance's approach to changing the industry. More broadly, his role was "trying to get the place re-organized to be a professional international NGO."[69] He had long in-person and email discussions about how the organization needed to be restructured, including the board of trustees: "If we want to play in the big leagues (and we are already), we have to play by the rules. And the rules on board membership for environmental NGOs are simple: The only staff member of an organization that can be on a board is the President, and he serves 'ex officio,' meaning 'by virtue of office.' Family members of senior staff, especially the president, cannot be on the board."[70] Once the financial issues surfaced, Barber served as a communication conduit between all IMA's funders and the leadership of the organization, often sending long, detailed memos about the status of funding from the East Asian Pacific Environmental Initiative, the Packard Foundation, the MacArthur Foundation, the Oak Foundation, and others, and advising Pratt on what needed to be done and what needed to be avoided to steer the organization through these difficult financial and reputational straits.[71] Having lived in the Philippines for years, he demonstrated both intercultural and cross-cultural understanding as well as the desire to act as a bridge. What he lacked was the power within the organization to make substantial changes. Despite all this effort, and consensus among other staff members that these changes needed to take place, his advice was not heeded and he eventually resigned.

Over the course of twenty years, the organization accumulated multiple staff members who were either local community members whose interest in global conservation made them eager to learn global capacities and norms, or global conservation or fisheries experts who were committed to local, community-based conservation. Like the funders who were eager to help IMA expand its programming beyond the Philippines, the globally oriented staff were also impressed by the organization's ability to affect change at the local scale, and thus committed to this approach. These globally and locally oriented staff pushed IMA to restructure to demonstrate global organizational norms while holding dear the local approaches to conservation. They worked to inform global debates with the organization's data and experience through its conservation efforts. They lobbied to bring global resources—media, funding, governance bodies—to the communities who adopted IMA's approach based on the trust they had built with the organization over time. Some of these efforts were welcomed by IMA's leadership. Others, however, were seen as an infringement on the approach that had made it successful in the first place.

IMA's strategic plan called for a revised management structure but former staff report that Pratt would disengage when the issue of restructuring was raised, since this meant removing his wife from office and other relatives from the board.[72] As the grip of the global scale became more powerful on the organization, the president's grip on the organization also became tighter, turning decision-making processes more opaque and starkly delineating the differences between how IMA operated and how the actors at the global scale wanted it to operate. When the organization found itself in a financial bind, Pratt would not reduce the core staff. Rather, he assumed that the better-compensated staff could sacrifice some of their salary so that the less salaried staff could still eke out a living.[73] One former staff member summarized his interactions with Pratt: "He'd go 'Well, what should I do? Fire people?' and I'd say 'Well, yeah! That's exactly what you have to do when you don't have any money and you can't pay them anymore! You should have fired me a long time ago since you can't pay me!'"[74] This loyalty to local, long-term employees precluded creating the management structure that employees, funders, and partners deemed necessary for IMA to function as a transnational NGO.

This is how the process of scaling up operations causes NGOs to break down. As IMA expanded into the global scale, its relationships with global actors triggered the paradox of scale. While global actors admired IMA's product and wanted to encourage the continuation of IMA's unique work, they needed IMA to conform to its procedural norms. Funders did not know, however, that IMA's success in achieving its mission was directly linked to the fact that its capacity and accountability relationships were *not* like global actors. IMA focused almost exclusively on the local scale and doing whatever necessary to achieve results—responding to fishers' needs even if it meant working outside of its original work plan; ignoring bureaucracy until a project was ready for implementation at a wider scale; including a broad definition of "stakeholders" that included children, teachers, the families of fishers, local NGOs, industries, and people from "all walks of life."[75] Its quick response was borne out of an understanding of the people who were tired of NGOs entering their communities without giving them any tangible or valuable results. IMA took uncomfortable risks. It had flexible financial practices. As a result, it was less bureaucratic and had more freedom to achieve its goals. Its primary stakeholders were not the most powerful actors; they were fishers and their families and neighbors, as well as the local staff hired to train fishers and administrate the organization. Where previously IMA enjoyed autonomy in its operations and programming as an entrepreneurial authority, these new global partners required a closer relationship and a more structured process. Frantically trying to free itself from this cobweb of demands, IMA's leadership made choices that led to the organization's demise.

From the beginning, IMA was known for its aversion to large meetings and workshops[76] and for creating short-term success on a low budget.[77] The two were related: Meetings cost time and money that could otherwise be used to solve a problem. The same was thought of creating office bureaucracy, and therefore no staff members with professional management experience or education were hired at IMA.[78] While IMA consistently avoided these markers of global organizational norms, it is important to state that IMA was encouraged by its funders to continue its renegade but effective activities. The NGO achieved results and it was given funds to do more of the same, without any major oversight or third-party reporting. IMA's successful history in conservation was what drew the attention of the global conservation actors, but it was also what served to inhibit the organization's long-term success at the global scale.

The story of the International Marinelife Alliance demonstrates one outcome of a locally focused organization scaling up operations. These locally focused NGOs find that when they are successful at implementing new rules for resource governance or enforcing those rules, they gain a reputation at the local level that spreads to organizations at the global scale. These local NGOs become legitimate authorities on the issue at the global scale, which gives them opportunity to expand to other localities. In this way, these organizations are pulled into the global scale and become transnational actors and must confront the paradox of scale: that the capacity and accountability practices that helped make them successful at the local scale (and thus garner attention in the global scale) will not help them be effective in the global arena; building their global capacity and operating with global norms of accountability will not help them be effective on the ground. The paradox in this case appears as an ultimatum to either prioritize the global scale at the expense of your local success, or prioritize the local-scale operations and jeopardize your chances of expansion and, perhaps, even survival. The president of the International Marinelife Alliance chose the latter, disempowering any potential bridges and rebelling against the global powers. The result of this rebellion: an organization that worked to reform the live reef fish trade for twenty years permanently closed its doors.

5 The Community Conservation Network in Palau: Exiting the Global Scale by a Local NGO Caught in the Paradox

Like much of the Western Pacific, Palau's resources are affected by the live reef fish trade's destructive methods and unregulated consumption. Far in the Philippine Sea, between Papua New Guinea, the Philippines, and Guam, Palau is a small country of fewer than twenty thousand citizens. Hatohobei ("Tobi") is an outlying state with a population of approximately two hundred citizens and housing the biodiversity treasure of the Helen Reef atoll. Because of its abundant resources and geographic isolation from the rest of Palau, the atoll is both valued and threatened by Indonesian and Filipino fishers working in the live reef fish trade. The Community Conservation Network was the transnational nongovernmental organization created for the unique purpose of facilitating local conservation of Helen Reef within the Hatohobei state. With a mission that demonstrated the norms of community-based conservation, CCN did not claim to implement conservation projects itself but rather "assist(ed) local communities and their partners to sustain vital ecosystems and resources by fostering relationships and building capacity that results in improved long-term conservation, management effectiveness, and human security" (Community Conservation Network 2003a, 1). In pursuing this mission, the organization exhibited several local accountability norms: its work was context-specific and flexible, where the stakeholders determined the goals of the project beforehand. Prior to incorporation, CCN's executive director worked for years in Palau on resource management issues as a consultant and student, ensuring that any NGO activities focused on the long-term relationships he built there.

But CCN did more than build local authority in Palau. By bringing global capacity to bear on the Helen Reef Resource Management Project and also by adhering to global accountability norms, the organization built broad-based authority for conservation. To balance these demands, CCN worked with the community members to develop project proposals, create a community action committee, and attract local and global experts to work on the project and bring global technical, political, and administrative capacity to Palau. It also assembled teams of global experts to train community members to perform resource assessments on Helen Reef. Their efforts secured funding from a broad range of international funders to train rangers to guard the resource from poachers. In 2003, resource management authority was delegated to CCN through a contract with the Palau government and the Helen Reef Management Board (HRMB) to create and implement a management plan for Helen Reef. Through this management plan, CCN demonstrated the authority to create, implement, and enforce the rules of resource governance. With fewer than one dozen staff members and expenses hovering around half a million USD (Community Conservation Network 2003a, 2003b, 2004a), CCN built its reputation in community-based conservation. As its local success grew, the organization began to operate with broad-based authority and eventually began to scale up its operations to work in Hawaii and Indonesia.

CCN implemented a division of labor and capacity that allowed it to neatly balance the global and local demands for a large portion of its existence. However, while the organization did exceptional work bridging local and global technical and political capacity, much attention was placed on what was missing: global administrative capacity. In response to this gap, CCN's leadership created organizational policy for smoother operations and in accordance with the norms of global organizational practice. It also applied for and received an organizational effectiveness grant to create a strategic plan and hired a part-time communications specialist to prepare its website, logo, and printed materials (Parras 2003). All this focused on global capacities and accountability norms. However, the local Tobian partners saw the organization's growth as an indicator of their losing local control over the project, including the project's funding. In response, CCN lobbied to transfer financial oversight to the local Helen Reef Management Board.

The pulls between being flexible and responsive to the local board and being systematic and consistent to the global funders created a constant struggle: the increased political capacity made the organization seem too global for its local partners, and the lack of administrative capacity reduced its ability to relinquish control over funding to local actors. In light of this perceived ultimatum, the organization's leadership and staff repeatedly prioritized local norms. Eventually, these choices reduced CCN's global authority to the point where it was unable to secure new funding. As a final act, the organization dissolved in 2009 with its project continuing through two community-based organizations: the Hatohobei Organization for People and the Environment and another focused solely on Hawaii. No longer a transnational NGO with global authority, CCN's staff and leadership exited the global scale to continued success as local organizations.

Like the International Marinelife Alliance case in chapter 4, this chapter explores how the paradox of scale develops in an NGO that begins at the local scale. However, the Community Conservation Network case is distinct from IMA in several ways. First, where IMA built entrepreneurial authority, CCN was delegated authority by the local traditional and bureaucratic governments. Even with this delegation, however, CCN had to work to legitimate its power with the local Tobian community and other Palauan agencies, indicating that delegation is not sufficient to legitimize power. Second, where IMA was a locally-focused national Filipino organization that worked with several local communities throughout the Philippines, CCN really worked with only one community and locale before it began to expand internationally. Third, the CCN case demonstrates how strong bridging capacity—actors with intercultural and cross-cultural understanding, power to change organizational operations, and a dedication to deliberately bridge scales—can help maintain broad-based authority within an organization. The IMA case represented a missed opportunity due to weak bridging capacity. Lastly, where IMA ceased operations altogether, CCN's work continued through newly created local organizations—organizations that seem designed to avoid global pressures to conform. All these differences help paint a richer understanding of how the paradox operates within transnational NGOs.

This chapter traces the organization's development and denouement over the course of CCN's ten years of operation (see figure 5.1). The organization's story is divided into three eras: (1) building and maintaining broad-based authority from 1998 to 2002; (2) calls to expansion and global professionalization from 2002 to 2007; and (3) the final dissolution of the organization from 2007 to 2011. This chapter first demonstrates how the organization strived to create broad-based authority by integrating local

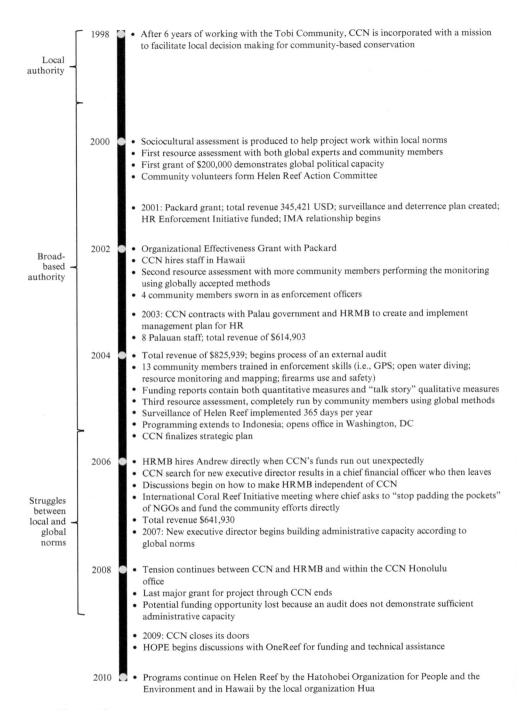

Figure 5.1

Community Conservation Network: How the paradox developed in Palau

and global accountability norms and capacities in the development of its program. The merging of the global and local norms and capacities is most evident in the organization's modus operandi, its monitoring and assessment program, and the creation of an enforcement plan and enforcement officers. Next, this chapter will trace the pulls to scale up its operations as well as the competing dynamics of the local actors wanting more control and the global actors wanting more structure. Lastly, this chapter will explore how these efforts to adhere to global norms of administrative and political capacity were undermined by the staff's passion for locally focused, flexible programming. Where there were individuals who had bridging capacity within the Helen Reef Resource Management Project, most of them eventually lacked the dedication to act as a bridge, creating a gap between scales. All of this will demonstrate how a small NGO with broad-based authority can be pulled into the dynamics of the paradox of scale without being able to maintain the very focus of work for which it gained global recognition in the first place.

Helen Reef and the Community Conservation Network

Before the Community Conservation Network started working with the Tobian community to manage the resources of Helen Reef, the atoll's abundant resources were hardly known to the international conservation world. Now, Helen Reef is recognized as an example of community-based conservation. While the Republic of Palau is an isolated nation, the Helen Reef atoll is even more remote, with 320 miles of sea between it and Palau's capital, Koror.[1] One of the most biologically diverse coral reef atolls in the Pacific (Birkeland et al. 2000), Helen Reef is 163 square kilometers of enclosed atoll with extensive reef flats and a small island (Pacific Initiative for the Environment 2002). The same remoteness that protected it from overexploitation in the past became reason for it to be targeted due to its abundant resources and lack of security.

Helen Reef is not only isolated from the main island of Palau, but also from the populated island of the Hatohobei state, which is one of Palau's smallest states. Located forty miles from Tobi's populated island, the traditional local use of Helen Reef's resources is limited. With almost all the Tobian people moving to Koror in search of economic opportunities, community reliance on the reef for cash income (trochus, live grouper) and consumptive catch (fish, sea turtle, sea birds, etc.) has been replaced by an annual or semiannual one-day field trip to harvest the atoll's resources in limited quantity as a cultural event.[2] The main threat to the resource then comes from outside the community. Since the 1990s, reef-fish poachers aboard Filipino, Indonesian, Taiwanese, and Korean vessels have frequented the reef unhindered by any enforcement[3] (Pacific Initiative for the Environment 2002). The state tried early on to protect the reef from poachers by placing enforcement agents on Helen Island, but these individuals often had insufficient provisions and no authorization or training to enforce regulations. Moreover, these enforcement officials were often accused of colluding with fishers to exploit the reef for personal gain.[4] Palau's national government made similar ineffective conservation attempts, as the Palau National Patrol Boat toured Helen Reef infrequently and insufficiently to ward off poachers. Both the state and the national governments were interested in developing further enforcement, but neither had the resources nor the capacity to do it unaided (Pacific Initiative for the Environment 2002). Some argue that the national government simply lacked the will to effect change, as the Tobi people ranked lowest in the Palau social order,[5] thus making Helen Reef conservation the lowest priority for the country. Several researchers and conservationists since the 1960s recommended creating a marine protected area of the atoll (Pacific Initiative for the Environment 2002), and while funds were promised to Tobi for such a purpose, they were never disbursed. The lack of national investment condemned conservation efforts from the start; as many state and national officials have stated, it is very difficult for a project that is not nationally driven to succeed in the long term.[6]

The Community Conservation Network was founded, in part, to fill the gap between conservation needs and national resources available by bringing global resources to Tobian community-based resource management. Like many smaller NGOs, CCN was created through the interests of one curious and dedicated person. In 1992, Michael Guilbeaux ventured to Palau for the first time as a research assistant working on sea turtle research with the University of Georgia's Institute of Ecology. Guilbeaux started interacting with the Tobi people, developing what would become a long-term relationship with the community. In the late 1990s, he started graduate school to continue his study of Tobian culture and resources. At that point, to enable him to fund bigger and longer-term projects with the

Tobi people in Palau, Guilbeaux set up a board of a few close colleagues and professors[7] and filed for nonprofit status, which was officially approved by the U.S. Internal Revenue Service in 2001. For the first three years, he was the organization's only paid employee. He worked and interacted with the Tobian community daily, learning about the uniqueness of Tobian culture.[8] In my interactions, many community members used Guilbeaux's name and "CCN" interchangeably.[9] He was seen as a "good listener"[10] and demonstrated local accountability norms by building relationships, regularly communicating face to face, and facilitating local conservation priorities.

Building Broad-Based Authority in Palau

From the beginning, CCN's community-based conservation approach ensured that the Tobian community was at the center of most of the processes of the project. A CCN staff member offered that the organization's strength was "getting people together and then standing in the background" while different actors worked together.[11] It hired local staff to facilitate the work and pulled together local volunteers to help determine the project area focus. It avoided globally accepted approaches to resource monitoring and assessment if they did not seem accessible to local communities.[12] As the Helen Reef Project developed, CCN continued this focus on communities, spelling out the timeline by which the community would be autonomously in charge of the entire project. The fact that CCN's leader worked with the community for almost a decade before implementing a resource assessment—and did so with the community determining many of the assessment's foci—cemented trust between the community and CCN. Even when questions arose about Guilbeaux's ability to administer a growing organization, or the speed at which the project would be completely turned over to the community, most community members, government officials, and traditional leaders saw Guilbeaux's arrival to Palau as a positive thing for both Tobian resources and the Tobian community.[13]

CCN had a clear vision focused on community-based resource management, where successful long-term solutions required empowerment of local communities, meaningful and mutually beneficial partnerships, and monitoring and evaluation standards that conformed to the global norms of conservation science (Community Conservation Network 2003a). This vision was demonstrated repeatedly over the course of ten years. As an

organization created to facilitate local engagement, the NGO was deliberate in bridging local and global capacities and norms, working first to
bridge the outer island community with the rest of Palau. Even as CCN
grew and attracted global experts, the new actors placed the same value on
community-based approaches and grassroots issues as CCN did.[14]

The organization's approach to planning was rooted in local accountability norms. As part of this relationship building, the organization aimed
to use "people skills more than anything else"[15] to determine what types of
trainings the communities themselves wanted and to bring those trainings
to fruition.[16] Community members mentioned that since Palau is such a
small community, an organization cannot work there alone but must coordinate with local groups.[17] While it took a while for the local community
to appreciate how partnerships and collaborations might benefit them, this
was one of the goals of long-term interaction.[18]

The Helen Reef Resource Management Project (known in this chapter
simply as "the project" or "the Helen Reef Project") resulted from a collaborative process with the Tobi community, the Helen Reef Action Committee,
the Hatohobei state government, and CCN. The group's very first proposals
spelled out clearly how community-based resource management was to be
done: "The overall goal of this research is to show how Western science
(natural science and management science) and CBM (community-based
management) can complement each other to mitigate the impediments to
effective CBM of resource limitations, uncertainty, and conflict" (Ridgely
and Guilbeaux 1999, 2). Furthermore, the project aimed to demonstrate
how Western scientific ideas can be communicated to non-scientist Palauans, and Palauan views to Western scientists, to facilitate cross-learning.
Together, the communities and scientists would determine the broader
aims, detailed objectives, and performance measures of coral reef management (Ridgely and Guilbeaux 1999, 3). In its reports and proposals, CCN
discussed its exit plan, aiming to have local control of the project completed by year eight (Guilbeaux 2002).

Like Conservation International's work in Milne Bay (see chapter 3),
one of the first activities of the project was an assessment not just of the
biological resources, but also of the sociocultural features of the Tobian
Community to help the organization follow local norms of engagement
and understand local customs, conflict, and communications (Black
2000). The sociocultural report and recommendations were written by an

anthropologist who had worked in and studied Palau cultures for more than thirty years. They flagged many important approaches, which Guilbeaux and CCN worked to exemplify from the beginning: the importance of sitting with conflict for extended periods of time instead of immediately trying resolve it; the depth and motivation of Tobian altruistic offers to "help the island" and "do your part"; the regular struggles of Palauans to reconcile the various approaches of leadership that have historically existed in the country (from the egalitarian approaches of the U.S. government, to the authoritarian approaches of the Japanese, to the benevolent and respectful oversight by traditional elders)[19] (Black 2000). In keeping with this book's definition of local accountability norms, the report encourages seeking out stakeholders whose nonattendance at meetings could be a means for voicing dissent about the project.

While not all of the recommendations of this report were followed, those that were helped the organization interact with the community appropriately and effectively. With the organization's first grants in 2000,[20] CCN not only performed assessments of the resources on Helen Reef but also started working with community members on the idea of conserving the atoll's resources.[21] With CCN's help, a group of nine men and women formed the Helen Reef Action Committee (HRAC) to get the project started.[22] A dynamic and active volunteer group, CCN saw the action committee as the basis for the local management authority for the reef and the legitimacy for any work to protect the atoll. The organization worked with this group to build local awareness and capacity for conservation and to develop and design the community-based marine conservation project that CCN shopped to funders (Pacific Initiative for the Environment 2002). This committee also worked to improve communication between the project and the community through daily interactions, events like the community trash clean-up days, and an annual summer program to bring youth and elders to the reef to explore and learn (HRRMP and CCN 2004). At this point, Guilbeaux and the HRAC hired an administrative assistant in Koror to help with the project finances and communications.[23]

While community news billboards and meetings were often used by the project to convey information, the preferred medium for communication for the Tobian community was face-to-face conversation. Even with cell phones and email, Tobians drive or walk to talk to another person to communicate (perhaps due to the small geography of Koror). Balancing the work he had to do at the organization's headquarters in Honolulu with this Tobian preference for face-to-face communications, Guilbeaux traveled often to Palau to work with project staff, community leadership, and government officials on issues large and small. This norm of accountability for the Tobi community thus had budgetary implications for CCN and its projects, as well as implications for leadership and administration of the organization. As CCN began to grow in Hawaii, staff looked to Guilbeaux to make decisions, lead meetings, and lend support for Hawaii-based efforts, but he was often called to Palau to work on the project.

There were many activities that blended local and global scales to create broad-based authority (see table 5.1). As the project moved from the planning phase to the implementation phase, two activities required this balance between local and global capacities: resource monitoring and assessment, and the creation of enforcement officers for the atoll.

Table 5.1
Evidence of CCN's broad-based authority

	Accountability (as an indicator of legitimacy)	Capacity (as an indicator of power)	Bridging capacity
Local	• Built long-term relationships and sociocultural report to support and inform work • Face-to-face reporting and communication • Board demanded project control and NGO works to help board attain legal control of funds • Community members decided what to monitor	• Volunteer board reflected local norm of each "doing their part for the island" (PC) • Influence helped pass legislation on atoll (PC&AC) • Local trainings for surveillance, monitoring, enforcement activities (TC&AC) • Understanding local culture through sociocultural studies (PC&TC)	• Funding reports include "talk story" sections to explain delays and learning in addition to quantifiable results • In-depth collaboration between local experts and global experts on resource monitoring • Seeking and converting control over funding to local actors
Global	• regular reports to global funders with quantifiable results based on Western scientific measures	• fundraising from global philanthropy (PC&AC) • scientific rigor of outside scientists brought in to monitor and map (TC&AC&PC)	

A = accountability norms; PC = political capacity; AC = administrative capacity; TC = technical capacity; B = bridging capacity

Monitoring and Assessment

The resource assessment and monitoring program was one clear demonstration of CCN's ability to bring global capacity to local communities in
appropriate and helpful ways. Reef monitoring assessments of existing and
threatened resources in the ecosystem were performed on Helen Reef in
the years 2000, 2002, and 2004, and each used globally accepted scientific
methods to determine the state of the reef. With each successive assessment, the membership of the survey team grew increasingly Tobian, with
the last assessment completed entirely by the community with no outside
experts. By contrast, the Milne Bay project performed a rapid assessment of
coastal resources without participation from local communities.

Starting with the first assessment in 2000, a survey team was commissioned by the project and the Hatohobei state governor with no reference
in the report about being led by CCN. In the foreword of the survey report,
the HRMB chair and Tobian governor thank Guilbeaux for editing the
document and indicate that, while the effort was led by a team of international scientists, the Hatohobei state government, community members,
and project staff "have always had access to the information within—from
the moment the expedition returned to Koror until today" (Birkeland et
al 2000, 1). The purpose was not only to assess the resources, but to produce recommendations for the state to act and to build the capacity of
the state and community through training in monitoring (Birkeland et al.
2000).

A large part of this first assessment focused on the pilot efforts of a
community-based monitoring program, through which the community
identified the species of concern (mainly economic products like giant
clams, trochus, sea cucumbers, turtles), were trained in monitoring methods, and performed the assessment. The program was planned, designed,
and undertaken largely by the members of the Tobi community, with members of the scientific team assisting and training local actors. A major recommendation of this process was that the state and community carry out
and expand community monitoring in the future, with the community
"remain[ing] involved in the selection of monitoring targets and methods,
so that efforts best suit community needs and interests. ... As community
members gain experience and skills in monitoring, it may be possible to
rely on local expertise to carry out some of the survey methods for some of
the target species" and consult with national and international scientists

with particular skills that may not be found at the local level (Birkeland et al. 2000, 51).[24] In this way, the international expertise that was brought to the project conformed to the norms of global conservation while focusing on the areas the community found most important. One report to funders regarding the monitoring expedition in 2000 included notes from the international experts, such as "I think you did a great job of keeping us aware that the purpose of our expedition was to help the Tobian people get back control of their heritage. I thought an outstanding aspect of our trip was our involvement and communication with the people from Tobi" (Guilbeaux 2000, 8). Another researcher quoted in this report noted, "You really are to be commended for reminding us, in patient and kind (albeit exhausted) tones, why we were there" (Guilbeaux 2000, 8).

In October 2002, the Tobi community completed the second survey of reef resources. With more than 330 surveys around the reef (Emilio et al. 2002), these monitoring activities also served as training for the community for future monitoring (Pacific Initiative for the Environment 2002). The survey team was supported in training and participation from the Locally Managed Marine Area Network (a network of organizations focused on empowering local resource owners in conservation), using guidelines by the World Commission on Protected Areas Marine Protected Area Effectiveness program sponsored by the World Conservation Union, the World Wide Fund for Nature, and the U.S. National Oceanic and Atmospheric Administration (HRRMP and CCN 2003). The resulting report, which was authored primarily by Tobians, demonstrated local actors' global scientific capacity. The report made recommendations about how the previous monitoring efforts could be improved (Emilio et al. 2002).

In October and November of 2004, local project staff performed another survey of the area, this time without any assistance from outside scientists or advisors (HRRMP and CCN 2004). To further improve local capacity, the project began a summer program to bring Tobians to the reef to learn about their resources and the local traditions association with them (HRRMP and CCN 2004). The progression of these monitoring efforts responded equally to global norms of conservation and the local demands both to understand more about the reef resources in a traditionally respectful way and to have the community remain in charge of the process.[25] As one former Tobi official noted, "They need to have the community in charge. They can't just say 'Science says this' and people believe it. So they need to educate the people to see what's happening with the reef themselves because they won't just take the scientists' word for it."[26] With these monitoring programs, CCN and the Helen Reef Project did just that.

Enforcement

Enforcement is another area where CCN seems to have been adept at its role as a catalyzer of both local and global resources. The Hatohobei state government had long had an interest in protecting the resources of Helen Reef, but the task proved too difficult to fund considering the politics of the national budget and the remoteness of the reef. The main threat to the area's biodiversity and ecosystem integrity was the roving live reef fisherman from the Philippines and Indonesia (Guilbeaux 2002). While the poachers were not aggressive, they often outnumbered the islanders, leaving the community feeling ineffective against them (Community Conservation Network 2003b).[27] In addition, the atoll is a forty-hour journey by boat from the mainland of Koror, and the Helen Reef Conservation Area is large, protecting 162 square kilometers of the atoll (HRRMP and CCN 2003). This made enforcement from the capital very difficult. As stated earlier, the state's efforts at placing enforcement officers on Helen Island were undermined by a lack of provisions, authorization, training, and communication (Pacific Initiative for the Environment 2002).[28] Meanwhile, the Palauan National Patrol boat could only visit Helen Reef sporadically. Without the capacity to address these issues of enforcement, the state and national governments turned to CCN, which prioritized creation of a temporary presence (about half of the year) on Helen Island with proper training, provisions, communication, and authority to deter illegal fishing (Pacific Initiative for the Environment 2002). Thus, in 2001, the Community Conservation Network, in partnership with the Helen Reef Action Committee and the Hatohobei state government, successfully solicited funding to create the Helen Reef Enforcement Initiative. This was designed to be a multi-stakeholder marine enforcement effort to safely and efficiently prevent poaching and over-harvesting of the resources (Community Conservation Network 2002).

This effort to create and implement an enforcement plan combined CCN's ability to frame the problem to global funders with multiple local partners' enforcement capacity. In partnership with the Palau Ministry of Justice, the Hatohobei state government, the Tobi communities, and the

Bureau of Public Safety (Palau's national government law enforcement agency), CCN created the Helen Reef Surveillance and Deterrence Plan, outlining key roles and responsibilities, logistics, and the processes for enforcement. The project identified four Hatohobeians to serve as conservation officers and gave them six months of on-the-job training with a multitude of partners (Pacific Initiative for the Environment 2002). Officers learned basic law enforcement and small arms handling at the Palau National Police Academy. They learned marine surveillance, enforcement, boarding, vessel approach, evidence gathering, and legal processes in a Marine Law Enforcement Conservation Officer Course at the Palau Marine Enforcement Division with the technical assistance of the Australian Royal Navy. CCN trained the officers on coral surveying, monitoring techniques, and SCUBA (Pacific Initiative for the Environment 2002). Rangers were sent to other Micronesian countries and Honolulu to learn firefighting and other essential skills for boat operations,[29] fish surveying, and turtle-tagging techniques.[30] The collaboration of this diverse set of actors was a clear indicator of CCN's ability to bridge across scales to achieve real results.

In 2002, the trainees were sworn in as conservation officers.[31] Since then, several more officers have been identified, trained, and deputized (Pacific Initiative for the Environment 2002). As of 2004, thirteen community members had been trained in enforcement skills, two in GPS training, two in open-water diving, and eight in resource monitoring and mapping. In addition, two Conservation Officers were trained in firearms use and safety (HRRMP and CCN 2004).

With the many agencies working to train conservation officers on the local scale, the local technical capacity was evident. What was missing prior to CCN's engagement was the funding for both the trainings and infrastructure for the patrols (e.g., boats, shelter on the island, regular shifts of the conservation officers). In this way, CCN used its global political capacity to fundraise to facilitate local partners' work—a clear example of getting people together and standing in the background. It used its global authority to create and implement a coherent enforcement plan, convening several actors to collaborate on its implementation. Since enforcement began, many community members and rangers said their presence has been an effective deterrent for foreign vessels (Pacific Initiative for the Environment 2002).[32] As of 2004, the reef had 365 days of surveillance and enforcement per year, and the project reported a lower number of infractions by foreign vessels (HRRMP and CCN 2004).

The Helen Reef Project's Tug-of-War between Global and Local Scales

The preceding section demonstrates how the Community Conservation Network was able to create local and then broad-based authority through its approach to conservation as a community-based endeavor. By pulling global experts and funding to the project, the organization bridged the divide between scales and facilitated local conservation. While this balance lasted for several years more, the evolution of two distinct but interacting bodies demonstrates the tug of war between global and local norms and capacity as well as how CCN responded to it.

On the community side, the transition from the volunteer Helen Reef Action Committee to the governmentally charged Helen Reef Management Board signaled a conversion from a local volunteer approach to conservation to a political and professionalized conservation body that demanded local control of the project, which highlighted the lack of administrative capacity of both partners.

On CCN's side, its internal management and organizational development increasingly struggled with reconciling the global norms of a professional conservation organization with the local norms that it strived to uphold. As these two entities developed and changed over the course of the project, power struggles over who had authority and responsibility for fundraising and the use of funds became more pronounced, exemplifying the struggle between prioritizing local and global scales.

Converting an Action Committee to a Board

The Helen Reef Action Committee was founded in the year 2000 by a group of self-selected Tobian individuals interested in conserving the resources of Helen Reef.[33] The action committee worked diligently, meeting three times per week and inviting other community members to give input.[34] This group of volunteers worked with CCN to create plans and priorities for the reef and to lobby government officials to make the reef a conservation priority. Instrumental in the project's success, this group worked with CCN to create the Draft Surveillance and Deterrence Plan for Helen Reef (Guilbeaux 2001), which became the basis of activities for conservation officers (Pacific Initiative for the Environment 2002). It also drafted and lobbied to pass the Helen Reef Management Act in 2001, on which details follow.[35] Through this action committee, CCN fulfilled its mission of community-based conservation.

The action committee's success with lobbying the government for leg-
islation was a bittersweet success. On September 13, 2001, the Hatohobei
state legislature passed Bill Number 5-IR-04, D2, otherwise known as the
Helen Reef Management Act. The goal of this act was "to established [sic]
the management and conservation of natural resources of the Helen Reef
and for other related purposes" (Hatohobei State Legislature 2001). This act
restricted access to the area for three years by declaring it a marine reserve
and required the governor to create the Helen Reef Management Board,
among other things. While significant for the conservation of Helen Reef,
this law had two elements that changed the project dynamics for better
and for worse. First, when consulted, the Tobi people and the HRAC recommended a multipurpose marine protected area for Helen Reef, not a no-take
marine reserve.[36] They based this proposal on both their desired use for
the reef and the recommendation of the resource assessment performed
in 2000. The state legislature's decision to create a three-year moratorium
on all resource use upset many of its citizens[37] who called for several meetings with project staff and government officials. While their concerns were
heard, these meetings did not change the outcome.[38]

A second element of change was less obvious at the time of its creation:
the establishment of the Helen Reef Management Board. Codifying this
board in place of the Helen Reef Action Committee temporarily decreased
community involvement in the project and created greater demands for
this group of individuals, but also empowered the community to seek even
further control over the project. The management board's membership
was much more restricted, structured, and, as a result, often less active.[39]
Where people had given their time and energy for the action committee
of their own volition, members of the management board were selected
and appointed by the state government (with representation required
from both traditional and state leadership), often more for their role in the
Tobian community than their interest in the project. Appointment to the
board was a political endeavor, causing community members who might
have previously volunteered to disengage due to personal disagreements
with the board members.[40]

Much like the Helen Reef Action Committee, the purview of the Helen
Reef Management Board reflected local accountability norms delineated in
this book, since both bodies had oversight not just on the implementation
of the project, but also on the goals the project set out to accomplish from

the beginning. Important to this case, the HRMB took ownership of the project in such a way that some of its members called for CCN's exit, with a transfer of project staff to the board. As one source stated, the "the HRAC were the 'do-ers' of the project, but now Andrew (the deputy manager of the project) is the voice and the do-er of the project."[41] The community had the impression that only those who were required by law[42] and/or paid to work on the project needed to be involved, and volunteer rates dropped, causing some community members to speculate that the project had lost some of its "magic or energy."[43]

Nevertheless, board members took their time-consuming job in this community-driven enterprise seriously. The board had bylaws, detailed meeting agendas, and minutes, and it deliberated on everything from the most minute financial decision to the overall strategy and direction of the project. It paid much of its attention to sustainable finance mechanisms for the project. However, the amount of work that needed to be done was daunting and led community members to question if it had the appropriate capacity to perform. One report to a funder stated, "Because the board operates on a volunteer (unpaid) basis and many of the members are busy, it is difficult for the board to process much of the internal or external information related to the project—this has lead [sic] to a few misunderstandings related to certain management issues or opportunities" (HRRMP and CCN 2004, 4). This same report requested capacity building to learn how to make the board more effective. As the following sections of this chapter demonstrate, this capacity building resulted in an increased focus on financial sustainability for the Helen Reef Project. This sustainability included not just financing the project, but also performing the related tasks as a community independent of all outside actors, including CCN. Before engaging with these details, it is important to see how CCN's internal management developed (or did not) in parallel with this board.

Management in the Community Conservation Network and the Helen Reef Project

At the same time that the Tobian actors working on the project went from a volunteer-based action committee to a more codified board, the Community Conservation Network underwent a similar evolution aimed at both expanding its purview to community conservation in other countries and meeting the global norms of a transnational nongovernmental organization. Much of CCN's organization—its structure, staff priority, and activities—functioned to bridge the global and local scales throughout the project. The broad-based authority CCN garnered also brought it increased global attention. While the field of conservation seemed pleased with the organization's technical and political outcomes, the organization's dearth of global administrative capacity created a considerable amount of consternation both within and outside CCN.

As documented earlier, CCN worked diligently to prioritize local capacity and accountability norms from the beginning of the project. Any former staff member will attest that CCN's priority focus was on community empowerment. CCN took on a "shepherd's role" in furthering conservation, facilitating communication, and creating space to connect various actors to achieve a community's conservation desires.[44] In order to empower communities for conservation, CCN trained them in organizing skills, meeting-facilitation skills, and technical skills about lobbying and conservation monitoring[45] (Community Conservation Network 2003a). If CCN was unable to respond to the community's needs itself, it found other individuals or organizations that could.[46] CCN staff distinguished themselves from other NGOs that might focus primarily on biodiversity, since CCN's first constituencies were communities[47] and first priorities were their interests.[48] One source mentioned specifically that CCN staff members "never change what the community wants in order to meet the niche of the donor,"[49] although they did consider donors a secondary constituency.

CCN's focus on enabling a local conservation agenda rather than creating an agenda itself invoked both admiration and annoyance from community members. While some members of the community wanted more control in decision-making, others reported feeling frustrated that CCN put the onus of decision-making on them. These community members wanted more guidance from CCN on project issues. Often, for short periods of time, neither actor would make a decision, stalling progress. The stalemate would only end when CCN staff and community leaders had face-to-face discussions to come to some consensus about the information needed to make decisions. While this conflict over the level of community autonomy and authority over the Helen Reef Project may have seemed at odds with participatory approaches (often conflated with local accountability norms), it made sense considering this context. Just as CCN's advisors on local culture indicated, these competing and contradictory ideas stemmed from the

Palauan history with various approaches of leadership, including the egalitarian approaches of the U.S. government, the authoritarian approaches of the Japanese, and the benevolent and respectful oversight by their traditional elders. CCN's ability to recognize this complex approach to leadership and address the issues in person was another demonstration of its facilitator role and local capacity.

The internal management of the project demonstrated varying levels of success in bridging local and global scales. Like Conservation International's project in Milne Bay (see chapter 3), the Helen Reef Project conformed to the global expectations that project leadership be academically credentialed. As such, the project hired Nick Pilcher—an esteemed biologist and turtle expert[50]—as project manager in 2001. Shortly after that, Tobian Wayne Andrew was hired as deputy manager. Wayne Andrew is an insightful individual who was much appreciated and liked by people from all walks of Tobian culture[51] and within CCN (Victor 2003b). The management board depended on him to get things done.[52] The project intended for the individual in Andrew's position to eventually take over as manager, but Andrew understood that his lack of education would prevent him from this eventual role. Though a quick and eager learner quite knowledgeable on issues of conservation[53], management, and leadership, his associate's degree in construction did not equip him for leadership positions. A teacher by profession, he was keen on sharing the skills he learned through his position (e.g., conflict resolution, leadership, team building) with his community. However, these skills did not substitute for a degree in conservation in the global conservation world, and the thought of moving his family to a country with a university to pursue a degree with little or no pay was a daunting prospect.[54] Much like the search for a project leader in the Milne Bay case study, global norms of capacity for project leadership limited both the pool of potential candidates to graduate degree holders and Andrew's power within the organization and community. When the project director left two years later, however, Andrew became acting director[55] and, as the project's top-salaried staff member in Palau, de facto decision-maker.[56] Since the management board did not have time to do all the work of the project, it depended on Andrew to inform their decisions and, at times, make decisions himself.[57] Considering his expanded role in the project, it seemed he was able to bridge this divide, as well. Through their use of bridging capacity, the project staff members were able to reconfigure the global norms of capacity and change expectations about qualifications for a project manager.

Fundraising to Bridge Global and Local Political Capacity

In some ways, CCN was able to gracefully maneuver between local and global accountability demands, using its political capacity to frame the issue and receive funding for the project. The first major grant from the David and Lucile Packard Foundation in 2001 almost doubled CCN's first year's income to a total of $345,421 USD and gave a much-needed jumpstart to the project, allowing it to hire another paid employee (the administrative assistant in Koror) and still carry over almost $100,000 USD for the next year's budget (Community Conservation Network 2001). This grant gave the organization some financial stability, demonstrating CCN's ability to operate successfully in the global political arena to raise funds and establish itself as *the* NGO working on Helen Reef conservation. The process of writing fundraising proposals and reports further demonstrated the organization's bridging capacity: Guilbeaux, Andrew, and Pilcher were able to translate the board's and community's priorities into a global fundraising context, complete with logical frameworks, quantitative indicators for each goal, and strategies for achieving these goals over the three- to five-year grant period. Funder reports were often authored by Guilbeaux[58] based on local staff reports, demonstrating both quantitative indicators and qualitative storytelling.

The Helen Reef Project balanced this adherence to global accountability norms with local norms in its reporting. In an eleven-page *End of Project Report* to the New England BioLabs Foundation, one entire page was dedicated to describing the difficulties encountered with the project and how they were solved (or not solved), which exposed to funders the flexibility and context specificity of local accountability norms. This particular report also asked for a no-cost extension to the project in order to attain goals in a more realistic timeline than was proposed initially (CCN 2000a). A report for the Packard Foundation had an entire section titled "telling the story" (CCN 2004a), which is a common concept in the Pacific that in this context included telling details that were not captured in two-plus pages of quantitative results. This narrative section of the report included a list of obstacles faced by the project that explained why progress in some areas was delayed or halted. These difficulties included the project manager's departure, the limited time available for board members to meet and complete tasks, an undisclosed personal event that delayed staff productivity, and a misunderstanding by management board members about how funding was to be spent. The narrative also reported that "Even with all this [sic] obstacles, the project managed to adapt to the needs of the management board, state government, community, staff and other partners to ensure transparency in financial accounting and reporting and to help in making decisions together" (CCN 2004b, 11), which led to an improved working relationship for all involved. The report also noted that a visit by the foundation representative proved helpful in addressing the misunderstanding and strengthening their relationship, indicating once again the local accountability norm of face-to-face communication to build long-term relationships and trust. These reports are another indicator of CCN's ability to bridge local and global norms and capacities.

CCN's Efforts to Build Global Administrative Capacity

While the Helen Reef Project was developing and starting to focus on its sustainability, the Community Conservation Network was also developing and expanding. Its reputation as an organization that facilitated community-based conservation with demonstrable results spread throughout the conservation world. More funders became interested in its work, as did global policy fora like the International Coral Reef Initiative and regional initiatives like the Locally Managed Marine Area Network. CCN continued to grow financially, showing its global political prowess by accumulating more and more revenue for the organization: in 2001 ($345,000 USD), 2003 ($614,903 USD), and 2004 ($825,939 USD) (Community Conservation Network 2003c). The organization began to consult for projects in Indonesia and create similar programs in Hawaii, which eventually grew to be the single-largest program of the organization.

With this scaling up, however, came more expectations about how the NGO would be organized and administered; more struggles to reconcile global and local differences (see table 5.2). CCN as an organization lacked the administrative capacity it needed to operate on the global scale. Funders voiced concern about sending such large grants to an organization so small and with such little administrative experience. CCN did not refute these concerns. Rather than becoming paralyzed by them, Guilbeaux exercised his political prowess and negotiated a partnership with a larger

Table 5.2
The struggle between global and local norms and capacities for CCN

Local norms and capacities …	… replaced by or competing with global norms and capacities
Face-to-face communication in Palau; budgetary implications for travel (A& PC&AC)	Competed with budgetary implications and needs for in-person administrative decision-making in Hawaii (A&AC&PC)
Desire for local control over finances (and the boat) (A&PC&AC)	Needed to keep the funding contract with the named organization, difficult to transfer (A&PC&AC)
Local volunteers decided the focus of monitoring and assessment (A&TC&PC)	(stays the same)
Flexible volunteer committee built on local trust and norms of "each doing our part" (A&AC&PC)	Codified into a board professionalized the work of conservation, perceived to be only for individuals with official posts (A&PC&AC)
CCN in shepherd's role (PC&TC)	CCN needed to be "in charge" since the grants went through them (PC&A)
Slow pace of decision-making (A&AC)	Still needed to report on regular progress (although some extensions granted) (A&AC&PC)

A = accountability norms; PC = political capacity; AC = administrative capacity; TC = technical capacity; B = bridging capacity

organization: the International Marinelife Alliance (IMA). For the cost of rent and overhead, CCN was able to share office space and administrative services with IMA, relieving any worry the funders had about its organizational capacity. Within a year, however, CCN and the funder's confidence in IMA's accounting operations was revealed to be misplaced. As chapter 4 of this volume indicates, IMA accessed CCN's funds without permission. CCN then decided to work on its own, with two IMA employees leaving to join CCN's ranks. These two acquired staff brought their global and local reputations as experts in community conservation. With the addition of an administrative manager in Honolulu, CCN began addressing its capacity gaps, demonstrating adaptability to funder demands and partnership disappointment.

While still a small organization, CCN saw more changes in 2002. After acquiring staff in both Honolulu and Palau, CCN solicited and received an Organizational Effectiveness grant from the David and Lucile Packard

Foundation. The grant aimed to "increase the effectiveness of grantee organizations and networks, to enhance their capacity to meet the Foundation's goals" (The David and Lucile Packard Foundation 2013). The funding undoubtedly jumpstarted the NGO, giving it the resources to deliberately design its mission and strategic plan. This grant allowed CCN to gather its board and staff in a retreat setting and clearly articulate the organizational focus to facilitate community conservation. The mission of the organization did not change very much from this process. However, other important recommendations were made.

Part of this strategic plan focused on the administrative shortcomings of the organization, including organizational structure and administrative capacity. At the beginning of my research on the organization, Michael Guilbeaux was both CCN's executive director as well as the substantive director of the Palau program. As the Hawaii program grew to be CCN's biggest, the demands on the executive director and program director also grew, leaving Guilbeaux with essentially two full-time jobs.[59] An executive director of a small but growing NGO needs to carefully manage the creation and implementation of office policies and processes, but the local accountability norms in Palau demanded Guilbeaux's attention and physical presence. It was as simple an issue as this: a person cannot be in more than one place at a time. And Guilbeaux prioritized the local work in Palau over the global work of becoming a transnational NGO, much to the frustration of the Honolulu staff.[60] Trying to replace CCN administrative staff with new hires, approving the purchase of office supplies,[61] and initiating regular staff meetings: all these efforts were delayed in part because the executive director was often in Palau, holding the face-to-face meetings required to keep that project moving forward.

This competition of priorities between local norms of face-to-face communication in Palau and global norms to transform the organization into a professionally structured and managed NGO epitomized the ultimatum NGOs often feel they face while scaling up. Organizations like CCN, where programs are fairly autonomous and compartmentalized, foster more context-specific actions that adhere to local accountability norms. However, without centralized processes and policies, the administrative and political work that facilitates local interactions often get duplicated or lost, making local actors work even harder. With CCN, this prioritization of the local norms resulted in programs never being fully informed of what other programs were doing across the organization. Without standard operating procedure or policy guides, there was no travel report or internal reporting requirements to capture and share learning; no group travel schedule to coordinate meetings; and inexplicable delays in simple actions like check distribution. These administrative issues directly impacted CCN's relationships with the Tobian community in 2005, when funding for the Helen Reef Project ran out three months before planned. Interactions like this jeopardized the organization's long-term relationships with communities. Thus, while the paradox of scale highlights the dangerous pressure to prioritize global accountability norms and capacities over local ones, operations on the global scale are not without merit. Indeed, they seem necessary for NGOs to function on a transnational scale. These questions are raised again in this book's conclusion: is there an optimum division of functions between scales? These cases and the literature on NGOs offer some insights that merit further examination.

Local Demand for Control

As both the local administration of the project and the global organization of the Community Conservation Network grew and became more codified and structured, a power struggle developed in the eyes of the Helen Reef Management Board. For the first several years of the project, all the funding went to and was administered by CCN. While its intentions were honorable, this power dynamic caused the most controversy in the project. As board members acknowledged, whoever controls the funding controls the project and, therefore, the resource. This understanding pushed the board to request more autonomy over finances.[62]

The power struggle became public at a 2005 International Coral Reef Initiative meeting that CCN helped sponsor in Palau. There, the Tobi chief publicly stated (much to the surprise of CCN and other participants) that if funders wanted to help the community, they should give it money and "don't pad the NGO pocket." This public declaration stemmed both from the larger argument of who controls the project finances (and therefore the project) as well as a feeling that the local need for face-to-face deliberation and decision-making was not being met. In the eyes of the chief, "long distance relationships do not work."

Part of the struggle over funding echoed the same concerns in the Milne Bay Project: when the Tobi community heard that a $500,000 USD grant was approved by the Packard Foundation, it assumed that the funds were enough to employ the entire community.[63] While the community benefited from resource conservation, it also wanted to benefit from the funding, and only about one dozen villagers (some of them the most elite villagers) received any monetary value from the project (in the form of employment). Community members asked: If funds are raised in the name of the community, why don't all the funds go to the community? There were concerns and rumors regarding the size of CCN staff salaries and overhead in Honolulu, and whether these line items came from funds intended for Palau-based work or CCN's funds for Honolulu activity (Victor 2003a, 2003b). This financial transparency demanded of CCN (and practiced by other conservation organizations working in Palau) required greater administrative capacity on the part of both CCN and the community.[64]

While questions about where funding goes seem typical for transnational NGOs, it is important to acknowledge several additional financial issues for the Helen Reef Project, including who wrote the proposals, who had the capacity to write them, and who was responsible for accounting and reporting, since proposals are how the rules for resource governance are shaped for the project area. For the first several years of the project, CCN wrote all project proposals.[65] While the board, the state government, and the community at large all sought more financial autonomy, few if any of these actors had the time or capacity to do the work of proposal writing and reporting;[66] none of them had the global administrative or political capacity. Indeed, it was only through the work of CCN that many community members were introduced to the concept of grants for conservation in the first place.[67] This did not mean that Tobians did not have a say in the content of the proposals; they were written based on issues and outlines supplied by the project staff and management board,[68] and proposals were sent to the management board for approval. Unfortunately, the board did not always have time to review them,[69] creating a dilemma for CCN of either submitting a proposal that had not been reviewed or missing funding deadlines altogether.

CCN headquarters exercised authority by controlling spending for the first several years. To receive funds, the Palau office administrator petitioned CCN headquarters monthly for a funds transfer to a Palauan account (Victor 2003a, 2003b). Except for sporadic funding reports from CCN, the board and community had no way of knowing how much of the

funds were remaining in Honolulu or how they were being spent.[70] Thus
the board sought more control over finances[71] and a closer relationship
with funders in order to create more financial autonomy.[72]

Two stories illustrate this power struggle between CCN and the management board. The first focuses on funds raised to purchase a boat for
the project. While Guilbeaux consulted the board before writing the proposal, the board did not have the time to read the final draft. When it was
time to purchase the boat, the board disagreed with the type of boat to be
purchased as described in the proposal. Moreover, it was concerned about
whose property the boat would be. Since the funds were raised in CCN's
name, it technically would have been CCN's boat. The Community Conservation Network was responsible for it and could not sign over the funds
or the boat to the project or the board. The board was adamant that the
boat be its property and contacted the funder directly to seek approval.[73]
The funder confirmed that the boat needed to be purchased in CCN's name
since the grant was in CCN's name, reflecting the global norms of contracts.
Further, the funders noted that the board needed CCN, since the board
did not have the administrative capacity to raise funds and manage its
own grant. As a result, the board asked for capacity building in fundraising
and accounting and started the process of registering as its own nonprofit
organization. In a clear demonstration of bridging capacity, CCN inquired
with other donors if grant agreements could be transferred into the board's
name. One funder, the U.S. Department of the Interior (DOI), agreed to
this, and that grant was transferred.

Another shift in authority and responsibility was less deliberate. In 2005,
CCN's accounts for the project dried up unexpectedly, leaving the deputy
director's salary in jeopardy. The Hatohobei state government took over
responsibility and paid the deputy director for several months, moving the
lines of authority from CCN to the Helen Reef Management Board. Also,
with the transfer of the DOI grant, the project deputy director became a
direct employee of the management board.[74] Both the board and the community took this financial miscalculation as a sign of CCN's inadequte
financial ability,[75] causing suspicion among the community members[76]
(HRRMP and CCN 2004). Tobians were concerned about funds running
out again and workers going unpaid[77] while CCN's staff maintained their
income. The board demanded assurance that the Helen Reef Project budget
would never again be in jeopardy, and that, in case of future accounting

problems, CCN's Honolulu-based budget should be cut rather than the Palau-based budget.[78]

This struggle is an example both of how CCN's lack of global administrative capacity hindered its progress, but also of how the organization worked to answer local demands. With its goal to facilitate community conservation, CCN did not resist reducing its role in decision-making and financial control. Indeed, it did the opposite and embraced the opportunity to connect local actors to global funders. The organization also sought funding to build local administrative capacity in financial management, accounting, budgeting, and reporting so that the board could better manage grants, but it encountered difficulty.[79] As sources from all three cases in this book complain, funding for the substantive outcomes of the project was much more available than funding for training in administration.[80]

Cognizant of its own capacity shortcomings, the management board recognized that if CCN left the project, the project would end.[81] But with long-term sustainability and local control as priorities, the project leaders looked for other ways to build capacity, like temporarily assigning staff to other Palau organizations.[82] The management board also explored other ways the reef could create economic security through ecotourism, clam aquaculture, and other mariculture initiatives (HRRMP and CCN 2003).

Internal Struggles for Administrative Capacity at CCN

The staff and leadership of the Community Conservation Network were well aware of their administrative shortcomings and made several unsuccessful efforts at building that essential global capacity. First, the organization embedded itself with the International Marinelife Alliance. Chapter 4 of this book demonstrates how that collaboration became detrimental to CCN. Then CCN advertised to hire an executive director to take the administrative burden off Guilbeaux, freeing him to lead the international programs. A person was hired but under a lesser leadership title (maintaining Guilbeaux as the executive director). In an attempt to build administrative capacity, this person created an employee handbook, which was never implemented, and then left the organization. Staff speculated that she was not given the authority to do her job.

Then, a group of employees in the Honolulu office tried to set up a cooperative system to rotate responsibilities of management so that they could do the management tasks in addition to their hired responsibilities.

However, this too was unsuccessful since no one employee had complete information on how the programs were running or authority to use the corporate credit card. Purchase orders and meeting times all piled up on Guilbeaux's desk as staff waited for him to return from his face-to-face meetings in Palau, where the relationship was starting to sour due to the dynamics detailed in preceding sections. Moreover, these efforts to build institutional structure for the organization were constricting: fewer processes and policies meant more flexibility to respond to the communities in which they worked. More rules and processes were often difficult to follow in the various contexts in which staff worked: how can you get documentation for purchases if the communities in which you work do not offer receipts? Which scale would prevail if the administrative norms of the global and local scales diverged?

In the meantime, CCN advertised again and hired an executive director who started in September 2007. She worked diligently to create policies and procedures for the organization and to secure long-term funding. She took on the difficult task of bringing the accounting system into conformity with global standards and submitted proposals to foundations to sustain and stabilize the organization so that it could build its global capacity further as a multisite, transnational NGO. One major grant for the Palau program was ending in 2008, and there were few prospects for future funding. Another of the organization's funders—the Oak Foundation—was keen to continue funding CCN but needed some assurance that CCN followed standard protocol with finances. It required the organization to pass an audit before approving the grant. Unfortunately, due to a delay in filing the organization's form 990, the auditors examined the books that were kept prior to this new executive director's efforts at standardizing. This inauspicious start to the audit did not raise funder confidence in the organization. The grant, which was essential for CCN to continue, was not awarded. With no funding to pay staff, office rent, or for programming, CCN's board held an emergency meeting and voted on January 15, 2009, to close the organization. Guilbeaux and the head of the Hawaii program were given until the end of the month to clean out the offices. Since the Hawaii program still had some funding and an organizational structure that seemed viable, it was allowed to continue by transferring its grants to a fiscal sponsor in Hawaii. CCN as a transnational NGO, however, closed its doors.[83]

Hawaii-based programming renamed itself the Hawaii Community Stewardship Network and found new homes with a series of organizations acting as fiscal sponsors. Finally, in 2013, the leadership of the program was able to file for nonprofit status as a Hawaiian nonprofit and changed its name to Kua'aina Ulu Auamo. This organization is not a transnational NGO; it is located in Hawaii, focused on Hawaiian communities and their resources, and funded by Hawaii-based funders. Moreover, it is rare that it brings in outside expertise to advise the communities on their resources or their use. It is truly a local organization.[84]

As detailed earlier, the Palau program had suffered since late 2006 from a deterioration of the relationship between the Community Conservation Network and the Helen Reef Management Board. This relationship had become even more strained in the next two years. The year 2008 was pivotal since the major grant that had funded the project ended, and no alternative funding was found. At the end of that year, the CCN-HRMB relationship officially ended (just a few weeks before the closing of CCN). Also in 2008, the HRMB approached another NGO—OneReef—for help to secure sustainable financing through a marine conservation agreement. The organization provided Helen Reef with technical support and funding. In 2009, the Hatohobei Organization for People and the Environment (HOPE) was created to serve as a bridge between the Tobi community and outside partners. In 2010, the Helen Reef Project joined the Palau Protected Areas Network, a nonprofit created by the Palau government to solicit funding for conservation projects. Thus, the Helen Reef Project still exists today, but in a locally focused organization with the community board in charge. Former CCN leadership and staff still advise the organization. In fact, three of CCN's former employees were coauthors of the *Helen Reef Management Plan 2011–2016* (Andrew et al. 2010). While they are still "getting people together and standing in the background," they are no longer doing it as an NGO.

Part of this strategic plan delineates the roles and responsibilities of each partner. HRMB and project staff are responsible for pursuing the mission, creating and achieving goals, reporting accomplishments and setbacks, and fundraising. National partners like government and nonprofit agencies in Palau are responsible for providing infrastructure (meeting facilities), local outreach, monitoring plans and training, community educational materials, staff time and governance, enforcement support, and prosecution of violators. International partners like transnational NGOs and funders are responsible for technical advice, organizational development training, research support, and funding (Andrew et al. 2010). This division of responsibilities by type of actor suggests a division by scale and capacity. As will be discussed in this book's conclusion, other NGOs are mirroring this division of governance tasks in their reorganizations: local organizations determine the objectives and tailor responses to context; national organizations perform the governance functions that foster mission; international organizations serve as technical advisors and funders. Thus, while CCN closed its doors, the Helen Reef Project morphed into a locally focused NGO that created broad-based authority while *not* becoming transnational but still determining what each actor would do in the scheme of things.

Why did all of CCN's efforts to build global administrative capacity fail? Some former staff cited "founder's syndrome," where the founder inadvertently sabotages the organization due to an inability to delegate and transition to new leadership. This often occurs due to the founder's unwavering dedication to the original vision of the organization (Schmidt 2013). While these traits seem present in the case of the Community Conservation Network, this book asserts that the concept of founder's syndrome is just one of the many ways that a local actor can respond to the paradox of scale. For CCN, delegating and transitioning to new leadership could have meant a shift from the local accountability norms that the original vision of the organization sought to uphold to the global accountability norms that would bring a different kind of inflexibility to the project. If the mission of CCN was to respond to the needs of local communities, then how should a leader respond to organizational changes that are seen as reducing that responsiveness? Rather than focus on one individual to shoulder the blame for programmatic or organizational failure, this book contends that the larger systemic dynamics of scaling up are to blame.

Exiting the Global Scale

This case study illustrates how a small but successful, locally focused NGO can build broad-based authority and resist the paradox of scale for years. On the local scale, these NGOs demonstrate strong capacity and ability to adhere to accountability norms. They are able to partner with other NGOs and local governments, as well as maneuver within both the local government framework and traditional leadership. They understand local resource use, resource status, governance structures, politics, communication, and conflict resolution processes, and they are respected for this by local community members.[85] NGOs such as CCN also demonstrate global capacities and norms. They have collegial, respected relationships with global funders and partners, helping them secure increasingly larger grants. Their technical expertise is impressive, with both social and natural scientists on their staff regularly participating in global and regional fora.

Most impressive among these kinds of NGOs is their ability to connect the local and global scales at a programmatic level. Like many NGOs, the bulk of CCN's work focused on technical capacity building for Palauans (Pacific Inititive for the Environment 2002). As a direct result of CCN's work, resource monitoring and enforcement are now done by community members (Emilio et al 2002).[86] Going beyond Western scientific capacity, the project also built capacity on traditional use of resources.[87] By bringing in local leaders to international meetings, bringing international meetings like the International Coral Reef Initiative to Palau, and helping the community secure its own funding for conservation, CCN connected local and global political capacities.[88] Through its relationships with funders, it both fulfilled the global norms of reporting quantitative short-term results and pushed these relationships to include the local norms of demonstrating the difficulty of meeting global demands and timelines.

More so than the other cases in this book, the Community Conservation Network was able to balance the demands of each scale. It not only balanced these demands, but it also linked and integrated the scales in a way to create progress in its work. Part of this success was due to the many potential agents of bridging capacity associated with this project. Palau had an advantage over many other countries in this respect; because of its recent history of being administered by the United States, the country had experience melding local and U.S. cultures. The Tobi chief, who had begun pursuing his master's degree from a U.S. university in the area of traditional resource management, had the skills and desire to serve as a bridge for the network. The project deputy director, Wayne Andrew, along with many other community members, demonstrated an awareness of the differences between cultures and made some changes in how the organization reported to funders, but without the power to make lasting change in the organization. In addition, Guilbeaux had worked in Palau and with the

Tobi people for almost a decade with a keen understanding of Tobi customs and resource use, a desire to act as a bridge between scales, and the power to make changes.

This is the story of how an NGO with broad-based authority was ultimately forced to choose between local and global norms in its daily work. For several years, CCN was able to facilitate programming that the community asked for either through the action committee or the management board. To do this, CCN staff brought in globally recognized experts to train community members in monitoring and evaluation, funded through global funders and in a manner respected by the global conservation community. The organization was even successful in bringing some local norms into the global realm of conservation by sending community delegations to international fora, working with funders to contract directly with the management board instead of a globally recognized interlocutor, and reporting to funders both the quantifiable results of the project and the qualitative, contingent reality of the local context. Like so many other NGOs, CCN's reputation for results on the local scale raised its profile on the global scale. The organization attracted a dedicated staff that began to apply CCN's approach to community-based conservation in Hawaii with interest in starting work in Indonesia, as well.

With this global attention came the need to meet global norms of capacity. While CCN demonstrated political and technical capacity on both global and local scales, its administrative capacity was lacking. CCN staff understood this shortcoming and tried several strategies to overcome it. Most of these strategies, however, also involved reducing the flexibility of the organization to respond to local needs. The mechanisms that would turn the organization into a globally professional organization were seen as both difficult and constraining. The mechanisms that brought the organization success in the first place were in conflict with the norms of NGO administration and management.

Accountability often creates more demand for accountability. As the questionable practices of a few NGOs come to light (like The Nature Conservancy, Conservation International, or the International Marinelife Alliance), the administrative burden from government agencies, funders, and other actors to document the work of the NGO increases. The growing requirements for accountability favor the global norms for accountability—the quantitative, short-term, end measurements of each project—and in conflict with the local accountability demands of building long-term relationships where local communities have a say in the programs before they are created (not just after the results are in). The Tobian community of Palau was demanding more face-to-face interaction and more control of the project. CCN found it difficult to comply with the norms of both scales.

When the Community Conservation Network could, it integrated and connected demands, norms, and capacities from the global and local scales. However, whether deliberately or unconsciously, when given the choice of continuing its modus operandi or converting to more global capacity and norms, key leadership repeatedly chose the local scale over the global. As a result, all of these efforts to create a critical mass of global administrative capacity that would allow the organization to operate transnationally were thwarted. When one last effort to stabilize CCN's funding was defeated by the auditing process, the organization could function no longer. The work continued, though, with the missions taken up by two local organizations: the Kua'aina Ulu Auamo and the Helen Reef Management Board. Exiting the process of scaling up allowed CCN's original mission of facilitating community-based resource management to continue.

6 Conclusion: The Paradox of Scale and Nongovernmental Organizations

Growth born of necessity does not always mean that it happens strategically.
—International Marinelife Alliance Strategic Plan (2006)

Why do seemingly powerful NGOs struggle to create lasting, large-scale change? I have argued here that transnational environmental NGOs have difficulty implementing their programs because in order to gain the authority they need in both the local and global scales, they have to meet different requirements. Programs built with authority—which is almost universally defined as legitimated power—are more durable than those built with the mere compliance of other actors. However, the paradox of scale means that the accountability and capacity that built authority for transnational NGOs in one scale will not help it build authority in the other scale. Indeed, the cases in this book indicate that the misapplication of these norms and practices harm NGO authority.

In these pages, I have endeavored to paint a richer picture for understanding nongovernmental organizations as authorities in governance. I have argued that to understand these complex actors, we must balance broad, multidisciplinary theoretical understanding with concrete, context-specific detailed knowledge. In using this approach, this book offers five distinct contributions to the study of nongovernmental organizations and environmental governance.

First, this book introduced the concept of the paradox of scale as a way to understand the dilemma I have described. In explaining this concept, I have explored how authority is created, maintained, and lost for NGOs. Recognizing that authority requirements might vary in different scales is an important step in understanding the complex nature of these actors. As described in chapter 2, the size of the environmental nongovernmental organization sector is growing in both the number of organizations and their revenues, making questions of NGO authority increasingly salient. Moreover, to address the enormity of the problems they seek to remedy, NGOs are expanding their operations to new locales, and operating at both the local and global scales. All this makes them susceptible to the paradox of scale. To explain authority in these case studies, I have created a four-part typology of power and authority based on scale—raw power, local authority, global authority, and broad-based authority—which will be reviewed in the next section. The paradox of scale for NGO authority gives us a new theoretical schema with which to understand the successes and failures of transnational environmental nongovernmental organizations and their role in environmental governance.

This book's central focus is NGO authority. If authority is legitimated power, how do we know an NGO has power and then how can we tell if this power has been legitimated? These are not new questions for scholars of governance. Building on both the literature of these concepts and the empirical data of this research, the second contribution of this book is a new methodological approach to assessing authority. Through these cases, I have demonstrated how NGO authority is built by using accountability as a proxy for legitimacy and capacity as a proxy for power. By using these proxies, and by offering typologies for both capacity and accountability based on scale, I first established how accountability and capacity change at different scales and, then how an actor can demonstrate legitimate power in one scale as well as how it can fail to demonstrate legitimate power in another. Instructive for the paradox of scale, the cases offered here show that applying accountability norms or demonstrating capacity from one scale to another is not helpful in building authority; it can actually reduce an NGO's authority. Thus, these typologies help answer the question of how NGOs can be seen simultaneously as legitimate and "illegitimate" actors in governance.

How does one balance what seems like competing criteria for creating authority? As these cases suggest, not only is it important for NGOs to establish both local and global authority, but they must also connect actors and demands from both scales. Thus, the third contribution of this book is a potential antidote for the paradox of scale: the concept of bridging capacity. Agents of bridging capacity not only know the differences between the norms of the scales in which they operate, but they also can translate and negotiate between the demands of these scales. Think, for example, of individuals from the local context who have represented local interests in global negotiations or fora; or of nonlocal actors who have lived in local communities for years and have returned to work with global funders or secretariats. These actors can change how the organization responds to competing demands and withstand pressure to systematically prioritize one over the other. They can demand more reasonable or flexible timelines for project completion and ensure true participation in project planning because of their long-term relationships in multiple arenas. These agents of bridging capacity seem essential for translating norms to both scales—explaining to local actors why an NGO must take overhead from grants, where the funding goes, and why this project is important in the global context; explaining to global actors how communities perceive the project, why targets may not be met, and the learning that is accumulated beyond the quantifiable results. If an organization can do all this, it is said to have broad-based authority.

Fourth, the theoretical framework discussed in this book breaks new ground in our efforts to understand NGOs because it uses ideas from multiple academic fields—international relations, management, public administration, development, and political science; these are fields that address similar concepts but rarely work together. This has both scholarly and practical implications. By inductively examining NGO authority, this book demonstrates how different disciplinary theories and concepts can be combined to create better understanding of these complex actors. What's more, this approach suggests not only new lines of scholarly inquiry, but also potential new areas for capacity building in NGOs.

Lastly, through case studies, I have traced how these disciplinary approaches, concepts, methods, and mechanisms intersect and interact as strands of the multifaceted cobweb in which environmental NGOs operate. In the thick description involved in telling the story of these three environmental NGOs, I have illustrated the development of these dynamics in order to generate theory. Since this is qualitative work, I do not claim broad generalizability of this theory, but I hope that the detail of these cases triggers interest in applying these typologies, concepts, and theory to other case studies and NGO types, to capture even more of the complexity of these governance actors.

In the pages that follow, I compare the cases in this book and draw lessons from them for the academic governance, management, development, and environmental communities as well as for the NGO practitioner. Following the contributions listed earlier, this chapter will draw on the experience of the case studies, examples from other cases, and the multiple disciplines that are helpful to explain NGO authority. First, it will review the theory and operationalization of the paradox of scale and how it developed in each case study. Second, this chapter will examine broad-based authority and the concept of bridging capacity, and how they were built, maintained, and then, over time, eroded in each case. Third, this chapter focuses a critical eye on this book's central theory to examine alternative explanations for problems of NGO authority and effectiveness. Fourth, this chapter will examine the implications that these cases, theory, and methods might have for the study of nongovernmental organizations across disciplines. This last section of the chapter will review diverse academic disciplines and studies to explain both why an interdisciplinary approach was necessary for this study, and how various disciplines can continue to inform each other in understanding transnational NGOs and governance.

Operationalizing the Paradox of Scale

To explain authority in the case studies included in this book, I have created a four-part typology of power and authority based on scale. NGOs that are policy entrepreneurs often exert *raw power* when they have not accumulated a critical mass of legitimacy on either global or local scales, but have a small but powerful group of actors consenting to their will. These actors demonstrate capacity at one scale or another, but have yet to adhere to the accountability norms of either scale. Recall the example from the introduction of this book, Project Snow Leopard in Pakistan, which works to protect the endangered snow leopard from goat herders who would hunt the big cats to prevent them from killing livestock. This innovative project protects the cats by offering insurance so that herders could recuperate any financial losses when the endangered species killed their livestock, thus reducing incentives to hunt the snow leopards (Ebrahim 2010). At first, it was considered a wild scheme; herders were hesitant to hand over 1 percent of their annual earnings for such protection. Project funders in the global arena were also curious if the idea would be financially sustainable while providing protection for the big cats. The Royal Geographical Society in London took the chance of funding the project in 1999, and three villages were persuaded to participate (Strauss 2016). This funding represented a new form of entrepreneurial governance with, at the time, buy-in from a very small group of global or local actors. As organizations like Project Snow Leopard begin to adhere to local norms of accountability by building long-term relationships with communities, creating context-specific and flexible responses to local demands, incorporating the views of hidden stakeholders, and soliciting input not only into its programs strategies but also its objectives, they begin to build local authority. As word spread throughout the villages that herders were being compensated, other villages joined the effort, which is administered by the villages themselves (Strauss 2016; Rosen et al. 2012). NGOs with *local authority* experience success on a local scale, based on the consent of local actors. However, these actors will not be able to expand their operations to other locales or impact global policy until they balance their local authority with global authority. Seven years after the initial funding, the project's founder won the prestigious Rolex Award for Enterprise. This funding and recognition allowed the project to expand. Since its founding, Project Snow Leopard has been able to demonstrate short-term, quantifiable results—the villages reported fewer killings of the endangered species despite losses to domesticated herds; over two hundred herders have been compensated for loss of livestock from leopard attacks. The project has expanded to cover over ten thousand families in nineteen villages in Northern Pakistan, with similar projects started in Nepal, Bhutan, India, China, and Afghanistan (Ebrahim 2010; Strauss 2016; Rosen et al. 2012). Thus, one novel idea from a policy entrepreneur was implemented through raw power, but through demonstrating both local and global norms, Project Snow Leopard gained legitimacy and authority for resource governance.

NGOs that begin with only *global authority*—say, for example, a conservation NGO whose geographic information system (GIS) lab highlights a remote area of great biological diversity under threat, and whose fundraising efforts gain it access to enter the area for a more detailed resource assessment—adhere to global accountability norms by reporting quantifiable, short-term results, focusing on the technical ex poste reporting to only the actors with the most power in their networks to make accountability demands. These NGOs are often delegated authority by successfully soliciting funding from national or intergovernmental organizations to implement the rules of conservation. Until this global authority is matched with local authority, these organizations work with the consent of global actors but encounter repeated controversy and thwarted attempts to achieve mission on the ground.

When an NGO successfully develops both global and local authority, it is said to have *broad-based authority*. The cases I have explored here suggest that broad-based authority is most durable when the demands and norms of each scale are integrated with each other and negotiated with the bridging capacity in the organization.

I do not assume that every NGO effort at achieving its mission qualifies as exerting authority. Discussions of NGOs are filled with other types of power displays, especially their efforts to influence global policy through diplomacy, information exchange, and media campaigns. I have demonstrated that exerting global influence is important, because it often demonstrates the NGOs' expertise, which is then called upon to implement conservation projects. Using this expertise, they design, implement, and sometimes enforce the rules of resource governance for that locale. With these specific actions—designing, implementing, and enforcing rules of resource governance—NGOs meet the definition of exerting authority. They plan programs to change how conservation happens, and use their influence to attain funding, but once their programs are funded, NGOs have moved beyond influence and into authority. To apply Green's (2014) typology of private authority, if NGOs are funded by states or intergovernmental organizations, they are delegated authority. If they create and implement the rules of conservation through private funding, they are exerting entrepreneurial authority. The cases presented here further clarify this typology by showing how NGO authority might be delegated in one scale and entrepreneurial in another, since each scale has its unique legitimizing criteria.

Maintaining broad-based authority in the face of the paradox of scale is no easy task. As figure 6.1 outlines, the broad-based authority in each of the cases was worn down over time by the challenges that comprise the paradox of scale. NGOs starting with global authority may find that the capacities and accountability norms that gain them access at the local level will make them impotent or even harmful there. Conservation International's ability to adhere to global norms of capacity and accountability—to

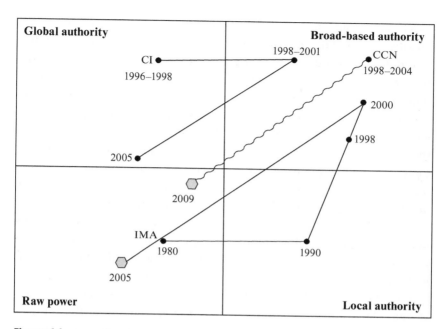

Figure 6.1
Case study authority over time

fundraise from leading philanthropic and UN agencies, to influence policy and discourse through international media outlets and scholarly publications, and to respond to requests for quantitative measures on its progress—did not help it to create long-term, meaningful relationships with actors in Milne Bay. Without these relationships, CI's programs not only risked irrelevance within their local context, but it eventually tarnished the NGO's reputation at both scales and decreased their global authority.[1]

NGOs that start with local authority often find their ability to respond to local accountability norms gains them recognition on the global scale. For example, the International Marinelife Alliance and the Community Conservation Network were both able to foster long-term relationships with local actors by responding to them and incorporating their ideas into the program in meaningful ways. Their success in doing this gained them recognition on the global scale as well as funding to replicate their successes elsewhere. However, in the process of scaling up their operations, they experienced pressure to prioritize the global scale by favoring and developing those capacities and adhering to those accountability norms. Both

NGOs faced a similar conundrum: they could abandon the processes that initially made the organization successful in order to compete for funding or influence global discourse and policy, or they could refuse to prioritize these forces and lose global authority. In both case studies, the organizations attempted the former, and when they faced repercussions for this choice, they then reverted to the latter, placing higher importance on the local scale. This prioritization risked IMA and CCN losing more than just the promise of expansion; it risked the very authority that brought their success in the first place. Once the choice to prioritize the local scale was made, the lack of global authority disconnected these organizations from many of the resources they needed to operate on either scale.

The difficulty for NGOs is that pressure to conform to and prioritize the norms of the global scale is more concerted than pressure to prioritize the local scale. It's easy to imagine why. Global-scale actors might demand different things, but are generally unified in the norms of what they demand: quantifiable, short-term reporting can be uniform in its format. To operate at multiple local scales, however, an NGO must understand the contexts of these localities—how actors in each context prefer to interact, how they define the terms of engagement with NGOs, and so on. These varied local demands are made in a cacophony of voices that can often drown each other out. Thus, the uniformity of the global scale is prioritized over the local one. This prioritization is the essence of the paradox of scale: not only are the requirements of legitimated power different in the local and global scales, but the prioritization of the global scale undermines maintaining local authority.

While the cases in this book bring to light this constrained choice set, they also indicate that this impossible choice does not necessarily have to be. To be sure, this broad-based authority seems difficult to maintain because the demands of each scale seem too often at odds with one another. I argue, however, that although further study is surely needed, these case studies suggest that it is not impossible. For years, each case was able to balance local and global demands. These cases indicate that the ideal scenario occurs when actors are able to manage the duality of operating at different scales. One example of how NGOs try to balance demands is through the use of a memorandum of understanding whereby either party could dissolve the partnership at any time. Although actors in the CI case demonstrate the flawed nature of this instrument, its use is a reflection of the tension on the one hand to be able to cease work that does not achieve benchmarks, and on the other hand to create long-lasting relationships that endure disagreements on project goals and implementation. Sustaining this broad-based authority, however, requires more than building capacity and accountability relationships on both the local and global scales; NGOs must also be able to connect these two scales of operation and balance their demands so that one does not overpower the other. Just as this book has identified the dynamics of the paradox of scale as a crucial limiting factor for NGOs, these case studies also point to a potential remedy: bridging capacity. This next section will examine how each case balanced the scales, presented elements of bridging capacity, and how that capacity was dismantled over time.

Developing and Maintaining Bridging Capacity in Papua New Guinea, the Philippines, and Palau

In each of the case studies explored in the previous chapters, the NGOs enjoyed broad-based authority for years. They were able to create and implement interventions with the consent of both global and local actors. They experienced progress toward their missions. They demonstrated global and local capacity and accountability norms and negotiated these differences regularly. Dismantling this broad-based authority was not quick; no single incident undermined it. Instead, the NGO in each case experienced an erosion of authority through a series of incidents and a variety of different actors.

The experience of these NGOs point to a specialized capacity that allows actors to negotiate between scales and balance the demands and norms of each: what I call bridging capacity. Three pillars of bridging capacity seem to emerge from these cases: (1) intercultural and cross-cultural (ICCC) understanding between the dominant and less understood cultures; (2) ability to change the way the organization operates; and (3) the dedication and focus—either at the individual or the organizational level—to act as a bridge and make changes even when they may be unpopular. Each case demonstrated elements of bridging capacity, but an unyielding prioritization of global norms by multiple actors eroded that capacity over time. This section will discuss how these pillars presented in each case.

Authority and Bridging Capacity in Milne Bay

Conservation International in Milne Bay demonstrated capacity and accountability at both scales. It was able to raise funds from multiple global sources, to influence discourse on conservation priorities through its research, and to become the first NGO accredited as a Global Environment Facility agency. CI reflected global accountability norms through reporting quantifiable results in a short-term five-year project with glossy, photo-filled reports.

Locally, the CI project planned to engage community members through Village Engagement Teams and oversight boards, and to mobilize several communities to move toward creating protected areas. It upheld local accountability norms by learning from the challenges other NGOs faced in Papua New Guinea as well as the difficulties and accusations CI endured about projects in other contexts (Grandia 2004; Chapin 2004). For the four years between 1998 and 2001, CI staff members incorporated local processes and demands into their plans and the organization's leadership empowered these processes. Initially, the project reflected local accountability norms by creating long-term engagement with communities through Village Engagement Teams, allowing communities to determine whether or not they wanted to create protected areas (and when), and following protocols that were culturally specific for the communities in which they worked. Moreover, the designers of the project were able to negotiate between local and global norms. In their project reporting they utilized both face-to-face interaction with local actors and text-heavy, logical frameworks with theories of change with global funders. In project planning they pulled together scientifically accepted protocols and the goals and desires of the resource-dependent communities. They built into their timelines a long period of relationship building with communities before discussing commitments toward changes in resource management. All of this worked not only to balance demands of global and local scales, but also to integrate them in one project.

This balance was undermined at multiple junctures starting in 2001. First, since very few staff members possessed the intercultural and cross-cultural understanding needed to act as bridges, the job of negotiating between scales fell upon the shoulders of few actors. Without widespread ICCC understanding, the bridging capacity was tenuous, at best. When several architects of the Community Engagement Process and visitor protocols left the project, the search for a new project leader, the chief technical advisor, made clear the prioritization of a PhD over local experience or even ICCC understanding. The local second in command—an official from the Milne Bay Provincial Government who was seconded to the project—had local understanding but was not empowered to make project decisions. Moreover, although this local leader could also have acted as a bridge, one community member noted that the learning was only one-way: "He got too carried away ... I'd get carried away too, I suppose, if I worked for a big NGO and wanted to have the American way here."[2] This accusation also points to a lack of incentives for local actors to be an agent for bridging capacity.

Next, during a trip for NGO leaders, funders, and board members to Milne Bay, those actors who did possess ICCC understanding were disempowered. During this trip to Kwawaira, powerful actors from CI's Washington, DC, headquarters allegedly asked the village leaders for a list of things they needed, raising expectations of a cargo-for-nature swap. This act demonstrated how organizational leadership prioritized the urgency of having quantifiable results over the culturally sensitive processes and rules of engagement with Milne Bay communities.

Finding nonlocal experts who have studied the local context of NGO work is another potential strategy for building ICCC understanding. In CI's case, this proved difficult, and created an eighteen-month delay in hiring a new chief technical advisor. Considering how quickly NGOs scale up operations to new geographic areas, this dilemma of finding a leader with both global and local expertise does not seem unique to the CI case. The question planted here for future research is: If *finding* actors with bridging capacity is so difficult, then how might the field *build* bridging capacity in environmental governance, to increase the number of actors who can act to maintain broad-based authority?

Even if there was sufficient ICCC understanding in Milne Bay, what ability and incentives do actors have to be agents of bridging capacity? For the CI project, the inflexible timelines of the project, driven by the urgency of their mission, acted as disincentive for bridging capacity. Funders required project timelines to remain intact, even after an eighteen-month delay in hiring a new project leader. This act not only maintained the global accountability norms of short-term, quantifiable results but also amplified their impact on the project. The urgency that NGOs, funders, and individual professionals all share to achieve their organization's mission is not trivial; without timely intervention, species will go extinct, democracies will be destroyed, and people will die of illness or violence from conflicts. In Milne Bay, the urgency to implement marine protected areas pushed project staff to create these areas in more locations than originally planned for the first phase of the project. It also resulted in increased spending that ended the project sooner than planned. In hindsight, this urgency acted as a disincentive to act as a bridge, and the resulting actions delegitimized Conservation International in the eyes of both global and local actors. Where initially the Milne Bay project exhibited local and global authority as well as the bridging capacity to integrate them in the project plan, over time the project lost much of its intercultural and cross-cultural understanding, the ability to communicate across difference, and the incentives the individuals and the organization needed to bridge scales in a meaningful way.

Authority and Bridging Capacity in IMA

The International Marinelife Alliance started out by creating entrepreneurial authority at the local scale. Between 1980 and the 1992 IMA focused on building long-term relationships with fishing communities and officials, and recognized hidden stakeholders throughout the fishing community by working with schools to create curriculum and with community members to create alternative income sources. The creation of the Coral Reef Education for Students and Teachers program throughout the Philippines is one example of IMA's local capacity. By avoiding collaboration with the Department of Education, Culture, and Sports in the Philippines, IMA staff members created and implemented their education program quickly, sidestepping bureaucratic processes and broader accountability norms. Starting in the mid-1990s, the organization brought global capacity onto the local scale in limited and compartmentalized ways by commissioning the creation of a scientifically rigorous cyanide detection test to enforce the ban on cyanide use in reef fishing, while designing implementation protocols to fit the context of fishing communities. Moreover, IMA leaders were not afraid to fail at these endeavors in order to answer the needs of their stakeholders, as their investment in the now-defunct coral farm indicates. All this demonstrated the organization's local and global authority.

As the NGO grew to operate transnationally, the demands for the organization to adhere to global norms also grew. Similarly, the number of potential agents of bridging capacity increased, reflected in the efforts of new employees, leadership, organizational partnerships, and funding relationships. Like many NGOs in other fields, IMA hired staff who cared about local context and understood global demands. The experience of these staff members evokes two lessons about the paradox of scale: first, the importance of organizational power for agents of bridging capacity; and second, the tendency of prioritizing global norms over the local. Such potential bridging capacity reminds us that actors can possess sufficient intercultural and cross-cultural understanding, but without the ability to change how an NGO operates, they cannot connect, interpret, and negotiate the differences in contexts, capacities, and accountability demands. Moreover, while these potential agents of bridging capacity understood the importance of global and local scales, they still prioritized global norms. To balance IMA's local authority from its first fifteen years, these new stakeholders advocated for a more professionalized board, a strategic plan, and systematic decision-making. What these advocates did not seem to understand was that their efforts prioritized global demands over local ones, making IMA less flexible and less able to respond to community contexts and demands. Thus, while these individuals had ICCC understanding, global norms undermined their efforts. One powerful actor who recognized this dynamic, the president of IMA, chose to disempower these potential bridging actors and prioritize the local scale. When the disbursement of funds from a major funder was delayed, the president broke global norms of accountability by keeping the organization afloat with restricted funds and destroyed the organization in the process.

This case demonstrates that broad-based authority built without robust bridging capacity is tenuous. While each of IMA's potential agents of bridging capacity demonstrated ICCC understanding, each lacked either the ability to create organizational decisions or the incentives to balance and integrate local and global demands. Without this capacity, the norms and capacities of each scale were upheld, but not integrated with each other. The importance of this integration, evident in the other two case studies of this book, should be assessed in future research on NGO authority.

Authority and Bridging Capacity in Palau

Similar to IMA's experience, the Community Conservation Network's capacity to engage Hatohobei elected government and traditional leaders, respond to the traditional users of Helen Reef, and advocate for locally managed approaches to conservation led to a demand for the organization to operate in other communities. Unlike IMA, CCN did not compartmentalize its local and global activities: it sought to integrate the two scales throughout its programming and leadership. This was evident in many activities and events. From the date of its incorporation in 1998, CCN was able to use its global capacity to fundraise and bring in scientists to assess resources and train community members to perform future assessments. The organization built long-term relationships with the Tobi community and empowered those actors to have a voice in the goals and implementation of the project, often bringing local actors to global fora to represent the program.

As the cases here indicate, acting as an agent of bridging capacity is a risky endeavor. It requires saying yes to one approach or process and saying no to others. Often it will require going against the global norms of accountability or capacity and making unpopular decisions. In doing this, agents of bridging capacity risk offending actors whose norms are not adopted by the project in question; or making the wrong choice, resulting in the project or organization not attaining measurable results. An NGO cannot encourage risk without acknowledging that failure might result. But the NGO will not acknowledge failure if it runs the risk of losing its funding (Jepson 2005). Thus, this process of incorporating failure as a part of regular and ongoing conversations about the project and organization is important for building broad-based authority. As the earlier section on CI discusses, the urgency of taking action often seems at odds with building local accountability, which entails considering specific contexts, building long-term relationships, and demonstrating a willingness to change the goals and process of an intervention based on local needs and perspectives. How can an organization reconcile these contradictory demands?

The Community Conservation Network's relationship with its funders suggests some answers to this question. In 2004, CCN published a funding report that used qualitative methods to mitigate these risks and to balance the urgent need of results with the relationship building of local accountability. While much of the report was filled with quantitative answers to the project's pre-established success measures, the authors also wrote a section entitled "Telling the story" immediately following these measures (HRRMP and CCN 2004). The numbers reflected delays in the project.

The "story" explained why these delays happened—based on obstacles in the form of staff changes, high time demands of its volunteer board, and misunderstandings about the purchase of necessary equipment. Most important in explaining these delays, the report pointed to the transparent and participatory way in which the project aimed to overcome these obstacles, which resulted in better understanding among all parties to the project, a sense of accomplishment with the measures that were met, and a visit by the funders to help resolve any outstanding issues. While the two pages of quantifiable measures demonstrated the global accountability norms of the project, these two paragraphs of "story" balanced those measures with local accountability practices of maintaining flexibility, developing long-term relationships, and allowing stakeholders the time to make true changes to the project. Another funder granted CCN a no-cost extension for its work, creating flexibility in the timeline of deliverables. In both cases, global accountability norms would have pointed to a failure to achieve predetermined results, but incorporating local accountability norms demonstrated learning that would ultimately help the project's cause.

Once the organization was pulled onto the global scale, gaps in its global capacity—in its administrative capacity and decision-making structure—came to light. With more administrative reporting requirements, CCN experienced less flexibility to interact with community decision-making, decreasing local authority for CCN. The organization's local authority created an environment where local leaders demanded more control of the program but also more face-to-face interaction with CCN's leadership. Global actors demanded that leaders spend more time at headquarters to build organizational structure and process. This resulted in the repeated denial of global norms and demands in favor of the face-to-face requirements of doing business in Palau. Without being able to maintain its broad-based authority, CCN was not financially sustainable. It closed its doors, and in its place two local organizations were established—the Hatohobei Organization for People and the Environment (HOPE) and the Kua'aina Ulu 'Auamo in Hawaii—which continued its work.

There is a great deal we can learn from these three nongovernmental organizations' struggles in scaling up their operations. Each organization balanced global and local accountability demands, demonstrated capacity and effectiveness on each level, and experienced the apex of its power for years. CI and CCN were able to maintain broad-based authority in a more robust way than IMA because of the active engagement of bridging capacity in Milne Bay and Palau. The creation of bridging capacity in CI and CCN began with the deliberate creation of intercultural and cross-cultural understanding. The Milne Bay project used qualitative research to create the original project plan, the Village Engagement Teams, and the Community Engagement Process. CCN hired a consultant—an anthropologist with thirty years' experience in the community—to produce a report on the sociocultural features of the Hatohobei culture. This effort helped project staff to understand the cultural context of its work, and to create rules and processes for respecting that context—an important element of programming—although the plans were undermined later on by either disempowering these actors or a lack of incentives for staff members to act as a bridge. That CI lost its authority after prioritizing global norms and yet is the only case study still operational might be an indicator of how global norms are prioritized in conservation governance.

These three cases imply that bridging capacity requires deep understanding of cultural differences and the ability to embrace risk to negotiate scales and to temper the urgency of the NGO mission with building relationships. Bridging capacity was not dismantled quickly, or by a single event or actor; rather it faced multiple, sustained challenges over time. The next section of this chapter will group these challenges together by theme in order to explore alternative explanations for the loss of NGO authority.

Alternative Explanations

The cases in this book demonstrate how broad-based authority is created, maintained, and undermined for nongovernmental organizations. I assert that one key causal mechanism for undermining NGO authority is the paradox of scale. In comparing and contrasting the development of this paradox in these case studies, their events and issues seem to cluster around potential alternative explanations for the authority problems of NGOs. Nonprofit management issues, principal-agent pressures from funders, and the prevailing standards and practices of the NGO country of origin might suggest simpler explanations for the difficulties of these NGOs. This section will briefly explore each individual theme to demonstrate that they are indeed plausible explanations that collectively are strands in the complex cobweb of issues in which NGOs operate. Acknowledging these themes does not take away from the paradox of scale as an explanatory concept. Each example supports the prioritization of global norms over local ones and taken together they indicate that these norms and capacities are prioritized not just by individual actors or in individual relationships, but also by the field as a whole. Succinctly put, these alternative explanations are not truly alternatives, but help explain the dynamics of the paradox with different focuses and disciplinary lenses than the ones I have employed.

Nonprofit Management: Financial Mismanagement

Those who study nonprofit management might see the difficulties of each case in this book as typical examples of financial mismanagement, or the struggle between founder's syndrome and strategic planning. These issues merit further examination. Financial mismanagement occurred in each case, whether through spending funds faster than was planned, or using funds outside of their restricted purposes. In Milne Bay, the funding was completely spent eighteen months prior to the project ending. The Community Conservation Network experienced difficulties paying staff with empty coffers, and the International Marinelife Alliance suffered from delays in funding, prompting management to reallocate restricted funds.

Evidence in all three cases illuminated how the increasing complexity of rules and processes for maintaining funding or nonprofit status restricted responsiveness to resource-dependent communities. Conservation International's troubles adhering to the different financial reporting requirements of each actor were experienced by both local and global staff in the project. The Community Conservation Network could not keep up with the increasing demands of accounting and structure to become a "professional" global conservation organization. And in each case study, leadership mentioned how these increasing administrative demands occur simultaneously with their stakeholders' disinterest in funding the overhead functions that are needed to respond coherently. Thus, leaders and staff who could have spent energy focusing on bridging the local and global scales were instead focused on trying to adhere to reporting structures with few resources to do so.

Indeed, scholars of nonprofit management might point to these examples as justification for financial management courses for nonprofit managers. But the dynamics of the paradox of scale is not at odds with ideas of nonprofit management; rather, it offers underlying causes for them. The urgency behind the funders' calls to achieve quantifiable, short-term results in the Milne Bay project proved to be overwhelming for the project managers. More administrative capacity in financial management could have directed them to spend faster without overspending, but this was overshadowed by (1) the complex and contradicting accounting and reporting methods required by the global partners (which also resulted in a high turnover rate for accounting staff within the project); (2) the inflexible, short-term deadlines for the project; and (3) the implicit message to the project management that they must spend the funds or funds might be lost. In this way, issues of low administrative capacity in the form of financial management converged with other forces that reflected the prioritization of global norms and capacities. If the organizations had the financial management capacity, it is likely it would still run into issues of the paradox of scale, since it was still required to spend and achieve on the short term, which caused it also to override any local or bridging capacity it had.

Financial management problems in the case of International Marinelife Alliance can also be seen as just one element in a series that undermined broad-based authority. What would have happened if the organization had not used restricted funds to survive while waiting for the USAID funds to come through? Unlike CI, which survived an eighteen-month delay in funding from the GEF because it had global capacity to access other funding for that time period, IMA had no such capacity. It would have had to shut down its operations, and risk losing its staff's specific capacity when they found jobs elsewhere. More importantly, loss of this staff would also represent a loss of local authority, since these were the individuals who had created long-term relationships with communities.

Even if the funding was disbursed along the original timeline, the development of the paradox of scale was progressing steadily before these events started to unfold, indicating that best practices in financial management would have been unlikely to help even in the best of situations. Struggles over institutionalizing rules, restructuring the board, creating new hierarchies of decision-making, and questioning the approach and modus operandi of the cyanide detection labs—all these were well underway regardless of funding.

Similarly, adhering to global norms of financial management might have required CCN to discontinue adhering to the local norms of face-to-face communications, since it would have cut the number of trips to Palau by the project leader. Thus, increased global financial management capacity would have led to decreased local accountability practices.

Nonprofit Management: Strategic Planning and Founder's Syndrome

In the International Marinelife Alliance and Community Conservation Network cases, one might assert that the strategic planning process marked the beginning of difficulties in balancing local and global demands. Moreover, multiple informants—former staff, board members, staff from partnering organizations—in these cases pointed to founder's syndrome as a cause of difficulties. Founder's syndrome occurs when a founder inadvertently sabotages the organization due to a grandiose ego, an inability to delegate, an inability to make a smooth transition to new leadership, and an unwavering dedication to the original vision of the organization (Schmidt 2013). Indeed, as detailed in chapters 4 and 5, IMA and CCN's strategic planning processes seemed to be in direct conflict with the leadership style and focus of the founding leaders of these NGOs.

Let's examine how strategic planning and the leadership style of a founding leader might work at odds with each other. While there is a plethora of different approaches to strategic planning, the process generally creates and institutionalizes rules and procedures within an organization toward achieving its mission. For IMA, that process included two short retreats with senior staff to create priorities for the next three to five years; establishing new operational policies and procedures; defining the roles, responsibilities, and authorities of all programs and their individual staff; establishing new programs in multiple countries; and restructuring the board of directors without many founding members of that board (Parks 2001). This process was funded by an organizational effectiveness program whose goal is to help their fund recipients "to enhance their capacity to meet the *Foundation's goals*" (emphasis added). In essence, this strategic planning process changed the modus operandi that made IMA successful in the first place. It prioritized the goals of the funders—the most visible stakeholders—and the global norms of short-term, quantifiable results over multiple geographic areas. This process would have IMA change its focus from local to global accountability norms.

In the case of the Community Conservation Network, delegating and transitioning to new leadership could have meant a shift from upholding local accountability norms toward prioritizing global accountability norms, which would bring a different kind of inflexibility to the project. If the mission of CCN was to respond to the needs of local communities, and the changes in the organization were seen as reducing that responsiveness, then perhaps the delays in implementing these changes—for example, choosing face-to-face communication with community leaders that required time away from the organization's headquarters where leadership was needed to make major decisions on policy and process—were warranted.

In each of the case studies in this book, many sources sought one individual to shoulder the blame for programmatic or organizational troubles. I assert that not one individual is to blame, but the larger systemic dynamics of transnational governance. For these organizations' founders, there was little choice but to make the changes that would ultimately dissolve their organizations. The paradox of scale created a constrained choice set: either transition and deny what made the organization successful in the first place or remain dedicated to those principals and processes regardless of global pressures. Some scholars of founder's syndrome caution that "silencing the person with the original vision is counterproductive" highlighting the irony "that donor intent has been accorded so much legal protection over the last few years, but founder intent is ignored" (Schmidt 2013). In IMA and CCN, this struggle between founder's syndrome and strategic planning exemplified the struggle between local and global norms, illustrating that tenets of nonprofit management and the concept of the paradox of scale are not mutually exclusive in their explanatory power. Moreover, since this particular struggle did not occur in the CI case, we know that issues besides founder's syndrome can contribute to these NGO predicaments, meaning that we cannot explain all the authority issues in these cases through the analytical lens of these nonprofit management theories. Had these founders submitted to the conclusions of the strategic planning process, they would have encountered the paradox in other ways, perhaps in the same ways that CI did.

Principal-Agent Problems

Others with more traditional backgrounds in political science or economics might suggest that the principal-agent relationship between the funder and the NGO can better explain these organization's struggles. The very primacy of this relationship is part and parcel of global accountability norms: the need to answer to the most powerful or visible stakeholders. One cannot deny that these NGOs felt pressure to adhere to the norms of short-term, quantifiable results, with very little room for flexibility, which was, in part, driven by funders.

However, each case also offers evidence of prioritizing global norms from other actors. Recall the small group of community members in Palau who asked for less responsibility to make project decisions in an effort to expedite results. They had little to no contact with funders and yet upheld the norms of short-term results with little *ex ante* input from the community. The second in command of the project in Milne Bay was observed by community members as learning the "top down" way of management from the chief technical administrator. Staff members in IMA and in partnering (and competing) organizations sought to facilitate community-driven conservation but still adhered to the prioritization of scientific certifications and professionalized boards. All these actors illustrate how global accountability norms and capacities are upheld beyond funder demands.

That the funders helped diffuse global norms throughout the network is important, to be certain. They are key players in prioritizing global norms over local ones and hold financial incentives for NGOs not just to scale up their operations, but also to reproduce these norms. When CCN approached its funders to ascertain if it could hand off financial responsibilities to the Helen Reef Management Board, the NGO was not allowed to transfer funds until global administrative capacity was built in the board. Because of this, future research that examines funder participation in creating bridging capacity throughout the conservation field would be helpful in understanding how to overcome the paradox of scale. However, the multiple actors in each case who prioritized global norms in a multitude of ways implies that the principal-agent relationship between funder and NGO is just one element of resource governance that upholds the paradox of scale.

Country of Origin

Since all three NGOs studied in this book have U.S. origins, the impact of NGO national origin on their effectiveness might be considered a potential alternative explanation. Sarah Stroup (2012) compared national regulatory environments, government-NGO relations, economic resources, and social networks in the United States, the United Kingdom, and France to explore these variables' impact on NGO effectiveness. She found striking differences on these fronts. In particular, she found that in comparison to their British and French counterparts, U.S.-based advocacy NGOs in human rights and humanitarian fields (1) work in partnership with government more, (2) are more "professionalized" and less voluntary, and (3) are funded more from government agencies than individual donations. Variation on these three particulars of U.S.-based NGOs appears in this book's cases—CI and CCN seemed to work in partnership with government while IMA deliberately avoided such partnerships; CI was the only NGO considered professionalized by global standards; and IMA had a history of operating through small private grants and individual funding until the USAID funding—perhaps making these cases significant for assessing the impact of country of origin. However, that is beyond the scope of this book.

To be sure, Stroup's theory raises interesting issues that should be explored further. However, the intention of my book's qualitative study is to build theory on NGO authority. The data from which the theory and frameworks were derived comes primarily from transnational environmental NGOs that originated in the United States, thus limiting their generalizability. Having the theory tested with data—from NGOs originating elsewhere—would be a natural continuation of this research. I encourage researchers from other fields or of NGOs from other countries of origin to assess this framework in other cases.

Alternative or Supporting Explanations?

All of these alternative explanations for problems with NGO authority— issues of nonprofit management, principal-agent relationships with funders, and practices associated with the NGO's country of origin—raise interesting questions for new lines of analysis across specialties. Exploring how these issues operate in the three cases presented in this volume suggests that these are not competing explanations about NGO authority and effectiveness; instead, they offer different disciplinary foci with which to explain the paradox of scale. The variation of these potential explanations in these specific cases raises questions as to whether or not these variables or others raised in this analysis are individually sufficient to explain each case's problems. Imagining the absence of these variables highlights the plethora of other actors and events that demonstrate the prioritization of global norms. These questions point to the importance of using causal mechanisms—suites of hypotheses that work together to explain a phenomenon (Checkel 2008)—rather than one individual causal relationship or disciplinary focus, to explain NGO authority. Each of these potential alternative explanations supports the dynamics within the paradox of scale, and thus, each can be considered an addition to the suite of assertions highlighted in chapters 1 and 2. The theory presented in this book incorporates multiple disciplines to explain NGO authority; the examination of these alternative explanations points to alternative but complementary areas of study that could offer additional understanding of the causal mechanism of the paradox of scale and the global norms that are prioritized within it.

Implications for the Study of NGOs across Multiple Fields of Scholarship

Examining nongovernmental organization activities across scales changes our understanding of these actors' roles in governance, further distinguishes different types of power and how they manifest, and pushes scholars to think not just of specific concepts in governance, but also of how the norms of those concepts change over scale. Questions have been raised for decades about how working on multiple scales creates dilemmas for NGOs, but until now there has not been this level of detail to explain them (Fisher 1997; Avant, Finnemore, and Sell 2010). To do this, I have had to reach across disciplines to knit concepts, definitions, and ideas from management, public administration, and development studies together with international relations in order to understand the empirical complexity of NGOs.

Through this analysis, I have introduced a new and detailed filter through which to look at nongovernmental organizations' roles in governance. Until recently, the field of international relations (IR) has regarded NGOs as a homogeneous group of actors. Additionally, IR seems to focus on NGOs in the global scale and their influence in rulemaking and negotiations (Betsill and Corell 2008), and development studies tends to focus on their local interactions with communities (Slim 2002; Edwards and Hulme 1996; Fisher 1997; Chambers 1983; Banks, Hulme, and Edwards 2015). Other scholars have also examined the interactions between local and global NGOs through networks (Bob 2005; Keck and Sikkink 1998).

But NGOs are not confined to either the local or the global scale. A growing number of them work globally to shape the rules of their fields and then work to implement these rules locally (Murdie 2014). Examining NGOs through the lens of scale adds this dimension to the field of NGO studies by connecting their global and local activities to see how these distinct scales interact. In this way, my work here has demonstrated that NGOs are not a homogenous group of actors, and that each NGO can have different goals, strategies, and impact depending upon the scale of action.

This book also contributes to the growing area of study that demonstrates the importance of management and public administration to international relations. Beginning with Ebrahim's (2005b) study of how external accountability impacted two of India's largest development NGOs, the importance of connecting an NGO's internal attributes and operations with its external effectiveness has become more salient.

The recent trend of global NGOs decentralizing functions and relocating offices presents a fertile testing ground for comparing authority across federated, confederated, networked and unitary forms of organizations (Brown, Ebrahim, and Batliwala 2012). In the past few years, large NGOs have made great efforts to reduce centralized offices located in the global north and relocate either offices or functions in the global south. ActionAid in the mid-2000s relocated its offices to South Africa. Amnesty International decentralized its research and advocacy functions. With the exception of its one headquarters office, Oxfam has closed its offices in the UK. Moreover, these large NGOs are morphing into "networked" NGOs— where the NGO's role is reduced from its traditional planning and implementation functions to one of supporting local organizations in their planning and implementation of interventions (Doane 2016). How does an organization's ability to build and maintain broad-based authority differ in these distinct forms of NGOs, and how does it change as the NGO changes form? The concepts and typologies I have outlined here suggest a framework and a method for answering these questions.

Beyond offering concepts and typologies, I present thick data for each case study, raising new questions about organizational structure and decentralization of decision-making. Wendy Wong (2012) asserts that for advocacy NGOs, there is an optimum balance of centralized versus decentralized agenda-setting functions: human rights NGOs must centralize power to introduce or veto items for the political agenda while leaving implementation strategies and tactics to local-level actors, who can adapt them to area contexts. Does this rule of thumb hold true for conservation and development NGOs—organizations more focused on service delivery than advocacy at the local scale? Contrasting with Wong's findings, the Helen Reef Project in Palau found it helpful to keep agenda setting at the local level, leaving only fundraising for technical support for the global scale actors. While more data needs to be collected to answer this question, the detail in these cases raise questions about functional divisions across other transnational NGO and networks.

To explain the experience of environmental NGOs in governance, I have created practical, applicable theory on the IR concepts of NGOs power and authority across scales by bringing management and public administration ideas of capacity and accountability to serve as observable proxies for these often ethereal concepts.

The field of international relations has long been fixated on the concepts of power, authority, and legitimacy. Indeed, these are the bedrock concepts of political science. Those studying nonstate actors are particularly interested in seeing how applicable traditional state-centered notions are to governance actors. This book advances our understanding of these concepts by connecting and operationalizing them for nongovernmental organizations. Building on Betsill and Corell's (2008) work on NGO diplomacy, I trace how influence can create authority for NGOs at the global level, arguing that authority is necessary for NGOs to be effective in the long term because consent is more durable than compliance, and these actors seek to make durable change on the ground. The framework on power and authority presented here informs the traditional ideas of power in political science with the lessons learned in the field of development studies, which focuses on empowerment of local communities (Slim 2002; Sumner 2006) and capacity problems of NGOs (Brinkerhoff and Morgan 2010). Moreover, building on Jinnah (2014), Betsill and Corell (2008), Avant, Finnemore, and Sell (2010), Green (2014), and others, I have augmented our understandings of influence and authority as distinct forms of power, giving texture to these broad concepts by explaining how they change across scale.

Because the study of private authority and power has developed so significantly since the turn of the millennium, I was able to look beyond the question "Do NGOs matter?" in international relations to dare ask, "When do NGOs try to matter, but don't?" These actors are indeed authorities who create the rules for conservation in the project areas where they work, who choose how to implement those projects, and who monitor and enforce how rules of conservation are implemented. They have delegated authority from states or intergovernmental organizations, or they create authority by securing private funding to create and implement rules. They demonstrate unique expertise about the resources they seek to protect and the communities in which they work. Why, then, do they face difficulties in exerting that authority? How does an NGO lose authority? How can an NGO be considered an authority by some yet illegitimate by others? From the data in the previous chapters, I have constructed answers to these questions not only by demonstrating how NGOs acquire authority, but also by tracing the processes of losing that authority as well.

While it seems standard practice now to define authority as legitimated power, a major methodological contribution of this book is the use of accountability and capacity as proxies for the concepts of legitimacy and power, respectively. Though these concepts have been connected in various ways in the discussions on legitimacy (Bernstein 2004; 2011; Cashore, Auld, and Newsome 2003), accountability (Avant, Finnemore, and Sell 2010; Balboa 2015), and power (Green 2014; Jinnah 2014; Koppell 2010; Baldwin 2002), this book explicitly demonstrates how the interaction of these concepts explain NGO authority.

Various discussions of these concepts have hinted at how they might manifest differently for different actors. Using this typology of capacity and accountability across scale particularly advances Green's (2014) typology of private authority by demonstrating that delegation at one scale does not mean that authority is delegated at the other; globally delegated NGO authority might require the organization to legitimate its authority at the local scale in similar ways to entrepreneurial authority.

The incremental and compartmentalized study of accountability for nonstate actors has left our understanding of NGOs incomplete. The complexity of NGOs and the various stakeholders to whom they answer is one reason for this. Much IR ink has elucidated our understanding of NGO relations with just one actor: intergovernmental agencies, the state, secretariats, industry, and other NGOs (Pattberg 2004; Betsill and Corell 2008; Bob 2005). Adding to this list, the area of development studies has focused on NGOs in relation to the communities they are meant to serve (Slim 2002).

While these studies have advanced our understanding of governance, mine is not the first study to assert that the single-relationship analysis of principal-agent theory cannot capture the complexity of the networks of actors to whom NGOs are accountable.

The fields of management, public administration, and development studies have expanded our understanding of NGO accountability, but with a different focus. These fields tend to focus on the mechanics of how accountability occurs instead of how it might function, if multiple stakeholders could reimagine it. This approach reduces the concept's ability to truly act as a check on power (Kearns 1994; Balboa 2015). This book expands the limits of our understanding through its multidisciplinary approach. Where its contributions, listed earlier, discuss how other literatures augment the field of international relations and its understanding of NGOs and power, I contend that the converse is true for the concept of accountability. That is, this book's presentation of accountability—a concept often evoked in management or development fields—is enhanced by applying the international relations concept of norms to instrumental ideas of accountability. In this way, the applying key concepts and approaches from one discipline to another helps paint the complex empirical picture of NGOs.

The typology of global and local accountability norms presented here builds on the literature that has begun to map out the dysfunctions of NGO accountability. In management and public administration, the idea that one's accountability relationships can paralyze the actor in achieving any mission was introduced in Koppell's "multiple accountabilities disorder" (2005). Brown confirms that the demands of different actors complicate any universal understanding of accountability, but stops short of asserting that these different actors might have common types of demands or forms of accountability (2008). Jordan and van Tuijl (2006) discuss how different understandings of accountability can create conflict on the ground while Avant and colleagues caution that actors are not as unaccountable as some assert—they are just accountable to the wrong actors (Avant, Finnemore, and Sell 2010). Kramarz and Park (2016) assert that different motivations for accountability have resulted in increased accountability but not in increased environmental outcomes. Ebrahim and Weisband (2007) critique the technocratic approaches to accountability and call for context-specific approaches to the issue, but do not offer a framework for how this might be done. In other work, I discussed how competing demands can lead to tech-nocratic self-preservation of NGOs through "single accountability disorder" (Balboa 2017).

All of these critiques, discussions, and disciplinary approaches informed the parameters I have used to operationalize global accountability norms and local accountability norms. By focusing on norms and not the details of each scale's and actor's demands, I have offered a framework that can be assessed in multiple contexts to demonstrate the unique attributes of each locale while still preserving broad applicability. In this way, the typology of accountability norms acknowledges the complexity of each context and each disciplinary approach while advancing our understanding to a meso-theoretical level.

In identifying trends in research for global environmental politics, Dauvergne and Clapp (2016) direct the next century of research by posing the question: how do we govern in ways that address the global scale of environmental issues? This book sheds considerable light on how NGOs might answer this question, and cautions against systemically prioritizing one scale over the other. This caution is not new: prioritizing this larger scale has been criticized by a myriad of scholars and NGO professionals (Dowie 2011; Hobbes 2014; Alcorn 1998; Fisher 1997). Unlike these cri-tiques, I assert that each scale serves important purposes in governance. As practitioners and scholars alike focus on discerning the optimum global-local division of labor and responsibility for transnational work, this book suggests that some functions, like fundraising and media campaigns, work better on the global scale (Ron, Pandya, and Crow 2016; Josiah 2001; Alcorn 1998; Wong 2012) and other functions, like protected area imple-mentation, must be done at the local scale. NGOs will need a broad per-spective of the field in order to create networks of local practitioners to share lessons learned on the ground as well as the state-of-the-art techni-cal advancements. Raising local issues to the attention of global actors for consideration on a policy agenda will also need facilitation by actors with global capacity (Bob 2005). Pressuring powerful local agents to consider the needs of marginalized communities will require global media campaigns and lobbying (Keck and Sikkink 1998). And to do all this, actors will need to report and communicate within the norms of global accountability. Thus, I do not claim that all interventions must be absolutely local endeavors. Both scales play a part in solving the world's most pressing problems. Both are essential to creating and maintaining broad-based authority and durable change.

The enormity of the world's problems—both environmental and otherwise—press NGOs to scale up their operations in order to make any discernable impact. To avoid the paradox of scale, NGOs must rethink how they operate. By explaining how authority works for NGOs, defining the paradox of scale and the bridging capacity needed to avoid it, and suggesting how diverse fields can contribute to our understanding of these dynamics, this book is an effort to help in this task. The way forward for these organizations will not be easy; it will take imagination, uneasy power shifts and operational changes, messy innovation, and synthesizing approaches. But creativity and flexibility are part of what have made NGOs governance authorities in the first place. With a better understanding of how to manage authority across scales, NGOs can ensure that their part in environmental governance is rooted in broad-based authority, and that their efforts to create change are more durable.

Notes

1 Introduction

1. "Snow Leopard," CITES, https://cites.org/eng/gallery/species/mammal/snow_leopard.html.

2. The Nature Conservancy, "About Us: Vision and Mission," https://www.nature.org/about-us/vision-mission/index.htm?intc=nature.tnav.about.

3. CARE, "Mission and Vision" statement, http://care.org/about/mission-vision.

4. Feed the Children, "About: Our Organization," http://www.feedthechildren.org/about/.

5. WWF, "WWF's Mission," https://www.worldwildlife.org/?utm_campaign=301-redirects&utm_source=wwf.org&utm_medium=referral&utm_content=wwf.org.

6. The concept of scale is not confined to the binary divisions of global and local. An organization can operate on global, regional, national, provincial, and local scales. To simplify an already complex argument, this book examines a unified, reasonably homogeneous global scale and a diverse local scale, which can include multiple geographies and contexts. Thus, I refer to "both scales" in this book when referring specifically to global and local scales and "multiple scales" to acknowledge general interscalar activity.

7. There is no shortage of terms used to describe these nonstate, not-for-profit, mission-driven organizations: civil society organizations, nonprofits, voluntary organizations, and nongovernmental organizations, to name a few. In addition, there are a myriad of specific types of these actors based on their sphere of influence, like international NGOs (INGOs), transnational NGOs (TNGOs), national NGOs, local NGOs. While the paradox is a barrier for national, federated nonprofits as well, this book focuses on transnational nongovernmental organizations, NGOs whose primary activity involves delivering services or advocacy across national borders. Thus, while I acknowledge the multitude of forms, scope, and descriptors often assigned to the term "NGO," for simplicity of the manuscript, "NGO" refers to transnational actors, unless the organization is specified as a local or national NGO.

8. For a full list of the metrics used to assess financial health by Charity Navigator, see https://www.charitynavigator.org/index.cfm?bay=content.view&cpid=35 (accessed April 4, 2018).

9. For an alternative definition, typology, and discussion of NGO authority, see Stroup and Wong 2017.

2   A Theory of NGO Authority

1. Transparency International, "Corruption Perceptions Index 2016," https://www.transparency.org/news/feature/corruption_perceptions_index_2016; J. Githongo, "Kenya's Rampant Corruption Is Eating Away at the Very Fabric of Democracy," *The Guardian*, August 6, 2015, https://www.theguardian.com/global-development/2015/aug/06/kenya-barack-obama-visit-anti-corruption-plan-democracy (accessed September 27, 2017); and S. Goldenberg, "Does Peru Need a Special Prison Just for Ex-Presidents?," *New York Times*, August 7, 2017, https://www.nytimes.com/2017/08/07/opinion/does-peru-need-a-special-prison-just-for-ex-presidents.html (accessed September 27, 2017).

2. Edelman Trust Barometer 2018, http://cms.edelman.com/sites/default/files/2018-02/2018_Edelman_Trust_Barometer_Global_Report_FEB.pdf (accessed April 4, 2018).

3. For a more expansive definition of "authority," see Avant, Finnemore, and Sell 2010. They include creating issues and setting agendas in their definition of "governing." Moreover, they assert that creating new preferences in actors who were previously indifferent or at odds with one's efforts could be seen as acts of governing and authority. My work on NGO authority follows the more restrictive definition of Green (2014) because (1) it is more easily observable and (2) NGOs still fulfill the criteria of this restrictive definition.

4. This is also one clear distinction between how authority is defined here and in other work on NGOs. For an alternative view on this, see Stroup and Wong 2017.

5. In conservation in particular, extreme cases have been documented where NGOs train or acquire armed forces to achieve compliance to conservation rules. In Cambodia, the U.S.-based NGO WildAid has trained and employed armed citizens to enforce wildlife trafficking restrictions through the Wildlife Protection Mobile Units. Within two years of its creation, the WPMU operated in seventeen provinces and reported an impressive list of accomplishments, including seizing animals and animal products, apprehending traders, waging fines, confiscating weapons and raiding suspects' houses (WildAid 2005). The World Wildlife Fund removed itself from working in the Democratic Republic of Congo's Garamba National Park, after determining its role in implementing conservation policy should not include hiring private mercenaries to enforce park rules (Avant 2004). Though extreme cases, both

of these instances demonstrate the use (or contemplated use) of force by an NGO to achieve its mission.

6. Oxfam, "About Oxfam," https://www.oxfamamerica.org/explore/about-oxfam/.

7. WWF Global, "WWF's Mission, Guiding Principles and Goals," http://wwf.panda .org/mission_principles_goals.cfm.

8. My previous work on this framework used the term "sphere of influence" instead of scale. While this framework is based on Steinberg's (2001, 2003) spheres of influence framework, this book expands, alters, and refines Steinberg's theory to be more applicable to nongovernmental organizations by including the local sphere, incorporating the language of capacity, and coupling it with the three types of capacity (political, administrative, and technical) I offer above. Lastly, it delineates the traits necessary to exhibit what I call "bridging capacity" (a variation of Steinberg's bilateral activists) between the global, national, and local spheres.

9. While the questions of to whom and for what an actor is accountable are fairly common, Koppell offers a typology to answer the question "accountability how?" He discusses how accountability is often falsely equated with controllability, and offers a more textured typology of accountability: first, the transparency dimension of accountability raises the question: Did the organization reveal the facts of its performance? Second, the liability dimension raises the question: Did the organization face the consequences of its actions? Third, control indicates that the agent did what the principal desired and that the principal can induce a certain behavior from the agent. Fourth, responsibility refers to an actor's following the constraints for rules and norms of the situation. And fifth, responsiveness raises the question: Did the actor fulfill a substantive expectation, be it the principal's demand or the principal's need? See Koppell 2003.

10. For an alternative view on legitimacy, see Brown 2008. Brown asserts that the diversity of actors in transnational work means that one cannot discuss transnational accountability demands as universal; accountability must be considered on a case-by-case basis.

11. For more on organizational learning, see Argyris 2004, Senge 1990, and Ebrahim 2005b.

12. LMMA, "Building Vibrant, Empowered, and Resilient Communities," http:// lmmanetwork.org (accessed April 2, 2018).

3   Conservation International in Milne Bay

Portions of this chapter were previously published as C. Balboa, "How Successful Transnational NGOs Set Themselves Up for Failure Abroad," *World Development* 54 (2014): 273–287.

1. The Global Environment Facility was founded in 1991 by the United Nations Development Programme, the United Nations Environment Programme, and the World Bank to fund efforts to protect the global environment and promote sustainable development. It has since become the financial mechanism to implement the Convention on Biological Diversity, the United Nations Framework Convention on Climate Change, the Stockholm Convention on Persistent Organic Pollutants, and the UN Convention to Combat Desertification. It is the largest public funder of environmentally focused projects around the globe (Global Environment Facility 2012).

2. The analysis in this book focuses on this particular timeframe. Since this time period, CI has worked again in Milne Bay, and recently transitioned its conservation work in PNG to a local organization called Eco-Custodian Advocates. This second tranche of work in the province will afford more data with which one can assess the paradox of scale, https://www.conservation.org/projects/Pages/community-driven-conservation-papua-new-guinea.aspx.

3. Total protein consumption is low in Milne Bay, and up to 80 percent of animal protein comes from coral reef species (Milne Bay Community-Based Coastal and Marine Conservation Project 2005). Over 62 percent of local people in Milne Bay are dependent on the marine and coastal resources of the Netuli Island Area (CI's first project site in Milne Bay) (Milne Bay Community-Based Coastal and Marine Conservation Project 2005) and an estimated 80 percent of the province depends on marine resources from the areas of highest conservation value for cash incomes and subsistence (Van Helden 2004).

4. Interviews 3, 78, 82, and 89.

5. Capacity would be built through formal training workshops, hiring or seconding individuals in the CI offices, and informally through basic interactions that expose actors to concepts, processes, and norms of the organization. Local actors like the provincial government, local-level government, village or ward leaders, local nongovernmental organizations (e.g., business associations, church development groups, and the newly formed resource owner associations) as well as individuals within the community would acquire skills to perform the administrative (e.g., management skills, priority setting, budgeting, time management, staff management), technical (land mediation, assessment, and establishment of marine protected areas, household gardens), and political (e.g., planning, policymaking and enforcement, intragovernmental communication and collaboration, leadership, conflict management) tasks of implementing the project in Milne Bay (ibid).

6. Interviews 1, 2, and 3.

7. Interview 3.

8. Interview 64.

9. Interview 69.

10. Interview 1.

11. Interviews 3, 69, and 96.

12. Google Scholar lists over 20,000 citations of this article from both scholarly and other sources (Google Scholar 2018).

13. These were not the first publications to discuss biodiversity hotspots by Myers or Mittermeier. However, the article in *Nature* has been cited almost an order of magnitude more often than any previous writing on the concept (Clarivate Analytics 2018).

14. These six conventions include the Convention on Biological Diversity, the Convention on the Conservation of Migratory Species of Wild Animals, the Convention on International Trade in Endangered Species of Wild Fauna and Flora, the International Treaty on Plant Genetic Resources for Food and Agriculture, the Ramsar Convention on Wetlands, and the World Heritage Convention (Liaison Group of the Biodiversity-related Conventions 2009).

15. CI's own website confirms this (Conservation International 2012b): "Every day, CI staff is on the ground in 28 countries building personal relationships with local people empowered to enact change. As a result, we're invited to the table when local, regional, and national leaders need guidance crafting environmentally friendly policies. We're ready to help them make responsible choices articulated with the most recent global guidance."

16. While the proposal was submitted by the Government of Papua New Guinea and the agreement is a legal instrument between the Government of Papua New Guinea and UNDP, Conservation International was the executing agency that would perform the tasks and manage the funds (Government of Papua New Guinea 2002).

17. Interview 3.

18. This funding indicated a delegation of authority from several governments to implement conservation, since it came from the GEF, the Japanese Human Development Trust Fund, the UNDP, the Government of PNG (in kind), CI, Australian National University, and ACIAR (Government of Papua New Guinea 2002).

19. Interview 3.

20. The stakeholder analysis cited resource users and owners as the primary stakeholders, those who indirectly benefit from the resources (businesses, etc) as secondary stakeholders, and last, others interested in the resources (Kinch 2001b).

21. Interview 61.

22. Interview 63.

23. Interview 61.

24. Interview 69.

25. Ibid.

26. Interview 1.

27. Ibid.

28. This also seems to typify the economic coercion discussed in chapter 2's section on theory.

29. The concept of "cargo" is rooted in historic cultural practices in Papua New Guinea aimed at gaining white man's wealth through incorporating modern features into existing magical practices (Callister 2006a).

30. Interview 2.

31. Interview 65.

32. In the villages of Yabam and Pahilele Islands, the local-level government agreed to close their coastline for three years as a sustainable management measure by a village vote of 77 to 100 (Bailasi 2005). Six communities were ready to move forward with delineation of marine protected areas as of 2005 (Interview 1).

33. Interviews 96 and 108.

34. Interview 74.

35. Interview 102.

36. Ibid.

37. Interview 72.

38. Ibid.

39. Ibid.

40. Interview 101.

41. Interview 65.

42. Interviews 72 and 102.

43. Interviews 74 and 98.

44. Interview 74.

45. Interviews 72 and 74.

46. Interview 98.

47. Interview 2.

48. Interviews 63 and 68.

49. Interview 65.

50. Perhaps a reflection of the pressure the project was under to achieve results, staff described MacKay as being very demanding—so much so that the last accounting person who was fired is rumored to have returned to the office and smashed the CTA's computer (Interview 69).

51. Interviews 69 and 74.

52. Interviews 72, 74, 101, and 102.

53. Interview 72.

54. Interview 41.

55. Interview 61.

56. Interview 107.

57. Ibid.

58. Interview 64.

59. Interview 67. Another community member stated, "They talked about conservation and tourism, but ended up spending money on other things, fancy cars and offices" (Interview 48).

60. Interview 3.

61. One local stated that the "GEF allowed only 12–15 percent overhead ... but there are estimates that CI takes up to 25 percent overhead—not an honest bunch in my estimate" (Interview 10). However, according to CI employees in DC, the GEF would not allow for the overhead rate allowed by USAID, so CI actually had to fundraise for its overhead separately to subsidize the GEF agreement (Interview 3). This contradictory information clearly indicates the absence of bridges.

62. Interview 3.

63. Interviews 2 and 3.

64. Interviews 64 and 74.

65. Interviews 69, 74, and 98.

66. Interviews 74, 96, and 102.

67. Interview 69.

68. Interview 96.

4   The International Marinelife Alliance in the Philippines

For a different discussion of accountability in this case study, see C. Balboa, "Mission Interference: How Competition Confound Accountability for Environmental Nongovernmental Organizations," *Review of Policy Research* 34 (1): 110–131.

1. Interview 20.

2. In 1986, Robinson documented also the use of cyanide to catch grouper for the live reef food fish trade—consumption of which is based in southern China where restaurant customers prefer to select fish for their meal as it is swimming in a tank (Rubec 1997).

3. Interview 36.

4. Ibid.

5. Interview 17.

6. Interview 4.

7. Ibid.

8. Ibid.

9. Interview 17.

10. Ibid.

11. Ibid.

12. Ibid.

13. Interviews 30 and 32.

14. Interview 17.

15. Interview 35.

16. Interviews 17 and 23.

17. Interview 17.

18. Interview 23.

19. Dali Pratt, wife of IMA's president, IMA's chief financial officer, IMA board member, and a business person on her own started one successful project working with the women in communities to create crafts out of found objects.

20. Interview 17.

21. Interview 21.

22. Whether the test was created by IMA founder Peter Rubec or an outside scientist is still a source of controversy (Holthus 1999; IMA 1999c; Rubec 1997; Interview 4).

23. Interview 4.

24. Ibid.

25. The process started when CDT officers—either Coast Guard, local government, or deputized IMA staff—confiscated fish for testing (Interview 25). The fish were then frozen (to stop them from metabolizing the poison) and shipped to the local lab where specimens were numbered to create blind testing. Within twenty-four to forty-eight hours, the lab results were faxed to Manila where another technician certified them (another check to ensure no bias or undue influence) (Rubec 1997). The certified results were then faxed back to the fishing city where a certificate was issued and the shipment of fish was released to the exporter (Department of Agriculture—Fisheries Sector Program Philippines et al., n.d.). In the early 2000s, a kilo of fish could cost up to $16 USD, but the fishers' reservations about surrendering the three pieces of fish for testing were not long-lived since the threat of tougher regulation or even a ban on the trade was even worse (Interview 25).

26. Interview 17.

27. Interview 4.

28. Interviews 4 and 8.

29. Interviews 4 and 33.

30. The CDT indicated backsliding in 2001, when reports indicate about 30 percent of the net-trained collectors had reverted to cyanide use. The financial incentives to sustainably harvest fish were not in place; cyanide was cheaper and supplied by the middlemen of the industry (Rubec et al. 2001).

31. Interviews 4, 8, 17, 18, and 33.

32. The Marine Aquarium Council review also complained that there were no routine quality assurance or quality controls for the labs (Holthus 1999). Independent review of the test demonstrated that it was unreliable and not sensitive enough for the purposes of certification and enforcement (Mak et al. 2005). The chemists working in the labs responded that the test is accurate and the process is internationally accepted. IMA did not take issue with the idea that the test was not sensitive enough, since they were still finding fish with cyanide in their systems and, therefore, could punish a few fishers and give the threat to others (Interview 4). Other critiques indicated the test was too sensitive—that it could give false positives (due to cyanide in agricultural runoff) and unjustly restrict the trade (Interview 18). One former IMA employee boasted that he caught fish himself, sent them to the labs, and they resulted in a positive test, proving to him that the test is too sensitive (Interview 8).

33. Interview 17.

34. Interviews 4 and 8.

35. Interview 18.

36. Interview 37.

37. Interview 4.

38. Although it was officially based in Hingham, MA (International Marinelife Alliance 1996).

39. Interview 4.

40. Interview 17.

41. Interview 37.

42. Interview 4.

43. Interview 36.

44. Interviews 4 and 36. Some former staff described IMA as Pratt's "imperial kingdom" (Interview 26).

45. Interview 17.

46. Most staff members had cell phones provided by IMA so that headquarters always knew what was going on and Pratt could be in constant contact with them (Interview 17).

47. Interview 4.

48. Interview 37.

49. Interviews 4 and 37.

50. Interview 37.

51. Interview 17.

52. Ibid.

53. CCN works on coral reef issues in Southeast Asia and the Pacific, but did not primarily address the issues of the live reef fish trade and, therefore, was not really an actor on this issue, apart from their organizational relationship with IMA. It is, however, the focus of another case study in this book.

54. Interview 4.

55. All USAID funding agreements have disclaimers that indicate funding can be delayed or withdrawn at any time, however, most of the time this disclaimer is not exercised.

56. Correspondence from Vaughan R. Pratt, president of IMA, to Barbara Wright, general counsel, The David and Lucile Packard Foundation, dated June 28, 2002.

57. Some sources dispute this amount, alleging that BFAR owed IMA closer to $100,000 USD (Peter Rubec, personal communication, August 2, 2009).

58. Letter from Vaughan Pratt, president of IMA, to Bernd Cordes, program officer, The David and Lucile Packard Foundation, dated September 19, 2002; attachment "CCN Funds Diversion and Replenishments."

59. Interview 4.

60. Ibid.

61. Interviews 4 and 37.

62. Interview 37.

63. Correspondence from Barbara Wright, Packard General Counsel, The David and Lucile Packard Foundation to Dr. Vaughan R. Pratt, International MarinelifeAlliance, dated November 14, 2002.

64. Correspondance from Vaughan R. Pratt, president of the International Marinelife Alliance to R. Michael Wright, MacArthur Foundation, dated November 30, 2002.

65. Interview 17.

66. CVBarber email communication to VRPratt, April 21, 2002.

67. CVBarber email communication to VRPratt, September 13, 2002.

68. While these reforms were big for IMA, they reflected the minimum requirements to be a legitimately operating NGO in the United States and it is assumed that all grantees meet this minimum requirement.

69. When asked why they stayed with IMA for as long as they did, staff members cite that they were assured funding was coming soon, they felt they were owed too much money to just walk away, and they felt that they had invested so much of their time, energy, and expertise into the organization that they would not leave it. There was also an ethical commitment to the cause: destructive fishing had not gone away just because their funding did.

70. Interviews 4, 36, 37.

71. Interview 4.

72. Interviews 4 and 37.

73. Interview 22.

74. Interview 4.

75. Interviews 30 and 32.

76. Interview 17.

77. Interview 4.

78. Ibid. Also, IMA encouraged this modus operandi not only within the organization but also with the communities in which it worked as well. A community in Coron, Palawan, announced to IMA that its members had acquired fifty tires to make an artificial reef. The scientific jury on artificial reefs was still out at the time. However, because the community was interested in doing *something*, they were encouraged to continue, regardless of whatever scientific assessment might declare in the future (Interview 17).

5   The Community Conservation Network in Palau

1. Interview 51.

2. Interview 58.

3. Interviews 46, 47, and 53.

4. Interview 58.

5. During my fieldwork in Palau, I received several unsolicited and hostile opinions about the Tobi people that confirmed this pecking order along with suspicion that any conservation or resources Tobians claim to protect cannot be so (Interview 58). On a less personal note, many non-Tobi Palauans stated that the reef was just too far to be practical for a resource management project (Interview 53).

6. Interviews 47 and 53.

7. Interview 38.

8. Interview 54.

9. Perhaps with the addition of one or two others: Scott Atkinson, and for a brief time, Andrea Bertoli. They saw the project office and even Andrew as part of the project and therefore part of the state, even though previously no support came from the state.

10. Interview 42.

11. Interview 38.

12. Ibid.

13. Interview 49.

14. Interview 38.

15. Ibid.

16. Ibid.

17. Interview 53.

18. Interview 38.

19. Interview 55.

20. Its revenue in 2000, its first year of funding, was just under $200,000 USD and its expenses were about half of its revenue (Community Conservation Network 2000a).

21. Interview 54.

22. Interview 40.

23. Interview 44.

24. Interview 51.

25. Interview 50.

26. Interview 54.

27. Interview 50.

28. Ibid.

29. Interview 43.

30. Interview 46.

31. There was some conflict about how much authority these rangers held (Interview 51; Victor 2003a, 2003b). A memorandum of understanding with CCN and the state indicated that the rangers were meant only to deter illegal activity, not to enforce laws. This was because their funding came from U.S.-based funders who did not fund law enforcement activities. Thus, they went on their patrols as a deterrent. At any time, however, they could have been called by the state to enforce state laws and, at that time, they would be compensated by the state (Victor 2003a). The rangers themselves stated that they did have the authority to arrest, but were encouraged to call the national patrol boat instead. In one incident where the rangers caught Indonesian fishers on Helen Reef, the rangers radioed for assistance from the national patrol boat, which came to enforce the law (Victor 2003a). However, some sources indicated that the patrol boat gave the rangers full authority to do what they thought best with the fishers (Interview 48).

32. Interview 51.

33. Interview 38.

34. Interview 41.

35. Ibid.

36. Interview 54.

37. Interviews 48 and 54.

38. Interview 52.

39. Interview 38 and 40.

40. Interview 60.

41. Interview 40.

42. Interview 38.

43. Interviews 38 and 40.

44. Interview 105.

45. Ibid.

46. Interview 103.

47. Interviews 56 and 103.

48. Interview 105.

49. Interview 103.

50. Interview 40.

51. Interview 43.

52. Interview 41.

53. Interview 40.

54. The second factor hindering Andrew's growth was financial. At the time of the field work for this case, his salary from CCN was about $4,000 USD more per year than the Governor of Tobi. Only four Tobians had salaries in this range (Interview 40). While he still was paid less than other conservation professionals in Palau, the state could not afford to keep him on salary if the project transferred to the state. For this reason, Andrew could not be considered for the permanent post. It is important to note that Andrew's salary was a calculated decision on CCN's part to make conservation an attractive livelihood alternative for Tobians. Also, they wanted to address salary disparities between U.S.-based experts and locally based experts. As a fairness issue, they wanted Tobians to be paid a wage that showed the value of their expertise and was more in line with Honolulu-based salaries. These salaries are not sustainable in the local economy.

55. Interview 40.

56. Ibid.

57. Interview 50. Also, perceptions on who was the leader of the project varied greatly, including Andrew, the governor (Interviews 43 and 46), the state (Interviews 46 and 47), the board (Personal Interview 47), CCN (Interview 44), Pilcher when he was with the project (Interview 41), the state delegate, and the HRMB chair.

58. Interview 40.

59. Interviews 56 and 105.

60. The executive director was the only one with a corporate credit card for ordering office supplies, often delaying supply replenishment. He also travelled often for his substantive work overseas, leaving the office without administrative authority (Interview 56).

61. Interview 56.

62. Interview 49.

63. Interviews 49 and 54.

64. While the board sought more control over and capacity for grant management, it also recognized that grant-based funding would not last forever. As such, board members focused on sustainable financing mechanisms for the protection of Helen Reef (Interviews 41, 46, and 47) (HRRMP and CCN 2004). Since Helen Reef is a very remote place, the costs of upkeep were too high for the state to maintain (Interviews 46 & 50). They were working both to trim expenses (Interview 41) and to find alternatives to grants like coral or teak farming (Victor 2003b) or tourism.

65. Interviews 50 and 53.

66. Interviews 54 and 59.

67. Interview 49.

68. Interview 40.

69. Interview 50.

70. Interviews 40 and 50.

71. Interviews 44 and 49.

72. Interview 40.

73. Ibid.

74. Interview 49.

75. Interview 60.

76. Interviews 41 and 50.

77. Interviews 41, 42, 44, and 48.

78. Interview 41.

79. Interview 49.

80. Interview 47.

81. Interview 49.

82. Interview 47.

83. The organization remained in existence on paper until 2011 in order to pass grant funds requests through to finish the work of the grant. But without the ability to secure new funding or function as an organization, CCN was essentially closed in 2009.

84. Interview 111.

85. Interviews 48, 49, and 52.

86. Interview 40. Also, some critics would like to see monitoring for more species in place (Interview 53).

87. Through summer programs, local youth experience traditional uses and views of their resource.

88. Interview 41.

6 Conclusion

1. For one example of this tarnished reputation, see the brief organizational summary of CI here: http://theredddesk.org/countries/actors/conservation-international -papua-new-guinea.

2. Interviews 64 and 65.

References

Alcorn, J. B. 1998. "Big Conservation and Little Conservation: Collaboration in Managing Global and Local Heritage." Keynote address. *Yale Forestry and Environmental Studies Bulletin*, no. 98. https://environment.yale.edu/publication-series/documents/downloads/0-9/98alcorn.pdf (accessed April 4, 2018).

Alotau Environment Ltd. 2006a. "Milne Bay Marine Conservation Project: Dead." *E-Version No. 19.*

Alotau Environment Ltd. 2006b. "Our Summary of the Final Evaluation Report of the Milne Bay Community-Based Coastal and Marine Conservation Project." Electronic journal.

Anasti, T., and J. E. Mosley. 2009. "'We Are Not Just a Band-Aid': How Homeless Service Providers in Chicago Carry Out Policy Advocacy." Chicago: University of Chicago School of Social Service Administration. https://allchicago.org/sites/default/files/archive_files/Mosley%20AdvocacyCommunityReport%202009.pdf (accessed April 4, 2018).

Andrew, W., S. Atkinson, M. Guilbeaux, and A. Wong. 2010. Helen Reef Management Plan 2011–2016. The Helen Reef Board. Palau: Hatohobei State Leadership and the Hatohobei Community.

Andrews, A. 2014. "Downward Accountability in Unequal Alliances: Explaining NGO Responses to Zapatista Demands." *World Development* 54:99–113.

Anheier, H. K. 2014. *Nonprofit Organizations: Theory, Management, Policy.* 2nd ed. New York: Routledge.

Ansula, A. C., and S. A. Evilio. 1998. *Training Manual: How to Catch Food Fish Alive.* Quezon City: International Marinelife Alliance—Philippines.

Argenti, P. A. 2004. "Collaborating with Activists: How Starbucks Works with NGOs." *California Management Review* 47 (1): 91–116.

Argyris, C. 2004. "Double-Loop Learning and Organizational Change." In *Dynamics of Organizational Change and Learning*, ed. J. J. Boonstra. doi:10.1002/9780470753408.ch19.

Attkisson, S. 2002. "Red Faces at the Red Cross." *CBS News*. https://www.cbsnews.com/news/red-faces-at-the-red-cross/ (accessed May 1, 2015).

Auld, G. 2014. *Constructing Private Governance: The Rise and Evolution of Forest, Coffee, and Fisheries Certification*. New Haven: Yale University Press.

Avant, D. 2004. "Conserving Nature in the State of Nature: The Politics of INGO Policy Implementation." *Review of International Studies* 30:361–382.

Avant, D., M. Finnemore, and S. Sell, eds. 2010. *Who Governs the Globe?* Cambridge, UK: Cambridge University Press. doi:10.1017/CBO9780511845369.014.

Bailasi, H. 2005. "Milne Bay Province: Milne Bay Project/Conservation International." *Wasa News*.

Baines, G., J. Duguman, and P. Johnston. 2006. *Final Evaluation of the Milne Bay Community-Based Coastal and Marine Conservation Project*. UNDP Terminal Evaluation. Port Moresby: UNDP.

Balboa, C. M. 2003. "The Consumption of Marine Ornamental Fish in the United States: A Description from U.S. Import Data." In *Marine Ornamental Species: Collection, Culture, and Conservation*, ed. James C. Cato and Christopher L. Brown, 65–76. Ames: Iowa State Press.

Balboa, C. M. 2009. "When Non-governmental Organizations Govern: Accountability in Private Conservation Networks." Ph.D. diss. New Haven, CT: Yale University.

Balboa, C. M. 2014. "How Successful Transnational NGOs Set Themselves Up for Failure Abroad." *World Development* 54:273–287.

Balboa, C. M. 2015. "The Accountability and Legitimacy of International NGOs." In *The NGO Challenge for International Relations Theory*, ed. W. DeMars and D. Dijkzeul, 159–186. New York: Routledge.

Balboa, C. M. 2017. "Mission Interference: How Competition Confounds Accountability for Environmental Nongovernmental Organizations." *Review of Policy Research* 34 (1): 110–131.

Balboa, C. M., and M. Z. Deloffre. 2015. "Policymaking in the Global Context: Training Students to Build Effective Strategic Partnerships with Nongovernmental Organizations." *Journal of Public Affairs Education* 21 (3): 417–434.

Balboa, C. M., A. Berman, and L. Welton. 2015. *International Nongovernmental Organizations (INGOs) in New York City: A Comparative Study*. New York: Baruch College—CUNY School of Public Affairs' Center for Nonprofit Strategy and Management. http://tinyurl.com/INGONYC (accessed May 1, 2015).

Baldwin, D. 2002. "Power and International Relations." In *Handbook of International Relations*, ed. W. Carlsnaes, T. Risse, and B. A. Simmons, 177–191. London: SAGE Publications Ltd. doi: 10.4135/9781848608290.n9.

Banks, N., D. Hulme, and M. Edwards. 2015. "NGOs, States, and Donors Revisited: Still Too Close for Comfort?" *World Development* 66:707–718.

Baquero, J. 1999. "The Trade of Ornamental Fish from the Philippines." *Reefs.org.* February 21, 1999, 7.

Barber, C., and V. Pratt. 1997a. *Poison Profits.* Washington, DC: World Resources Institute.

Barber, C., and V. Pratt. 1997b. *Sullied Seas.* Washington, DC: World Resources Institute.

Barber, M., and C. Bowie. 2008. "How International NGOs Could Do Less Harm and More Good." *Development in Practice* 18 (6): 748–754.

Beattie, K. 2012. "Whose Accountability? A Case Study of NGO Accountability to Recipients of Aid in South Sudan." Master's thesis. Bedford, UK: Carnfield University.

Beehler, B., and G. Kula. n.d. "Conservation Without Border (part 1): Biodiversity Conservation in Melanesia." Unpublished.

Beisham, M., and K. Dingwerth. 2008. "Procedural Legitimacy and Private Transnational Governance. Are the Good Ones Doing Better?" SFB-Governance Working Paper Series, No. 14. SFB-Collaborative Research Center. Freie Universität Berlin.

Benjamin, L. M. 2008. "Account Space: How Accountability Requirements Shape Nonprofit Practice." *Nonprofit and Voluntary Sector Quarterly* 37 (2): 201–223.

Bennett, A., and J. T. Checkel. 2015. "Process Tracing: From Philosophical Tools to Best Practices." In *Process Tracing. From Metaphor to Analytic Tool,* ed. A. Bennett and J. T. Checkel, 3–38. Cambridge, UK: Cambridge University Press.

Bernstein, S. 2004. "Legitimacy in Global Environmental Governance." *Journal of International Law & International Relations* 1 (1–2): 139–166.

Bernstein, S. 2011. "Legitimacy in Intergovernmental and Non-state Global Governance." *Review of International Political Economy* 18 (1): 17–51.

Betsill, M. M., and E. Corell, eds. 2008. *NGO Diplomacy: The Influence of Nongovernmental Organizations in International Environmental Negotiations.* Cambridge, MA: MIT Press.

Birkeland., C., A. Green, M. Guilbeaux, T. Donaldson, D. Emilio, L. Kirkendale, J. Mangel, R. Myers, K. Weng, and R. van Woesik. 2000. *Helen Reef Marine Resources in the Year 2000.* Koror, Palau: Helen Reef Marine Resource Management Program.

Black, P. 2000. *Planning for the Future of Helen Reef: Socio-cultural Features of the Tobian Community and Their Implications.* A Report and Recommendations. Koror, Palau: Community Conservation Network.

Bob, C. 2005. *The Marketing of Rebellion: Insurgents, Media, and International Activism.* New York: Cambridge University Press.

Bornstein, D. 2011. "Grameen Bank and the Public Good." *Opinionator* (blog). *New York Times*, March 24.

Bradach, J. L. 2003. "Going to Scale." *Stanford Social Innovation Review* 1:18–25.

Brinkerhoff, D. W. 2005. "Public Administration and Iraq's Reconstruction." *PA Times* 28 (12) (December).

Brinkerhoff, D. W., and P. J. Morgan. 2010. "Capacity and Capacity Development: Coping with Complexity." *Public Administration and Development*. Special Issue: Symposium on Capacity and Capacity Development 30:2–10.

Brown, L. D. 2008. *Creating Credibility: Legitimacy and Accountability for Transnational Civil Society.* Sterling, VA: Kumarian Press.

Brown, L. D., A. Ebrahim, and S. Batliwala. 2012. "Governing International Advocacy NGOs." *World Development* 40 (6): 1098–1108.

Burger, R., and T. Owens. 2008. "Dishonesty in the Charitable Sector." Center for African Economies conference, Barcelona, Spain, 9–12. http://www.truevaluemetrics .org/DBpdfs/NGOs/Dishonesty-in-the-charitable-sector.pdf.

Burke, L., Y. Kura, K. Kassem, C. Revenga, M. Spalding, D. McAllister, and J. Caddy. 2001. *Pilot Analysis of Global Ecosystems: Coastal Ecosystems.* Washington, DC: World Resources Institute.

Burke, L., E. Selig, and M. Spalding. 2002. *Reefs at Risk in Southeast Asia.* Washington, DC: World Resources Institute.

Bush, S. S. 2015. *The Taming of Democracy Assistance: Why Democracy Promotion Does Not Confront Dictators.* Cambridge: Cambridge University Press.

Callister, G. 2006a. *Re-learning Learning: Dynamics of Integrated Conservation and Development in Two Donor Funded Projects in PNG.* Canberra: Australia National University.

Callister, G. 2006b. *Woes in Paradise: An Analysis of the Milne Bay Community Based Coastal and Marine Conservation Project.* Canberra: Australian National University.

Casey, J. 2016. *The Nonprofit World: Civil Society and the Rise of the Nonprofit Sector.* London: Kumarian Press.

Cashore, B. 2002. "Legitimacy and the Privatization of Environmental Governance: How Non-State Market-Driven (NSMD) Governance Systems Gain Rule-Making Authority." *Governance* 15:503–529. doi:10.1111/1468-0491.00199.

Cashore, B. W., G. Auld, and D. Newsom. 2004. *Governing through Markets: Forest Certification and the Emergence of Non-state Authority*. New Haven: Yale University Press.

Cervino, J. M., R. L. Hayes, M. Honovich, T. J. Goreau, S. Jones, and P. J. Rubec. 2003. "Changes in Zooxanthellae Density, Morphology, and Mitotic Index in Hermatypic Corals and Anemones Exposed to Cyanide." *Marine Pollution Bulletin* 46:573–586.

Chamberlain, C. G. 2002. "Community-Based Non-profits Pressured by Corporate Culture, Says Speaker." *Advance on the Web*, April 15. http://advance.uconn.edu/ 2002/020415/02041508.htm (accessed July 23, 2015).

Chambers, R. 1983. *Rural Development: Putting the Last First*. Harlow: Prentice Hall.

Chambers, R. 2014. "Knowing in Development: A Radical Agenda for the Twenty-First Century." *Forum for Development Studies* 41 (3): 525–537.

Chapin, M. 2004. "A Challenge to Environmentalists." *World Watch*, November/ December, 17–31.

Checkel, J. T. 2008. "Process Tracing." In *Qualitative Methods in International Relations*, ed. A. Klotz and D. Prakash, 114–127. London: Palgrave Macmillan UK.

Choudry, A. 2003. "Tarzan, Indiana Jones and Conservation International's Global Greenwash Machine 2003." http://www.scoop.co.nz/stories/HL0310/S00154/tarzan -indiana-jones-a-global-greenwash-machine.htm (accessed April 22, 2008).

Clarivate Analytics. 2018. Web of Science Core Collection. https://clarivate.com/ products/web-of-science/web-science-form/web-science-core-collection/ (accessed June 15, 2018).

Collier, D., J. Mahoney, and J. Seawright. 2004. "Claiming Too Much: Warnings about Selection Bias." In *Rethinking Social Inquiry: Diverse Tools, Shared Standards*, ed. H. Brady and D. Collier, 85–102. Lanham, MD: Rowman and Littlefield Publisher Inc.

Community Conservation Network. 2000a. "IRS Form 990." Washington, DC: Internal Revenue Service.

Community Conservation Network. 2000b. *New England BioLabs Foundation Award to the Community Conservation Network for Community-Based Marine Conservation at Helen Reef Palau End of Project Report*. October 17.

Community Conservation Network. 2001. "IRS Form 990." Washington, DC: Internal Revenue Service.

Community Conservation Network. 2002. *Strengthening Community-Based Conservation in Helen Reef, Palau and the Solomon Islands: A Proposal to the Homeland Foundation from the Community Conservation Network*. May. Honolulu: CCN.

Community Conservation Network. 2003a. *Community Conservation Network: 2004–2006 Strategic Plan Summary*. Honolulu: Community Conservation Network.

Community Conservation Network. 2003b. "IRS Form 990." Washington, DC: Internal Revenue Service.

Community Conservation Network. 2004a. "IRS Form 990." Washington, DC: Internal Revenue Service.

Community Conservation Network. 2004b. *Conservation & Resource Management in the Southwest Islands of Palau, Micronesia: Annual Interim Report (January 1–November 30, 2004) to the David and Lucile Packard Foundation*. December. Honolulu: Community Conservation Network.

Conservation International. 2003. *Sustainable Land Use and Nutrition Program: Adaptation on Farming Methods on Small Islands in the Samariai-Murua District of the Milne Bay Province, Papua New Guinea*. Alotau, PNG: Conservation International.

Conservation International. 2005. *2005 Annual Report*. Arlington, VA: Conservation International.

Conservation International, ed. 2010. *People Need Nature to Thrive*. Washington, DC: Conservation International.

Conservation International. 2012a. "Working with Governments." https://www.conservation.org/how/policy/Pages/intl_policy.aspx (accessed September 25, 2012).

Conservation International. 2012b. "International Conferences and Workshops." https://www.conservation.org/conferences/Pages/main.aspx (accessed September 25, 2012).

Conservation International. 2013a. "Harrison Ford and CI." https://www.umsl.edu/~hwec/WEArecipients/fordci.html (accessed April 4, 2018).

Conservation International. 2013b. "Corporate Partners." https://www.conservation.org/how/partnership/corporate/Pages/walmart.aspx (accessed April 4, 2018).

Conservation International. 2015a. Conservation International 2014 Annual Report. Washington, DC: Conservation International.

Conservation International. 2015b. "Rapid Assessment Program." https://www.conservation.org/projects/Pages/Rapid-Assessment-Program.aspx (accessed April 3, 2016).

Conservation International. n.d. *CI Facts: Milne Bay, Papua New Guinea*. Washington, DC: Conservation International.

Cooley, L., and R. Kohl. 2006. *Scaling Up—From Vision to Large-Scale Change: A Management Framework for Practitioners*. Washington, DC: Management Systems International.

Cuttelod, A., N. García, D. Abdul Malak, H. Temple, and V. Katariya. 2008. "The Mediterranean: A Biodiversity Hotspot under Threat." In *The 2008 Review of the IUCN Red List of Threatened Species*, ed. J.-C. Vié, C. Hilton-Taylor, and S. N. Stuart. Switzerland: IUCN Gland.

Dauvergne, P., and J. Clapp. 2016. "Researching Global Environmental Politics in the 21st Century." *Global Environmental Politics* 16 (1): 1–12.

Deloffre, M. Z. 2016. "Global Accountability Communities: NGO Self-Regulation in the Humanitarian Sector." *Review of International Sudies*: 42 (4) 724–747.

DeMars, W. 2015. "Follow the Partners: Agency and Explanation in the Color Revolutions." In *The NGO Challenge for International Relations Theory*, ed. W. DeMars and D. Dijkzeul, 237–262. New York: Routledge.

DeMars, W., and D. Dijkzeul. 2015. *The NGO Challenge for International Relations Theory*. New York: Routledge.

Department of Agriculture—Fisheries Sector Program Philippines. n.d. *Towards a Cyanide-free Fishing Tradition: The Cyanide Detection Test*. Manila: Bureau of Fisheries and Aquatic Resources Philippines, International Marinelife Alliance, and Presidential Committee on Anti-Illegal Fishing and Marine Conservation of the Philippines.

Dhume, S. 2002. "Jurassic Showdown: It Feels Like the Most Ancient Place on Earth, but Komodo National Park Is Being Swept up in a Very Modern Debate: Is Private Better Than Public When It Comes to Preserving Unique Habitats?" *Far Eastern Economic Review*, May 16. http://www.feer.com/articles/2002/0205_16/p050current .html (accessed May 20, 2002).

Diamond, N. 2002. "Scaling Up Participatory Conservation" (English). The World Bank. http://documents.worldbank.org/curated/en/844591468316432285/ pdf/35233.pdf (accessed April 4, 2018).

Doane, D. 2016. "Do International NGOs Still Have the Right to Exist?" *Guardian*, March 13. https://www.theguardian.com/global-development-professionals-network/ 2016/mar/13/do-international-ngos-still-have-the-right-to-exist (accessed March 14, 2016).

Dowie, M. 2008. "Wrong Path to Conservation in Papua New Guinea." *The Nation*. September 10. https://www.thenation.com/article/wrong-path-conservation-papua -new-guinea# (accessed February 15, 2013).

Dowie, M. 2011. *Conservation Refugees: The Hundred-Year Conflict between Global Conservation and Native Peoples*. Cambridge, MA: Massachusetts Institute of Technology.

Ebrahim, A. 2005a. "Accountability Myopia: Losing Sight of Organizational Learning." *Nonprofit and Voluntary Sector Quarterly* 34 (1): 56–87.

Ebrahim, A. 2005b. *NGOs and Organizational Change: Discourse, Reporting, and Learning*. Cambridge, UK: Cambridge University Press.

Ebrahim, A., and V. K. Rangan. 2014. "What Impact?" *California Management Review* 56 (3): 118–141.

Ebrahim, A., and E. Weisband, eds. 2007. *Global Accountabilities*. Cambridge: Cambridge University Press.

Ebrahim, Z. 2010. "Endangered Snow Leopard Clawing Its Way Back." *The Guardian.* August 12. https://www.theguardian.com/environment/2010/aug/12/endangered -snow-leopard (accessed September 27, 2017).

Eckhart-Queenan, J., A. Gindle, H. Hadley, and R. Thompson. 2015. "Designing for Transformative Scale: Global Lessons in What Works." *Rotman Management*, Wicked Problems III (Winter 2015). Toronto: University of Toronto. http://www.rotman .utoronto.ca/Connect/Rotman-MAG/Back-Issues/2015/Back-Issues---2015/Winter -2015---Wicked-Problems-III/Winter-2015-Free-Feature-Article---Designing-for -Transformative-Scale-by-Eckhart-et-al (accessed April 2, 2018).

Edwards, M., and D. Hulme. 1996. "Too Close for Comfort? The Impact of Official Aid on Nongovernmental Organizations." *World Development* 24 (6): 961–973.

Elbers, W., and B. Arts. 2011. "Keeping Body and Soul Together: Southern NGOs' Strategic Responses to Donor Constraints." *International Review of Administrative Sciences* 77 (4): 713–732.

Elgert, L. 2011. "The Politics of Evidence: Towards Critical Deliberative Governance in Sustainable Development." Ph.D. diss. Department of International Development. The London School of Economics and Political Science.

Emilio, D., R. Emilio, R. Victor, M. Andrew, F. Andy, K. Tarkong, and N. Pilcher, N. 2002. *Helen Reef Community Resource Monitoring Report—October 2002*. Koror: Helen Reef Resource Management Project.

Fenton, D. 2010. "HuffPost's Greatest Person of the Day: Kirsten Lodal, Combating Poverty with LIFT." *Huffington Post.* https://www.huffingtonpost.com/2010/11/29/ huffposts-greatest-person_12_n_789442.html (accessed June 26, 2016).

Feuchtwang, A. 2014. "Broken Promises: Why Handing over Power to Local NGOs Is Empty Rhetoric." *The Guardian.* February 7. https://www.theguardian.com/global -development-professionals-network/2014/feb/07/power-international-ngos -southern-partners (accessed April 29, 2015).

Finnemore, M., and K. Sikkink. 1998. "International Norm Dynamics and Political Change." *International Organization* 52 (4): 887–917.

Fisher, W. F. 1997. "Doing Good? The Politics and Antipolitics of NGO Practices." *Annual Review of Anthropology* 26 (1): 439–464.

Fleming, P., and A. Spicer. 2014. "Power in Management and Organization Science." *Academy of Management Annals* 8 (1): 237–298.

Ford Foundation. 2004. "Asset Building for Social Change: Pathways to Large-Scale Impact." http://www.racialequitytools.org/resourcefiles/fordfoundation.pdf (accesssed April 4, 2018).

Fritzen, S. 2007. "Can the Design of Community-Driven Development Reduce the Risk of Elite Capture? Evidence from Indonesia." *World Development* 35 (8): 1359–1375.

Fukuda-Parr, S., C. Lopes, and K. Malik. 2002. "Institutional Innovations for Capacity Development." In *Capacity for Development: New Solutions to Old Problems*, ed. S. Fukuda-Parr, C. Lopes, and K. Malik, P1–P23. New York: Earthscan Publications Ltd.

Geddes, B. 1990. "How the Cases You Choose Affect the Answers You Get: Selection Bias in Comparative Politics." *Political Analysis* 2:131–150.

George, A. L., and A. Bennett. 2005. *Case Studies and Theory Development in the Social Sciences*. Cambridge, MA: MIT Press.

Giddens, A. 1984. *The Constitutions of Society: Outline of the Theory of Structuration*. Cambridge, MA: Polity Press.

Global Environment Facility (GEF). 2012. "What Is the GEF?" https://www.thegef .org/about-us (accessed September 17, 2012).

Google Scholar. 2018. "Hotspots." *Google Scholar*. https://scholar.google.com/scholar ?start=10&q=Hotspots+&hl=en&as_sdt=0,33 (accessed June 15, 2018).

Gottlieb, H. 2004. "Founder's Syndrome: Who Me?" http://www.help4nonprofits .com/NP_Bd_FoundersSyndrome_Art.htm (accessed June 24, 2017).

Gourevitch, P. A., and David A. Lake. 2012." Beyond Virtue: Evaluating and Enhancing the Credibility of Non-governmental Organizations." In *The Credibility of Transnational NGOs*, ed. P. Gourevitch, D. Lake, and J. Gross-Stein, 3–34. Cambridge: Cambridge University Press.

Government of Papua New Guinea. 2002. *Community-Based Coastal and Marine Conservation in Milne Bay Province*. Port Morseby: United Nations Development Programme.

Government of Papua New Guinea. n.d. *Funding Proposal: Community-Based Coastal and Marine Conservation in Milne Bay Province*. Port Morseby, PNG.

Grandia, L. 2004. "Letter to the Editor re: Mac Chapin." *World Watch Magazine*. Unpublished.

Gray, R., J. Bebbington, and D. Collison. 2006. "NGOs, Civil Society and Accountability: Making the People Accountable to Capital." *Accounting, Auditing & Accountability Journal* 19 (3): 405–427.

Green, J. F. 2014. *Rethinking Private Authority: Agents and Entrepreneurs in Global Environmental Governance.* Princeton, NJ: Princeton University Press.

Guilbeaux, M. 2000. *Collaborative Reef Monitoring EDF Minigrant Project Final Report for Collaborative Resource Monitoring and Conservation at Helen Reef Atoll, Republic of Palau.* October 10.

Guilbeaux, M. 2001. Grant Progress Report Homeland Foundation Grant 4-00-137: Community Based Marine Resource Enforcement and Management, Helen Reef, Palau (a Community Conservation Network Initiative). May 15. Honolulu: Community Conservation Network.

Guilbeaux, M. 2002. *Conservation and Resource Management in the Southwest Islands of Palau, Micronesia.* A proposal to the David and Lucile Packard Foundation Program on Conservation. September 16.

Gunter, M. M. 2004. *Building the Next Ark: How NGOs Work to Protect Biodiversity.* Hanover, NH: Dartmouth College Press.

Gunther, M. 2006. "The Green Machine." *Fortune* 154. July 31, 2006. http://archive.fortune.com/magazines/fortune/fortune_archive/2006/08/07/8382593/index.htm (accessed August 4, 2013).

Hance, J. 2016. "How Big Donors and Corporations Shape Conservation Goals." *Mongabay Series: Evolving Conservation.* https://news.mongabay.com/2016/05/big-donors-corporations-shape-conservation-goals/ (accessed September 8, 2016).

Hardin, G. 1968. "The Tragedy of the Commons." *Science* 162 (3859): 1243–1248.

Harrison, M. 2001 "Coercion, Compliance, and the Collapse of the Soviet Command Economy." *Economic History Review* 55 (3): 397–433.

Hartmann, A., and J. Linn. 2007. "Scaling Up: A Path to Effective Development." 2020 FOCUS BRIEF on the World's Poor and Hungry People. International Food Policy Institute. https://idl-bnc-idrc.dspacedirect.org/bitstream/handle/10625/37196/127844.pdf?sequence=1 (accessed June 26, 2016).

Hartmann, A., and J. Linn. 2008. Scaling Up through Aid: The Real Challenge. Brookings Institution. https://www.brookings.edu/research/scaling-up-through-aid-the-real-challenge/ (accessed June, 16, 2016).

Hatohobei State Legislature. 2001. Helen Reef Management Act. Bill Number 5-IR-04, D2. Third Session.

Healy, S., and S. Tiller. 2014. "Where Is Everyone? Responding to Emergencies in the Most Difficult Places." Médecins Sans Frontières (Doctors Without Borders). http://www.msf.org/sites/msf.org/files/msf-whereiseveryone_-def-lr_-_july.pdf (accessed June 23, 2017).

Hedström, P., and R. Swedberg, eds. 1998. *Social Mechanisms: An Analytical Approach to Social Theory*. Cambridge, UK: Cambridge University Press.

Helen Reef Resource Management Program (HRRMP) and Community Conservation Network (CCN). 2003. *Sustaining Conservation at Helen Reef, Palau: A Summary of Current Costs and Sustainable Financing Needs*. HRRMP: Hatohobei.

Helen Reef Resource Management Program (HRRMP) and Community Conservation Network (CCN). 2004. *Conservation and Resource Management in the Southwest Islands of Palau, Micronesia*. Hatohobei: The David and Lucile Packard Foundation.

Henderson, S. 2003. *Building Democracy in Contemporary Russia: Western Support for Grassroots Organizations*. Ithaca: Cornell University Press.

Hinton, L., and R. Groves, eds. 2013. *Inclusive Aid: Changing Power and Relationships in International Development*. Sterling, VA: Earthscan.

Hobbes, M. 2014. "Stop Trying to Save the World: Big Ideas Are Destroying International Development." *New Republic*, November 17. https://newrepublic.com/article/120178/problem-international-development-and-plan-fix-it (accessed October 10, 2015).

Holthus, P. 1999. *Peer Review of Cyanide Detection Testing Methods Employed in the Philippines*. Honolulu: Marine Aquarium Council.

Honadle, B. 1981. "A Capacity-Building Framework: A Search for Concept and Purpose." *Public Administration Review* 41 (5): 575–580. doi:10.2307/976270.

Hrabe, J. 2014. "Haiti Earthquake Aid: Champagne, Cruise Ships and Cholera." *Huffington Post*. https://www.huffingtonpost.com/john-hrabe/haiti-earthquake-aid_b_1202392.html (accessed April 29, 2015).

Hudock, A. C. 1999. *NGOs and Civil Society: Democracy by Proxy?* Malden, MA: Polity Press.

Hudson, A. 2001. "NGOs in Transnational Advocacy Networks: From 'Legitimacy' to 'Political Responsibility'" *Global Networks: A Journal of Transnational Affairs* 1 (4) 331–352.

Hussain, S. 2000. "Protecting the Snow Leopard and Enhancing Farmers' Livelihoods." *Mountain Research and Development* 20 (3): 226–231.

Igoe, J., and T. Kelsall. 2005. *Between a Rock and a Hard Place: African NGOs, Donors and the State*. Durham, NC: Carolina Academic Press.

International Marinelife Alliance. 1996. "IRS Form 990." Washington, DC: Internal Revenue Service.

International Marinelife Alliance. 1998. "First Asia-Pacific Seminar/Workshop on the Live Reef Fish Trade." Paper presented at First Asia-Pacific Seminar/Workshop on the Live Reef Fish Trade, August 11–14, Manila.

International Marinelife Alliance. 1999a. *The Indo-Pacific Destructive Fishing Reform Initiative (DFRI)—1999–2001. Proposal by the International Marinelife Alliance to the John D. and Catherine T. MacArthur Foundation.* September.

International Marinelife Alliance. 1999b. *The Indo-Pacific Destructive Fishing Reform Initiative (DFRI) 1999–2001 Program Proposal Submitted to the United States Agency for International Development East Asia and Pacific Environmental Initiative (EAPEI).* EAPEI.

International Marinelife Alliance. 1999c. *Response to the Review of the IMA Cyanide Testing Standard Operating Procedures Prepared by the Marine Aquarium Council.* Pasig, PHL: International Marinelife Alliance.

International Marinelife Alliance. 2001a. *IMA Strategic Plan 2001–2006.* Honolulu: International Marinelife Alliance.

International Marinelife Alliance. 2001b. "IRS Form 990." Washington, DC: Internal Revenue Service.

International Marinelife Alliance. 2002a. *The R/V Alliance: The Research Vessel of the International Marinelife Alliance.* Honolulu: International Marinelife Alliance.

International Marinelife Alliance. 2002b. *R/V Alliance Management Strategy and Committee.* Honolulu: International Marinelife Alliance.

International Marinelife Alliance. 2002c. *International Marinelife Alliance Financial Status Report and Business Plan, 2002–2004.* Honolulu: International Marinelife Alliance.

International Marinelife Alliance. 2002d. *RV/Alliance Research Ship Project Proposal to the Oak Foundation.* Honolulu: International Marinelife Alliance.

International Marinelife Alliance. 2002e. *Statement of Sources of Organization Funds."* Honolulu: International Marinelife Alliance.

International Marinelife Alliance. 2003. *The East Asia-Pacific Coral Reef Conservation Initiative 2002–2003 Progress Report to USAID.* EAPEI. February.

International Marinelife Alliance. 2006a. "About the International Marinelife Alliance 2006." IMA website (accessed January 18, 2006).

International Marinelife Alliance. 2006b. "Coral Reef Rehabilitation Project." IMA website (accessed January 18, 2006).

Jepson, P. 2005. "Governance and Accountability of Environmental NGOs." *Environmental Science & Policy* 8:515–524.

Jinnah, S. 2014. *Post-treaty Politics: Secretariat Influence in Global Environmental Governance.* Cambridge, MA: MIT Press.

Johnson, S. 1999. "Microfinance North and South: Contrasting Current Debates." *Journal of International Development* 10 (6) 799–810.

Jones, S. 2015. "Aid, Cholera and Protest: Life in Haiti Five Years after the Earthquake." *The Guardian,* January 11. https://www.theguardian.com/global -development/2015/jan/12/haiti-earthquake-five-years-on-village-solidarite (accessed September 27, 2017).

Jordan, L., and P. van Tuijl, eds. 2006. *NGO Accountability: Politics, Principles and Innovations.* Sterling, VA: Earthscan.

Josiah, S. J. 2001. "Approaches to Expand NGO Natural Resource Conservation Program Outreach." *Society & Natural Resources* 14 (7): 609–618.

Kaldor, M., H. K. Anheier, and M. Glasius. 2003. *Global Civil Society Yearbook 2003.* Oxford: Oxford University Press.

Kamat, S. 2003. "The NGO Phenomenon and Political Culture in the Third World." *Development* 46 (1): 88–93.

Kareiva, P., C. Groves, and M. Marvier. 2014. "Review: The Evolving Linkage between Conservation Science and Practice at the Nature Conservancy." *Journal of Applied Ecology* 51:1137–1147. doi:10.1111/1365-2664.12259.

Kassem, K., and E. Medeja. 2014. *The Coral Triangle: Saving the Amazing Undersea World of Indonesia, Malaysia, Papua New Guinea, the Philippines, Solomon Islands, and Timor Leste.* Oxford: John Beaufoy Publishing.

Katz, J. M. 2013. *The Big Truck That Went By: How the World Came to Save Haiti and Left Behind a Disaster.* New York: Macmillan.

Kearns, K. 1994. The Strategic Management of Accountability in Nonprofit Organizations: An Analytical Framework. *Public Administration Review* 54 (2): 185–192. doi:10.2307/976528.

Keck, M. E., and K. Sikkink. 1998. *Activists Beyond Borders: Advocacy Networks in International Politics.* Ithaca: Cornell University Press.

Kennedy, C., D. Miteva, L. Baumgarten, P. Hawthorne, K. Sochi, and S. Polasky. 2016. "Bigger Is Better: Improved Nature Conservation and Economic Returns from Landscape-Level Mitigation." *Science Advances* 2 (7) (July 1): 1–9.

Khare, A., and D. B. Bray. 2004. *Study of Critical New Forest Conservation Issues in the Global South.* New York: Ford Foundation.

Kinch, J. 2001a. *Social Evaluation Study for the Milne Bay Community-Based Coastal and Marine Conservation Program.* Port Morseby: UNDP/Conservation International.

Kinch, J. 2001b. *Stakeholder Participation Plan for the Milne Bay Community-Based Coastal and Marine Conservation Program.* Alotau, PNG: UNDP/Conservation International.

Kinch, J. 2003. *What Has Been Happening with the Milne Bay Community-Based Coastal and Marine Conservation Program?* Alotau, PNG: Conservation International.

Kohn, A. 1993. *Punished by Rewards: The Trouble with Gold Stars, Incentive Plans, A's, Praise, and Other Bribes.* Boston: Houghton Mifflin.

Koppell, J. 2003. *The Politics of Quasi-Governments: Hybrid Organizations and the Dynamics of Bureaucratic Control.* Cambridge, UK: Cambridge University Press.

Koppell, J. G. 2005. "Pathologies of Accountability: ICANN and the Challenge of 'Multiple Accountabilities Disorder.'" *Public Administration Review* 65 (1): 94–108.

Koppell, J. G. 2010. *World Rule: Accountability, Legitimacy, and the Design of Global Governance.* Chicago: University of Chicago Press.

Kramarz, T., and S. Park. 2016. "Accountability in Global Environmental Governance: A Meaningful Tool for Action?" *Global Environmental Politics* 16 (2): 1–21.

Krieger, L. 1977. "The Idea of Authority in the West." *American Historical Review* 82:249–270.

Kula, G. R. 2002. "Conservation and Environmental Management: Social and Ecological Issues for Poverty Reduction in Milne Bay, Papua New Guinea." *Development Bulletin* 58:72–75.

Lacey, M. 2010. "10 Americans in Haiti Are Charged with Abduction." *New York Times.* February 4, 2010.

Leiman, R. 2002. "Letter to the Editor." *Far Eastern Economic Review.* May 16.

Liaison Group of the Biodiversity-related Conventions. 2009. *Report of the Seventh Meeting of the Liaison Group of the Biodiversity-related Conventions.* Liaison Group of the Biodiversity-related Conventions, Paris. BLG/7/2.

Longhofer, W., and E. Schofer. 2010. "National and Global Origins of Environmental Association." *American Sociological Review* 75 (4): 505–533.

Lukes, S. 1974. *Power: A Radical View.* London: Macmillan.

Mak, Karen K. W., Hideshi Yanase, and Reinhard Renneberg. 2005. "Cyanide Fishing and Cyanide Detection in Coral Reef Fish Using Chemical Tests and Biosensors" *Biosensors and Bioelectronics* 20:2581–2593.

Maxmen, A. 2015. "How the Fight against Ebola Tested a Culture's Traditions." *National Geographic,* January 30. https://news.nationalgeographic.com/2015/01/150130-ebola-virus-outbreak-epidemic-sierra-leone-funerals/ (accessed March 28, 2018).

Mazor, R., S. Giakouma, S. Kark, and H. P. Possingham. 2014. "Large-Scale Conservation Planning in Multinational Marine Environments: Cost Matters." *Ecological Applications* 24 (5): 1115–1130.

McCray, J. 2014. "Is Grantmaking Getting Smarter? A National Study of Philanthropic Practice." *Grantmakers for Effective Organizations.* https://www.geofunders.org/resources/is-grantmaking-getting-smarter-703 (accessed December 12, 2015).

McKeever, Brice, and M. Gaddy. 2016. "The Nonprofit Workforce: By the Numbers." *Nonprofit Quarterly.* https://nonprofitquarterly.org/2016/10/24/nonprofit-workforce-numbers/ (accessed December 12, 2016).

Melanesia Centre for Biodiversity Conservation. 2001. *Guidelines for Staff, Donors, and Affiliated Researchers or Visitors to the Melanesia Centre for Biodiversity Conservation (CBC) Project Sites.* CI CBC Melanesia.

Milne Bay Community-Based Coastal and Marine Conservation Project. 2001. *Community-Based Coastal and Marine Conservation in Milne Bay Province, Papua New Guinea.* Alotau, PNG: Conservation International.

Milne Bay Community-Based Coastal and Marine Conservation Project. 2005. *Management and Community Development Options for a Marine Protected Area in the Netuli Island Area, Milne Bay Province, Papua New Guinea.* Alotau, PNG: Conservation International.

Ministry of Environment and Forests, Government of India. 2009. *India's Fourth National Report to the Convention on Biological Diversity,* ed. A. Goyal and S. Arora. New Delhi, Ministry of Environment and Forests, Government of India.

Minkoff, D. C. 2002. "The Emergence of Hybrid Organizational Forms: Combining Identity-Based Service Provision and Political Action." *Nonprofit and Voluntary Sector Quarterly* 31 (3): 377–401.

Mishra, C., P. Allen, T. McCarthy, M. D. Madhusudan, A. Bayarjargal, and H. H. T. Prins. 2003. "The Role of Incentive Programs in Conserving the Snow Leopard." *Conservation Biology* 17:1512–1520. doi:10.1111/j.1523-1739.2003.00092.x.

Mitchell, D., J. Peters, J. Cannon, C. Holtz, J. Kinch, and P. Seeto. 2001. *Sustainable Use Options Plan for the Milne Bay Community-Based Coastal and Marine Conservation Program.* A report to the United Nations Development Program (PNG/99/G41). Port Moresby, Papua New Guinea: Conservation International.

Mitchell, G. 2012. "The Construct of Organizational Effectiveness: Perspectives from Leaders of International Nonprofits in the United States." *Nonprofit and Voluntary Sector Quarterly* 42 (2): 324–345.

Mitchell, G. 2015. "Fiscal Leanness and Fiscal Responsiveness: Exploring the Normative Limits of Strategic Nonprofit Financial Management." *Administration & Society* 49 (9): 1272–1296.

Mittermeier, R. A., N. Myers, C. G. Mittermeier, and G. Robles. 1999. *Hotspots: Earth's Biologically Richest and Most Endangered Terrestrial Ecoregions.* CEMEX, SA, Agrupación Sierra Madre, SC.

Mulgan, G. 2007. "Technology and Globalisation Have the Power to Transform Communities—But Not Always for the Good." *The Guardian*, October 24. https://www.theguardian.com/society/2007/oct/24/communities.guardiansocietysupplement (accessed May 1, 2015).

Murdie, A. 2014. *Help or Harm: The Human Security Effects of International NGOs*. Stanford, CA: Stanford University Press.

Murray, P. 2013. "The Secret of Scale: How Powerful Civic Organizations Like the NRA and AARP Build Membership, Make Money, and Sway Public Policy." *Standard Social Innovation Review* (Fall). https://ssir.org/articles/entry/the_secret_of_scale (accessed June 23, 2016).

Myers, N., R. A. Mittermeier, C. G. Mittermeier, G. A. Da Fonseca, and J. Kent. 2000. "Biodiversity Hotspots for Conservation Priorities." *Nature* 403 (6772): 853.

Niesten, E. n.d. *Observations on Conservation Incentive Agreements under the Milne Bay Project, Following Visit May 18–23*. Conservation Economics Program. Milne Bay: Conservation International.

Okorley, E., J. Dey, and R. Owusu. 2012. "A Ghanaian Case Study of Strategies of Ensuring Accountability by Nongovernmental Organizations." *Journal of Sustainable Development in Africa* 14 (7): 43–54.

Orosz, J. J. 2000. *The Insider's Guide to Grantmaking: How Foundations Find, Fund, and Manage Effective Programs*. San Francisco: Jossey-Bass.

Ostrom, E. 1990. *Governing the Commons: The Evolution of Institutions for Collective Action*. Cambridge: Cambridge University Press.

Oxfam-Monash Partnership. n.d. "Briefing Paper 2: Strengthening the Accountability of NGOs." https://www.monash.edu/__data/assets/pdf_file/0006/428325/Briefing-Paper-NGO-accountability-1.pdf (accessed May 5, 2015).

Pacific Initiative for the Environment. 2002. Protecting the Outstanding Biodiversity and Marine Resources of Helen Reef, Palau: Creating an Effective Enforcement Program. Project Progress Report. Honolulu: Helen Reef Project.

The David and Lucile Packard Foundation. 2013. "Organizational Effectiveness: Program Overview." https://www.packard.org/wp-content/uploads/2014/02/OE-Program-Overview-FINAL.pdf (accessed July 23, 2015).

Padilla, J. E., John Pontillas, Brian Gonzales, and Rolando P. Orozco. 2004. *Briefing Paper on Cyanide Fishing in the Philippines*. Manila: World Wildlife Fund.

Page, S. E. 2008. *The Difference: How the Power of Diversity Creates Better Groups, Firms, Schools, and Societies*. New ed. Princeton: Princeton University Press.

Pallas, C. 2010. "Revolutionary, Advocate, Agent, or Authority: Context-Based Assessment of Democratic Legitimacy in Transnational Civil Society." *Ethics & Global Politics* 3 (3): 217–238.

Pallas, C. L., D. Gethings, and M. Harris. 2015. "Do the Right Thing: The Impact of INGO Legitimacy Standards on Stakeholder Input." *Voluntas* 26 (4): 1261–1287.

Pandya, C. 2006. "Private Authority and Disaster Relief: The Cases of Post-tsunami Aceh and Nias." *Critical Asian Studies* 38 (2): 298–308.

Parks, J. E. 2001. *Strategically Planning for a New Direction on Marine Conservation in Southeast Asia and the Pacific by the International Marinelife Alliance: Final Report to the International Marinelife Alliance and the David and Lucile Packard Foundation.* Washington, DC: World Resources Institute.

Parras, T. 2003. "December 3 Entry." *Community Conservation Network: Updates on CCN's Conservation Work in the Pacific Islands* (blog). http://ccn-blog.blogspot.com/2003/10/2003/12/ (accessed January 15, 2004).

Pattberg, P. 2004. "Private Environmental Governance and the Sustainability Transition: Functions and Impacts of NGO-Business Partnerships." In *Governance for Industrial Transformation: Proceedings of the 2003 Berlin Conference on the Human Dimensions of Global Environmental Change*, ed. K. Jacob, M. Binder, and A. Wiexzorek, 52–66. Berlin: Environmental Policy Research Centre.

People Against Foreign NGO Neocolonialism. 2003. *Institutionalized Neocolonialism in International NGOs Operating in Papua New Guinea.* http://ces.iisc.ernet.in/hpg/envis/doc99html/biodpeo230524.html (accessed January 15, 2004).

Philippine Headline News Online. 1998. "Padlocked: Puerto Princesa Exporter of Cyanide-Caught Fish." *Philippine Headline News Online*, December 6.

Pontiu, Modi. n.d. *Community Engagement as a Tool to Support Conservation Outcomes in Milne Bay, Papua New Guinea.* Alotau, PNG: Conservation International.

Pratt, V. R. 2004. *Establishment of Regional Network of Cyanide Detection Test (CDT) Laboratories in the Philippines, Vietnam, Sabah Malaysia.* Honolulu: International Marinelife Alliance.

Rapid Assessment Program (Conservation International), and L. E. Alonso. 2011. *Still Counting: Biodiversity Exploration for Conservation: The First 20 Years of the Rapid Assessment Program.* Rapid Assessment Program. Washington, DC: Conservation International.

Ribot, J. 2002. "African Decentralization: Local Actors, Powers and Accountability." Democracy, Governance and Human Rights. Paper no. 8. Geneva: UNRISD and IDRC.

Ridgely, M., and M. Guilbeaux. 1999. *Collaborative Resource Monitoring and Conservation at Helen Reef Atoll, Republic of Palau, Micronesia.* Proposal to the EDF Environmental Minigrant Program. Honolulu: Community Conservation Network.

Risby, L. 2008. *GEF Country Portfolio Evaluation: Madagascar (1994–2007). Evaluation Report.* Washington, DC: GEF Council.

Risby, A. 2009. GEF Country Portfolio Evaluation: Cameroon (1992–2007) (English). Evaluation report, no. 45. Washington, DC: World Bank. http://documents .worldbank.org/curated/en/516001468228545965/GEF-country-portfolio-evaluation -Cameroon-1992-2007 (accessed April 11, 2016).

Risse, T. 2005. "Global Governance and Communicative Action." In *Global Governance and Public Accountability*, ed. D. Held and M. Koenig-Archibugi, 164–189. Malden, MA: Blackwell Publishing.

Rodgers, L. 2013. "Haiti Quake: Why Isn't Aid Money Going to Haitians?" *BBC News*. http://www.bbc.com/news/world-latin-america-20949624 (accessed May 1, 2015).

Romero, F. G., L. Kadlecik, C. B. Dumadaug, A. Alvarez Jr., and V. R. Pratt. 1996. *CREST: Coral Reef Education for Students and Teachers Manual*. Manila: International Marinelife Alliance—Philippines.

Ron, J., A. Pandya, and D. Crow. 2016. "Universal Values, Foreign Money: Funding Local Human Rights Organizations in the Global South." *Review of International Political Economy* 23 (1): 29–64.

Rosen, T., S. Hussain, G. Mohammad, R. Jackson, J. E. Janecka, and S. Michel. 2012. "Reconciling Sustainable Development of Mountain Communities with Large Carnivore Conservation: Lessons from Pakistan." *Mountain Research and Development* 32 (3): 286–293.

Rubec, P. 1997. Testimony for US Subcommittee on Fisheries Conservation, Wildlife and Oceans Concerning House Resolution 87, Washington, DC. http://www.house .gov/ resources/105cong/fishery/may06.97/rubec.htm (accessed June 1, 2001).

Rubec, P. J., Ferdinand Cruz, Vaughan Pratt, Richard Oellers, and Frank Lallo. 2001. "Cyanide-Free, Net-Caught Fish for the Marine Aquarium Trade." *Aquarium Sciences and Conservation* 3:37–51.

Schmidt, E. 2013. "Rediagnosing 'Founder's Syndrome': Moving Beyond Stereotypes to Improve Nonprofit Performance." *Nonprofit Quarterly*. https://nonprofitquarterly .org/2013/07/01/rediagnosing-founder-s-syndrome-moving-beyond-stereotypes-to -improve-nonprofit-performance/ (accessed July 20, 2015).

Schmitz, H. P., P. Raggo, and Tosca Bruno-van Vijfeijken. 2012. "Accountability of Transnational NGOs: Aspirations vs. Practice." *Nonprofit and Voluntary Sector Quarterly* 41 (6): 1176–1195.

Scholte, J. A. 2004. "Civil Society and Democratically Accountable Global Governance." *Government and Opposition* 39 (2): 211–233.

Seeto, P. 2001. *Conservation Needs Assessment Report*. Port Morseby: UNDP.

Seligmann, P. A. 2005. "Ecosystem Services Are Central to Our Mission." *Conservation Frontlines*, Summer. Washington, DC: Conservation International.

Senge, P. M. 1990. *The Fifth Discipline: The Art and Practice of the Learning Organization*. New York: Currency Doubleday.

Siegel, S. 2003. "Conservation at All Costs: How Industry-Backed Environmentalism Creates Violent Conflict among Indigenous Peoples." *Corporate Watch*. https://corpwatch.org/article/conservation-all-costs (accessed October 15, 2007).

Slim, H. 2002. "By What Authority? The Legitimacy and Accountability of Nongovernmental Organisations." The International Council on Human Rights Policy International Meeting on Global Trends and Human Rights—Before and after September 11. Geneva, January 10–12. https://www.gdrc.org/ngo/accountability/by-what-authority.html (accessed January 10, 2005).

Steinberg, P. 2001. *Environmental Leadership in Developing Countries*. Cambridge, MA: MIT Press.

Steinberg, P. 2003. "Understanding Policy Change in Developing Countries: The Spheres of Influence Framework." *Global Environmental Politics* 3 (1): 11–32.

Stephens, J., and D. B. Ottaway. 2003. "Nonprofit Land Bank Amasses Billions; Landing a Big One: Preservation, Private Development; Nonprofit Sells Scenic Acreage to Allies at a Loss; Developers Find Payoff in Preservation." *Washington Post*. http://www.washingtonpost.com/wp-dyn/content/article/2007/06/26/AR2007062600803.html (accessed May 1, 2015.)

Stern, M. 2008. "Coercion, Voluntary Compliance and Protest: The Role of Trust and Legitimacy in Combating Local Opposition to Protected Areas." *Environmental Conservation* 35 (3): 200–210.

Strauss, G. 2016. "The Snow Leopard's Best Friend." November 30. https://news.nationalgeographic.com/2016/11/shafqat-hussain-explorer-moments-pakistan-eco-tourism-to-protect-snow-leopards/ (accessed September 27, 2017).

Stroup, S. S. 2012. *Borders Among Activists: International NGOs in the United States, Britain, and France*. Ithaca: Cornell University Press.

Stroup, S. S., and W. H. Wong, 2017. *The Authority Trap: Strategic Choices of International NGOs*. Ithaca: Cornell University Press.

Subregional Steering Committee: CITES/MIKE–South Asia 2004. *Minutes of the 1st Steering Committee Meeting*. Subregional Steering Committee: CITES/MIKE-South Asia, Negombo, Sri Lanka.

Suchman, M. C. 1995. "Managing Legitimacy: Strategic and Institutional Approaches." *Academy of Management Review* 20 (3): 571–610.

Sumner, A. 2006. "What Is Development Studies?" *Development in Practice* 16 (6): 644–650.

SustainAbility. 2001. *The 21st Century NGO in the Market for Change*. SustainAbility, UN Global Compact, and UNEP.

Syed, Nabiha. 2005. "Factors of Success: A Comparative Study of Kashf Foundation and Grameen Bank." Thesis, Department of International Relations. Baltimore, MD: Johns Hopkins University.

TNC (The Nature Conservancy). 2004. *Conservation That Works: 2004 Annual Report*. Arlington, VA: The Nature Conservancy.

TNC (The Nature Conservancy). 2015. *Our World: 2015 Annual Report*. Arlington, VA: The Nature Conservancy.

Towns, D. R. 2007. *Islands Biodiversity Program: New Zealand Case Study*. Te Papa Atawhai: Department of Conservation: Te Papa Atawhai.

Van Helden, F. 2004. "'Making Do': Integrating Ecological and Societal Considerations for Marine Conservation in a Situation of Indigenous Resource Tenure." In *Challenging Coasts: Transdisciplinary Excursions into Integrated Coastal Zone Development*, ed. L. Visser, 93–118. Amsterdam: Amsterdam University Press.

Victor, R. 2003a. *Helen Reef Resource Management Board Meeting Minutes January 29, 2003*. Koror: Helen Reef Resource Management Project.

Victor, R. 2003b. *January 24, 2003 Minutes of the HRMB*. Koror: Helen Reef Resource Management Project.

Wallace, R., A. Fine, and M. Atkinson. 2010. "Scaling up Conservation Success with SCAPES: A USAID Cooperative Agreement with the Wildlife Conservation Society (WCS)." Wildlife Conservation Society. https://www.google.com/url?sa=t&rct=j&q=&esrc=s&source=web&cd=1&ved=0ahUKEwi3sdCckKHaAhUqrlkKHTg5CrgQFggsMAA&url=https%3A%2F%2Fprograms.wcs.org%2FDesktopModules%2FBring2mind%2FDMX%2FDownload.aspx%3FEntryId%3D9746%26PortalId%3D110%26DownloadMethod%3Dattachment&usg=AOvVaw2dZU67lMaVMGpwHVkDhqgu (accessed April 2017).

Werner, T. B., and G. R. Allen. 1998. *A Rapid Biodiversity Assessment of the Coral Reefs of Milne Bay Province, Papua New Guinea*, vol. 11. Washington, DC: Conservation International.

West, P. 2005. "Translation, Value, and Space: Theorizing an Ethnographic and Engaged Environmental Anthropology." *American Anthropologist* 107 (4): 632–642.

West, P. 2006. *Conservation Is Our Government Now: The Politics of Ecology in Papua New Guinea*. Durham, NC: Duke University Press.

Westley, F., N. Antadze, D. J. Riddell, K. Robinson, and S. Geobey. 2014. "Five Configurations for Scaling Up Social Innovation: Case Examples of Nonprofit Organizations from Canada." *Journal of Applied Behavioral Science* 50 (3): 234–260.

WildAid. 2005. *Cambodia's Mobile Unit Apprehends Wildlife Trader.* Report. WildAid, San Francisco.

WildAid. 2016. *2016 Annual Report.* San Francisco: WildAid.

Wong, W. H. 2012. *Internal Affairs: How the Structure of NGOs Transforms Human Rights.* Ithaca: Cornell University Press.

Wood, E. 2001. "Global Advances in Conservation and Management of Marine Ornamental Resources." *Aquarium Sciences and Conservation* 3 (1–3): 65–77.

World Bank. 2010. World Bank Statement: Fifteenth Meeting of the Conference of Parties to the Convention on International Trade in Endangered Species of Wild Fauna and Flora. CoP15 Doc 61. Doha, CITES.

World Resources Institute (WRI), The World Conservation Union (IUCN), and the United Nations Environment Programme (UNEP). 1992. *Global Biodiversity Strategy: Guidelines for Action to Save, Study, and Use Earth's Biotic Wealth Sustainably and Equitably.* Washington, DC: WRI.

World Resources Institute (WRI) in collaboration with United Nations Development Programme, United Nations Environment Programme, and World Bank. 2008. *World Resources 2008: Roots of Resilience—Growing the Wealth of the Poor.* Washington, DC: WRI.

WWF (World Wildlife Fund). 2005. *2005 Annual Report.* Gland, Switzerland: Andrew White Creative Communications.

WWF (World Wildlife Fund). 2015. *2015 Annual Report.* Gland, Switzerland: Andrew White Creative Communications.

Union of International Associations. 2014. *The Yearbook of International Organizations.* New Milford, CT: Brill.

Interview Sources

Source#	Date	Description
1	10/14/05	Former employee, Conservation International, Washington, DC
2	10/14/05	Employee, Conservation International, Washington, DC
3	10/14/05	Employee, Conservation International, Washington, DC
4	11/18/05	Former employee, International Marinelife Alliance, Washington, DC
5	2/10/06	Official, U.S. Coral Reef Task Force, Washington, DC
6	2/10/06	Employee, Conservation International, Washington, DC
7	2/22/06	Former employee, Conservation International, telephone conversation
8	3/9/06	Employee, Marine Aquarium Council, Manila, Philippines
9	3/9/06	Employee, Marine Aquarium Council, Manila, Philippines
10	3/14/06	Official, United States Agency for International Development, Manila, Philippines
11	3/14/06	Official, United States Agency for International Development, Manila, Philippines
12	3/14/06	Employee, ReefCheck, Manila, Philippines
13	3/14/06	Employee, ReefCheck, Manila, Philippines
14	3/14/06	Employee, Marine Aquarium Council, Manila, Philippines
15	3/15/06	Official, Philippine Bureau of Fisheries and Aquatic Resources, Manila, Philippines
16	3/15/06	Official, Philippine Bureau of Fisheries and Aquatic Resources, Manila, Philippines
17	3/19/06	Former employee, International Marinelife Alliance, Boracay, Philippines

228228228228

Source#	Date	Description
18	3/21/06	Philippine aquarium trade business owner, Manila, Philippines
19	3/21/06	Employee, Marine Aquarium Council, Manila, Philippines
20	3/21/06	Employee, Conservation and Community Investment Forum, Manila, Philippines
21	3/27/06	Former employee, International Marinelife Alliance, Batangas City, Philippines
22	3/27/06	Former employee, International Marinelife Alliance, Manila, Philippines
23	3/24/06	Official, Philippine Department of Education, Puerto Princesa, Philippines
24	3/23/06	Official, Palawan Council on Sustainable Development, Puerto Princesa, Philippines
25	3/24/06	Official, Philippine Bureau of Fisheries and Aquatic Resources, Puerto Princesa, Philippines
26	3/24/06	Official, Philippine Bureau of Fisheries and Aquatic Resources, Puerto Princesa, Philippines
27	3/23/06	Community member, municipality of Nara, Puerto Princesa, Philippines
28	3/27/06	Former employee, International Marinelife Alliance, Batangas City, Philippines
29	3/27/06	Official, Philippine Bureau of Fisheries and Aquatic Resources, Manila, Philippines
30	3/24/06	Former employee, International Marinelife Alliance, Puerto Princesa, Province of Palawan, Philippines
31	3/23/06	Official, Office of the Provincial Agriculture, Puerto Princesa, Province of Palawan, Philippines
32	3/24/06	Employee, local Palawan conservation nonprofit, Puerto Princesa, Province of Palawan, Philippines
33	3/24/06	Employee, local Palawan conservation nonprofit, Puerto Princesa, Province of Palawan, Philippines
34	3/27/06	Former employee, International Marinelife Alliance, Batangas City, Philippines
35	3/23/06	Official, Department of Education, Puerto Princesa, Province of Palawan, Philippines
36	5/4/06	Former employee, International Marinelife Alliance, telephone conversation
37	5/18/06	Former employee, International Marinelife Alliance, New Haven, Connecticut
38	7/1/06	Employee, Community Conservation Network, Honolulu, Hawaii

Source#	Date	Description
39	6/29/06	Former employee, Community Conservation Network, Honolulu, Hawaii
40	7/6/06	Employee, Community Conservation Network, Koror, Palau
41	7/6/06	Member, Helen Reef Management Board, Koror, Palau
42	7/6/06	Member, Helen Reef Management Board, Koror, Palau
43	7/7/06	Employee, Helen Reef Resource Management Program, Koror, Palau
44	7/7/06	Employee, Helen Reef Resource Management Program, Koror, Palau
45	7/7/06	Employee, local Palauan conservation nonprofit, Koror, Palau
46	7/7/06	Employee, Helen Reef Resource Management Program, Koror, Palau
47	7/7/06	Official, Hatohobei state government, Koror, Palau
48	7/7/06	Community member, Hatohobei, Koror, Palau
49	7/7/06	Member, Helen Reef Management Board, Koror, Palau
50	7/7/06	Official, Hatohobei state government, Koror, Palau
51	7/8/06	Officer, Palau Marine Enforcement, Koror, Palau
52	7/10/06	Former member, Helen Reef Action Committee, Koror, Palau
53	7/12/06	Official, Bureau of Marine Resources, Koror, Palau
54	7/12/06	Former official, Hatohobei State Government, Koror, Palau
55	7/12/06	Hatohobei expert, Koror, Palau
56	7/13/06	Employee, Community Conservation Network, Koror, Palau
57	7/12/06	Community member, Hatohobei, Koror, Palau
58	7/8/06	Palauan citizen, Koror, Palau
59	7/12/06	Official & former member, Hatohobei State Government & Action Committee, Koror, Palau
60	7/16/06	Former member, Helen Reef Management Board, Koror, Palau
61	11/29/06	Former employee, Conservation International, Port Moresby, Papua New Guinea
62	11/30/06	Official, national government, Port Moresby, Papua New Guinea
63	12/1/06	Official, United Nations Development Programme, Port Moresby, Papua New Guinea

Source#	Date	Description
64	12/5/06	Community member and local business owner, Alotau, Papua New Guinea
65	12/5/06	Former employee, Conservation International, Alotau, Papua New Guinea
66	12/6/06	Official, Milne Bay Church Development Fund Association, Alotau, Papua New Guinea
67	12/7/06	Community member and local business owner, Alotau, Papua New Guinea
68	12/7/06	Community member and environmentalist, Alotau, Papua New Guinea
69	12/7/06	Employee, Conservation International, Alotau, Papua New Guinea
70	12/7/06	Volunteer, Australian Agency for International Development, Alotau, Papua New Guinea
71	12/8/06	Board member, Milne Bay Church Development Fund Association, Alotau, Papua New Guinea
72	12/8/06	Official, Milne Bay provincial government, Alotau, Papua New Guinea
73	12/8/06	Volunteer, Australian Agency for International Development, Alotau, Papua New Guinea
74	12/8/06	Former employee, Conservation International, Alotau, Papua New Guinea
75	12/9/06	Former employee, Conservation International, Alotau, Papua New Guinea
76	12/9/06	Community member, Netuli, Milne Bay, Papua New Guinea
77	12/9/06	Community member, Netuli, Milne Bay, Papua New Guinea
78	12/10/06	Community member, Netuli, Milne Bay, Papua New Guinea
79	12/10/06	Community member, Netuli, Milne Bay, Papua New Guinea
80	12/10/06	Community member, Netuli, Milne Bay, Papua New Guinea
81	12/10/06	Community member, Netuli, Milne Bay, Papua New Guinea
82	12/11/06	Community member, Nuakata, Milne Bay, Papua New Guinea
83	12/11/06	Community member, Nuakata, Milne Bay, Papua New Guinea
84	12/11/06	Community member, Nuakata, Milne Bay, Papua New Guinea

Source#	Date	Description
85	12/11/06	Community member, Nuakata, Milne Bay, Papua New Guinea
86	12/11/06	Community member, Nuakata, Milne Bay, Papua New Guinea
87	12/12/06	Community member, Nuakata, Milne Bay, Papua New Guinea
88	12/12/06	Community member, Nuakata, Milne Bay, Papua New Guinea
89	12/12/06	Community member, Nuakata, Milne Bay, Papua New Guinea
90	12/12/06	Community member, Nuakata, Milne Bay, Papua New Guinea
91	12/12/06	Community member, Nuakata, Milne Bay, Papua New Guinea
92	12/12/06	Community member, Nuakata, Milne Bay, Papua New Guinea
93	12/12/06	Community member, Nuakata, Milne Bay, Papua New Guinea
94	12/12/06	Community member, Nuakata, Milne Bay, Papua New Guinea
95	12/13/06	Milne Bay community member and local business owner, Alotau, Papua New Guinea
96	12/13/06	Former volunteer, Australian Agency for International Development, Alotau, Papua New Guinea
97	12/13/06	Employee, Conservation International, Alotau, Papua New Guinea
98	12/13/06	Former official and community member, Milne Bay Provincial Government, Alotau, Papua New Guinea
99	12/13/06	Milne Bay community member and local business owner, Alotau, Papua New Guinea
100	12/15/06	Employee, United Nations Development Programme, Port Moresby, Papua New Guinea
101	12/15/06	Employee, The Nature Conservancy, Port Moresby, Papua New Guinea
102	12/15/06	Employee, The Nature Conservancy, Port Moresby, Papua New Guinea
103	9/1/06	Employee, Community Conservation Network, telephone conversation
104	9/2/06 and 5/17/16	Board member, Community Conservation Network, telephone conversation

Source#	Date	Description
105	9/3/06 and 5/2/16	Employee, Community Conservation Network, telephone conversation
106	12/13/06	Milne Bay community member and environmentalist, Alotau, Papua New Guinea
107	12/9/06	Board member, Milne Bay Church Development Fund Association, Alotau, Papua New Guinea
108	12/13/06	Former volunteer, AUSAID, Alotau, Papua New Guinea
109	4/29/16	Former board member, Community Conservation Network, telephone conversation

Index